The Outdoor Woman's Guide
to
Sports, Fitness and Nutrition

The
Outdoor Woman's Guide
to
Sports, Fitness
and Nutrition

Jackie Johnson Maughan
with Kathryn Collins, M.D.

Stackpole Books

THE OUTDOOR WOMAN'S GUIDE TO SPORTS, FITNESS AND NUTRITION

Copyright © 1983 by
STACKPOLE BOOKS

Published by
STACKPOLE BOOKS
Cameron and Kelker Streets
P. O. Box 1831
Harrisburg, PA   17105

Printed in the U.S.A.

Library of Congress Cataloging in Publication Data

Maughan, Jackie Johnson, 1948–
    The outdoor woman's guide to sports, fitness and nutrition.

    Includes index.
    1. Outdoor recreation for women.   2. Physical education for women.   3. Physical fitness for women. 4. Women—Nutrition.   5. Sports for women.   I. Collins, Kathryn.   II. Title.
GV191.64.M38
1983   796'.088042   83–355
ISBN 0–8117–1157–9

Trailbreaking is hard, hazardous, sometimes thankless work. This book is dedicated to all those women and men who have the courage to do it. This includes two editors—Ruth Dennison-TeDesco and Alison Brown—and my brother, William E. "Bodie" Johnson, for his unconventional and very appropriate skills. You were sure there when I needed you.

Contents

Acknowledgments

This book is the result of collective curiosity—my own, my editor's, my consultants', would-be and actual outdoorswomen; and the hundreds of scientists who've done the research about woman, her physiology, and her adjustment to the great, untamed, grandmother earth.

Perhaps acknowledgment pages such as these should be the first rather than the last thing an author writes. The summing up seems nearly impossible once the gigantic mass of words has been corralled and put on paper. Nevertheless, in sum then, this book is about fitness for outdoor sports and, conversely, how those sports will keep you fit. There's also a fair amount of quality information about nutrition and injury treatment, not to mention stories and inspirational passages from a good number of admirable women. It's intended to be a book you can just sit down and read, and then go back to as a reference. There's plenty of science here, but also enough anecdotes and true-life stories to get you emotionally involved. We (meaning Kathryn and I) wanted to give you what always seems to be needed—information and motivation.

Even with Kathryn's excellent credentials, I felt that the book needed a physiologist and a nutritionist. Alex Urfer, who has a Ph.D. in exercise physiology and is presently planning an expedition to the Himalayas, was my most important consultant second to Kathryn. Mary Echo, a registered dietician, amateur archaeologist, and assistant professor of consumer economics, was the consultant for the chapter about nutrition. Similarly, Tom Whittaker, a kayaker, and former climber who is pioneering work with the handicapped in the outdoors, reviewed the chapter about paddle sports; and Janene Willer a former national class bicyclist, the section about bicycling.

In addition, there are the women and men specifically mentioned in the text. As you will see, the advice of experts like Irma and Per-Olof Astrand, international pathfinders in the field of work physiology, was sought, as well as those whose only credentials are an abiding love for things wild and free.

So, here's to the wind in your hair, the spray on your lips, the sweat on your brow, and an inner vision undimmed by self-doubt or societal restraints.

> Alone I walked the mists that hung over the summit of Sainte-Victoire, and trod along the ridge of the Pilon de Roi, bracing myself against a violent wind which sent my beret spinning down into the valley below. Alone again, I got lost in a mountain ravine on the Luberon range. Such moments, with all their warmth, tenderness, and fury belong to me and no one else.
>
> Simone de Beauvoir, *The Prime of Life*

Chapter 1

Training for Endurance and Strength

Incentives

The woman who wants to become or already is active in the outdoors is a step ahead of others who keep fit for its own sake. She has extra motivation when good health, good looks, and satisfaction aren't enough to overcome the inertia of the armchair. The trips themselves are immediate goals, and the love affair with nature can be a lifetime union. Since her own body is as valuable as a wild stretch of whitewater, a great blue heron, or a flowered mountain meadow, she should have an added incentive to take care of it. A love of the outdoors should induce fitness in those who find the medical arguments about as compelling as a cold stethoscope. Most outdoorswomen realize that they must make a lifetime commitment to physical fitness, if only to prolong the quality of their outdoor careers.

For the outdoorswoman the call of the wild does not lie in jostling bait can to bumper at a Bureau of Reclamation reservoir with every motorized sportsman in the county. Nor is there any spiritual wine in posting prefabricated scenics from the lobby of a Motel Six. While fitness has its own rewards, many of them lie in the ability to get off the beaten path. So the thudding of the pulse in your neck while you jog to the top of a long grade near home is rewarded by the racing of your heart as the mountain cairn comes into view. On the summit at last, as the wind whips through your hair, you stand, hands on hips, surveying a frozen sea of Precambrian waves.

Carol Alice Liska, who has been mountaineering for almost thirty years, enjoys everything from picnics to expeditions. She and her husband also downhill and cross-country ski and bicycle. "I just love the outdoors. It doesn't have to be a summit every time," she says. The desire to get away from civilization is a great American tradition. No explanation is required when you announce that you need to get away from it all.

"My favorite spot in the whole world happens to be halfway in the Canyon," writes Marji "Slim" Woodruff, a professional guide, about the Grand Canyon. She continues:

> I love the feeling of hanging suspended between the rim and the River. Gravity is such a salient force. I can feel it pulling me down into the earth. I fought it all day: While I was hiking uphill it tried to keep me planted. While going down a steep incline it was always there, waiting, if I slipped. Gravity helped forge the Canyon. The River dug it deep, erosion and gravity carved it wide. I have heard gravity at work. Rocks would loosen, slowly, over long years and many frosts and thaws, many spring meltings, many summer thundershowers. Ultimately they would get just loose enough, gravity would suddenly grab them and they would hurtle down, whizzing through the quiet air and landing with a splatter near my sleeping bag. I would jerk away and listen, but the act was finished.

This spiritual oneness with geological immortality is a special sanctuary in itself. The Grand Canyon Slim lovingly describes is not so valued by others. They would see the river dammed, developed, and diverted. The Grand Canyon is one of the most heavily used and supervised national parks in the country. Yet you can find the serenity Slim describes by simply going in at a less popular trailhead: Line the rim with condos, populate the river with large commercial river-running outfits and the sanctuary is destroyed in favor of yet another noisy, expensive tourist trap.

What does the preservation of wilderness have to do with physical fitness? Plenty. Just as medical practitioners have begun to look to prevention of illness as preferable to an expensive cure once the body is already diseased, so too is preservation a form of preventive medicine for the ecosystem. Joggers, distance runners, backpackers, cross-country skiers, and others who like to get out and work their bodies are often asked what they think about. Most generally the answer is "nothing," or nothing that can easily be put into words. The mind clears. You think about your next step, the approaching storm, the feel of the oar rubbing your palms, the color of the river, the crystal refraction of sunlight on the powdered snow.

For women, physical fitness has certain rewards in itself. Here is a literal application of "taking control of your own body." It's up to you totally. Few other things in life are like that. It also has the rewards of direct cause and effect. You can see the results of your labor. You can set specific goals and actually reach them.

A training diary is one means of doing this goal setting. With it you can avoid self-deception and have a tangible way of answering to yourself. And it's more rewarding to be able to have such a concrete monitor of your progress over time. A training diary might be a spiral notebook, a memo pad, or an actual diary. It might look like this:

June 20 Sunday Weight 166	Weekly goals: I intend to run 45 minutes three times a week. I intend to weight lift 30 minutes three times a week. I want to lose two pounds this week by consuming only 1,400 kcalories a day and by exercising.

Exercise
Run/ 4 miles/ 40:27.7 (outside, three hills)
Thoughts/events
Felt good running; saw flock of barn swallows as I crossed Portneuf bridge.

Nutrient Intake	
B-complex vitamin	
Calcium (750 mg.)	
Iron (50 mg.)	
tea and honey	60
bread (2 slices)	200
pineapple (8 oz.)	150
egg	81
yogurt (fruit)	280
V-8 juice (6 oz.)	35
macaroni and cheese (4 oz.)	400
spinach and lettuce salad	—
diet dressing	64
crackers (3½ oz.)	350
watermelon (2 lb. wedge)	111
milk, skim (8 oz.)	99
	1830
run -	400
	1430

At the end of the week, assess your goals and see how close you came to meeting them. Once you reach your weight objective, whether it be a gain or loss, you won't need to devote so much space to calories. If you're trying to overcome poor eating habits, the diary can help you monitor your nutrition.

Endurance Training

Aerobic capacity has held the limelight over muscular strength because it does the most for long-term fitness. However, it is not sufficient if you wish to do well at most self-propelled outdoors sports and avoid injuries. Too many programs for women don't put enough emphasis upon strength, especially upper-body strength, to prepare them for the demands of the outdoors. A high oxygen capacity won't help prevent a shoulder dislocation. And it won't protect your calves and quadriceps from the strain of carrying a heavy pack down a steep grade. You can jog forty miles a week and still not do as well as you would like at cross-country skiing. All outdoors sports require both power and endurance. The basic triumvirate of injury prevention is a high aerobic capacity to prevent fatigue, strong muscles that are not easily strained and help protect the joints, and flexibility great enough to allow the body to go through its natural range of motion.

However, all of the self-propelled outdoor sports require more proportionate aerobic than anaerobic power. (Anaerobic energy is delivered in short-term, explosive movements, as in sprinting. It is called anaerobic because it does not use oxygen.) This is so if only for the fact that you must move your own body to get to your destination. The best choice among the many aerobic training methods is the one that comes closest to your outdoor activities. This is because of several factors, which together add up to *specificity of training*. This means that the nerves and muscles "learn" to perform better with practice. Therefore, a hiker should run, a canoer should swim or use a rowing machine, and so forth. Of course there's no better training than doing the sport itself. Studies have shown that when a cyclist is tested for her ability to use oxygen on a treadmill she won't do as well as she would if tested on a stationary bicycle. This is because the muscles she uses while cycling are different than the ones she uses while running or walking, and they're better trained to use oxygen.

To improve aerobic capacity, you need to train for at least twenty minutes at a heart rate that is at least 70 percent of your maximum. Your maximum heart rate can be estimated by subtracting your age from 220. If you are thirty, for example, your maximum heart rate would be 190, and 70 percent of this would be 133 beats per minute. You can get results by training at less than 70 percent if you are presently inactive, but it will take longer and the level of $\dot{V}O_2$ max reached won't be as great. ($\dot{V}O_2$ max means literally the maximum amount of oxygen ventilated per minute. For a further explanation, see chapter 6.)

Before you actually set out to run, bicycle, or whatever, get to know what it feels like to exercise at a certain heart rate. Then you won't have to stop to monitor it with a watch and lose your concentration. To determine your heart rate while exercising, find your pulse and count it for six seconds immediately after you have stopped exercising. Add a zero to the six to determine the per-minute rate. It may take several trials. Good pressure points are those in your wrists, neck, and the side of your forehead. Persons over sixty who are beginning a program or persons who are overweight or extremely inactive may have to train at a lower heart rate. One study showed that those sixty and older got the same results training at 30 to 45 percent of maximal heart rate as at 60 percent.[1]

Seeing improvement is harder as you get in better shape, and you may become dissatisfied with your progress. To improve, you will have to "overload" your system by exercising at a more demanding level. It is at this point that you will wonder if increased intensity, duration, or frequency is the answer. If you want simply to ease the task of travel in the outdoors, you can increase either the duration or frequency of your workouts. Increasing your jogging mileage from two miles to four, for example, will improve your endurance ability. It should also indirectly increase your overall speed because you won't tire as easily and won't require as many rest stops while hiking. Both increased duration and frequency reduce the work of the heart by increasing stroke volume. They thus do more for long-term fitness than high intensities.[2] Two miles, by the way, is a respectable distance for those who want to do ordinary backcountry trips. If you want to climb mountains or cover more than eight miles a day backpacking, you should try to increase your mileage beyond this.

Studies indicate that frequencies of more than three times a week will do little to increase $\dot{V}O_2$ max directly. However, if you're training aerobically to maintain or produce a weight loss, frequency is important. The three or four hundred kcalories used during a forty-minute workout will be hard to eliminate from your diet on off days. Since excess fat is a deterrent to oxygen metabolism (see chapter 6), losing fat by aerobics will in itself increase $\dot{V}O_2$ max.

At first, aerobic sessions should be only every other day to allow the body time to recuperate from stress/overload. The majority of stress/overload injuries occur with increased training frequency. In general, the older you are, the slower the tissues recover. This is also true if you are recovering from an illness. So you may need to wait longer than forty-eight hours. Once your body becomes accustomed to a certain level of stress, you can train more often. But you can't expect to increase duration, frequency and intensity all at the same time. High-mileage days should be followed by less demanding days. If you don't allow time for recuperation, you can train yourself into a state of fatigue, increase your chances of injury, and decrease rather than build muscle. This is known as the overuse syndrome. For example, if you're having chronic knee and back problems as a result of running, or shoulder pain from swimming or rowing, definitely allow a forty-eight-hour rest period between sessions.

You can maintain and even gain aerobic strength with as little as two workouts per week. However, losses begin if you slip under two. For example, one group of women trained for eight weeks, then went into a once-a-week detraining program. In ten weeks they had lost 40 percent of the VO_2 max gains they had made. Those who didn't exercise at all lost all of the gains they had made.[3] The rate of decline is not so rapid among those who have been exercising for several years, and losses of 15 percent in twelve weeks are reported when training stops completely.[4] If you are confined to bed, the decline in VO_2 max, stroke volume, and cardiac output is about 1 percent per day. The rate of detraining increases with age.

Just as your aerobic strength can decline drastically with little effort, so can it increase greatly with a little effort if you are presently sedentary. One study showed a 16 percent increase in VO_2 max in young inactive women who trained for only ten-minute sessions two days per week for eight weeks at only 60 percent maximal heart rate.[5] So even if you have been neglectful, you can do something to get in shape for an outing with as little as two months' minimal preparation.

If you want to become faster and do your particular activity with greater power, include high-intensity workouts in your program. If you are in your forties or fifties, allow at least one month to work these into your program. Dr. Joan Ullyot, a distance runner who writes a monthly column for *Women's Sports* magazine, suggests starting with just one intense workout a week, then two, then at most three. Two such workouts a week are sufficient to gain speed and power. These work sessions can be shorter: If you work at 80 percent of maximal heart rate, you can get the same results with ten to fifteen minutes of exercise as you would at 70 percent for twenty to thirty minutes.

Although high-intensity workouts are known to increase short-term power and speed, it is not known when more intensity ceases to be better for increasing aerobic capacity. Speculation places the maximum at 85 percent. Some elite marathoners advocate training at this intensity, but there is no scientific evidence to back them up. High-intensity training should not be undertaken if you have heart problems unless closely supervised by a sports-aware physician. It also may pose hazards to pregnant women because of overheating and possible fetal oxygen deprivation.

Interval training is a compromise method of developing both energy systems. With it you can maintain an intensity of exercise that you couldn't normally. During interval training you alternate brief periods of maximum effort with rest periods. If you want to develop the immediate energy system—that operating from 15 to 90 seconds—the ratio would be one unit of exercise for every three units of rest (1:3). The ratio for the intermediate energy system (90 to 180 seconds) would be 1:2. To train by the aerobic system, the ratio would be 1:½.

The rest periods used during interval training allow severe loads to be put on the energy systems of specific muscles without fatigue. During the rest periods slow your pace to the equivalent of a slow jog or brisk walk. The suggested intervals given here can be used for any aerobic activity. Each workout is divided into sets. Take a complete rest of several minutes between each set. Within each set are repetitions/intervals that should be repeated for the specified number of times. This program is simplified from work done by Edward L. Fox, director of the Laboratory of Work Physiology at Ohio State University.

Energy System	Workout Time (minutes/seconds)	Ratio	Rest Time	Reps	Sets	Total Time
ATP-PC (15–90 seconds)	30–1:00	1:3	1:30–3:00	5	2–5	not less than 30 minutes
Lactic Acid (90–180 seconds)	1:30–3:00	1:2	3:00–6:00	4	1–2	36 minutes
Aerobic	3:00–5:00	1:½	1:30–2:30	3	2–3	30–45 minutes

Fartlek training, from the Swedish word meaning *speed play,* is a modified version of interval training. With this system, you can alternate fast and slow speeds according to your pleasure. For example, if you are running outside and your route includes hills, you're most likely already doing fartleks.

There are numerous methods of aerobic training. Advocates of almost every sport will claim that their particular endeavor is "aerobic." No doubt most of them are, in the sense that you must breathe in order to perform them. But if an activity does not keep your heart rate elevated to 70 percent for at least twenty minutes, you won't get much of an aerobic effect. While golf, tennis, karate, roller skating, and the jitterbug may each have its benefits, appreciable levels of aerobic fitness are not among them.

Among methods of aerobic training that you can do indoors without any major investment in equipment are jumping rope, running in place, and chair/stair stepping. Any of these can be done to music or while watching TV to ease the boredom. Chair stepping, in which you step on and off a chair or step, is versatile because you can use a higher chair as you get in better shape. Jumping rope can be hard on your feet and shins and should be done only every other day at first. If you must make any one of these harder to achieve the training effect, you can either raise your knees higher or wear a pack to which you add weight, such as rock salt, sand, or water-filled plastic bags. Although most indoor exercises are not the first choice of most people because they are so dreadfully boring, they're an alternative should you be unable to do your regular aerobic training on a particular day.

Among indoor exercises that do require an investment is stationary cycling. Because it is a nonweight-bearing exercise, it is good for overweight, aged, or pregnant women. It is also excellent for those who find that running is too hard on the weight-bearing joints, or for those who may have suffered stress injuries. Stationary cycles cost between $100 and $400. Top-of-the-line ergometers cost just over $500. Ergometers allow you to regulate and measure the force of your pedaling. Before you purchase a cycle, make sure that it fits you, adjusts easily, pedals smoothly, and is easy to assemble and maintain. Some seem to be built for people with short legs. Check *Consumer Reports* (January 1982) for a good critique of these machines.

The small trampolines, or rebound exercisers, have been found to be an inferior aerobic-exercise device. They will not give you the same training effect as jogging, skipping rope, and similar exercises unless you exert strenuous effort by lifting your knees to your waist with each bounce. The heavier you are, the more the rebound will lessen the difficulty of the exercise. The devices do reduce the stress upon the joints, ligaments, and tendons that results from vertical pounding. But the rebound causes side-to-side stress of these tissues similar to the wobbling ankles of a beginning ice skater. Consequently, they are not a remedy or alternative exercise for those with ankle or knee problems, calf-muscle strains, or Achilles tendinitis. These devices cost between $50 and $200.

A treadmill, which costs $350 and upward, has a number of advantages. Most have both odometers and speedometers. The more sophisticated ones can be adjusted to increase the grade and consequent intensity of the exercise. These start at $840 and can run into thousands of dollars. Many people find that they don't get the sore knees, back, and other maladies associated with running on a hard surface when they use a treadmill.

A rowing machine is excellent for building aerobic strength. It is of special value to women because it exercises the neglected large muscle groups in the shoulders, arms, back, and abdomen—all areas in which women tend to lose a disproportionate amount of strength as they age. Because so many large muscle groups are exercised when you use this machine, it promotes a high rate of subcutaneous fat loss. The machines cost about $350.

The principles in this chapter, such as specificity of training, overload, the aerobic effect, maximum heart rate, and intensity all apply to the stationary methods of aerobic exercise. They apply as well to bicycling, swimming, and running—the triathlon of endurance exercise. But these three need further comment because the tradeoffs are not direct, and each presents its own benefits, applications, and drawbacks.

Swimming

Theoretically, women could hold most of the world records in swimming, including speed, if we developed our maximal aerobic and anaerobic power to the same degree as men. Women can swim a given distance with about 30 percent less energy expenditure. This is probably because of our greater fat content, which makes it easier to stay afloat. Our greater fat placement in the thighs helps keep the legs higher in the water, which makes the body more streamlined and reduces drag. Swimming is second only to cross-country skiing as an overall body conditioner. It forces you to use your upper body, and it builds strength in the abdominal muscles and, to a lesser extent, the leg muscles. If you use several different strokes during a workout, which you should, you can do more to build overall strength than you would by cycling or running.

Since you don't bear your own weight while swimming, the task will be too easy unless you consciously work at it, especially if you are overfat. On the other hand, the relative weightlessness takes stress off vulnerable areas such as the lower back, spine, knees, and ankles. It is an ideal exercise for the aged, handicapped, obese, or those recovering from an injury. Unlike cycling or running, it increases flexibility. This is because water supports the body and allows a greater range of motion while decreasing the chance of straining a muscle. This is why it is often used as physical therapy for stiffened or atrophied muscles.

The energy cost of swimming is about four times greater than running the same distance. Doing a crawl (freestyle) stroke for a quarter-mile (440 yards) is roughly equal to jogging one mile. Most public pools in the United States are twenty-five yards long; thus you must swim eighteen lengths to equal a quarter-mile. The maximal heart rate while swimming is about thirteen beats slower than normal per minute. This may be the result of the cooling effect of the water and possibly the horizontal position of the body. To determine a swimming heart rate for training, subtract thirteen plus your age from 220 and figure the percentage of your maximal heart rate at which you are working from this. Keep a stopwatch in a plastic bag at the end of the pool to take your pulse so that you can get to know what it feels like to swim at a certain heart rate. It is harder to get air while swimming, and doing this efficiently is one of the results of becoming a good swimmer. If you are a poor swimmer, regardless of your level of fitness, you won't do as well aerobically in the water. If you want to increase your swimming stamina, do it in the water.

Different strokes take varying amounts of energy. The percentage of power delivered by the arms versus the legs also varies with the stroke. The less taxing strokes are those that distribute power more equally between the arms and legs.

	Kcal per Minute	Percent of Power from Arms	Percent of Power from Legs
Butterfly	12	70	30
Freestyle (crawl)	9	80	20
Backstroke	8	75	25
Breaststroke	7	50	50
Sidestroke	6	50	50

A quarter-mile is a good distance per workout to aim for if you are a beginning swimmer or relatively unfit. An intermediate distance would be between half a mile (880 yards) and a mile (1,760 yards). Above one and a half miles would be considered advanced. This adds up to roughly (at ten minutes per quarter-mile) ten minutes of swimming for the beginner, between twenty and forty minutes for the intermediate, and sixty minutes or more for those doing advanced endurance training.

You do sweat when you swim, and water is lost through breathing. Fluids should be replaced as they would during and under the same conditions as other exercise. (See chapters 8 and 9 for more information on fluid replacement.) The urge to urinate upon contact with water is common enough to have given rise to medical speculation but no definite answers. Accidents in the pool usually result from collisions or mistakes made while diving. It is customary to swim counterclockwise within one lane in the pool. Let faster swimmers pass when you near the end of the pool in order to avoid collisions. Drowning is most common in open water when a person swims out too far and then panics or swims in water that is too cold.

For a swimmer to be advanced enough to get out of the pool and attempt the ocean, rivers, or lakes, she should be able to: (1) swim a continuous mile, (2) do 440 continuous yards each of the crawl, breaststroke, sidestroke, and backstroke, (3) keep afloat for an indefinite period by a combination of treading water, backfloat, and the technique of drownproofing.[6] (For an explanation of drownproofing, see chapter 4.)

Swimming caps and suits without decorative paraphernalia are the best for efficiency in the water because they cause less drag. Goggles are your main protection from eye irritation, and they are a must if you wear contact lenses. Chemically treated water and saltwater can cause the cornea of the eye to swell, which in turn causes light rays to bend as they pass through the cornea. This creates the halos you see around lights when you have been in the water for some time. The outer cells of the cornea may actually begin to shed after repeated exposure to chlorine. It will feel like you have something in your eye. Goggles can prevent this, and a day or two of rest should cure it.

To prevent goggles from fogging, apply saliva to the inner surface of the lenses. Special products consisting of a thick, oily substance can be used instead and don't have to be constantly reapplied.

Sensitive skin can be partially protected from water and chemicals by a light coating of petroleum jelly. Taking a shower after swimming will wash off the chemicals in the water.

Swimmer's ear, a fairly common ailment, comes about when skin oil and some layers of skin are washed away from being in the water for a long period. You will have an earache, and if you tug gently on the ear, it will hurt and pus may ooze from the skin. Mild cases can be treated with vinegar used full strength or diluted with an equal amount of water. If symptoms are severe, such as fever, swelling, extreme pain, and heavy discharge, or if the vinegar doesn't work, see a physician.

One of the primary assets of pool swimming is the low injury rate. Although it does not present the hazards to the lower back, knees, and ankles as weight-bearing exercises do, you will probably have some muscle and joint pain if you are a beginner or increase the difficulty of your training. The most common complaint is shoulder pain, followed by knee problems and occasionally a back problem. The primary culprit is the butterfly stroke when it comes to actual injuries such as shoulder dislocation. The lower back may also be injured by this stroke, especially if you do the stroke infrequently. Shoulder pain is to the swimmer as knee pain is to the runner and skier. The primary ways to avoid it are to increase slowly and do strength training and warm-up/warm-down stretching.

The following strength-training exercises for swimmers are arranged so that you can do them according to whatever system is available to you. Pick the ones you want, but be sure to do the number suggested for each muscle group. The numbers beside each exercise refer to the number of the muscle groups that are worked by each exercise.

1. Hips, lower back, buttocks (two exercises)
2. Chest, upper arms (two exercises)
3. Thighs, hamstrings (one exercise)
4. Calves, shins, ankles (one exercise)
5. Shoulders, triceps (two exercises)
6. Abdomen (one exercise)
7. Biceps (two exercises)
8. Forearms, wrists (one exercise)

Free Weights	*Universal or Nautilus*	*No Weights*
Clean and press (1,2,3,4,5,6,7,8)	Bench press (2,5,7)	Bent-leg sit-up (1,6)
Hyperextension (1)	Calf raise (4)	Calf raise (4)
Leg raise (1,6)	Leg curl (1,3,4)	Dip (2,5,7)
Pullover (2,5,6)	Leg press (3)	Leg raises (1,6)
Quarter-squat (1,3,4,6)	Overhead press (5,7)	Lunge (1,3)
Shoulder fly/side-arm raise (2,5)	Pulldown behind neck (1,5,7)	Pullup (2,5,7,8)
Upright rowing (2,5,7)	Shoulder shrug (5)	Pushup (2,5,7)
	Tricep extension (5,8)	Quarter deep-knee bend (1,3,4)

The basics of warm-up/warm-down stretching are given later in this chapter. The stretches recommended for swimmers are head/neck rotation, hyperextension (standing), lunge, pulldown behind neck, standing V, and toe touch.

Bicycling

The acceptance and progress of women in distance cycling can be measured by the fact that the 1984 Olympics in Los Angeles will include a thirty-two-mile women's road race for the first time. At the same time, the interest in bicycle touring and commuting has created a general public for cycling that hasn't existed before. The women's open-frame bicycle is becoming less common as women opt for the stronger men's closed frame. With the more stable structure of the closed frame comes less need to add pounds by reinforcing the frame. An open frame may make mounting more convenient if you have a child carrier attached to the back. (A child carrier that can be mounted on the top bar of men's bikes is available for about $19 from Elliott Industries, Inc., Box 4491, Dept. O, Boulder, Colorado 80306. This carrier is for older children who know enough to hang on to the handlebars.)

Cycling can be an excellent aerobic conditioner. Because it is

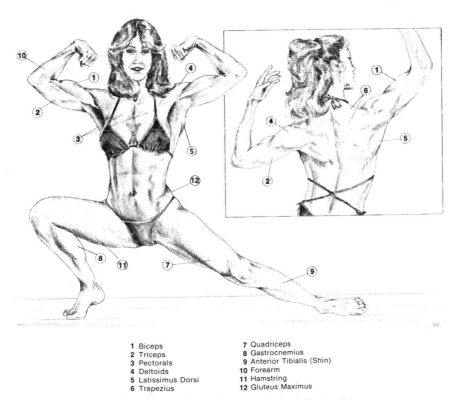

1 Biceps	7 Quadriceps
2 Triceps	8 Gastrocnemius
3 Pectorals	9 Anterior Tibialis (Shin)
4 Deltoids	10 Forearm
5 Latissimus Dorsi	11 Hamstring
6 Trapezius	12 Gluteus Maximus

Female musculature. Drawing by Janis Rockwell.

nonweight bearing, it also avoids some of the hazards of lower-body stress and injuries, and it is a good alternative if you find that running causes excessive jarring of the back and knees. However, in cycling, like swimming, there's the temptation to not work hard enough to get the training effect.

"I find that I have to triple both cycling distance and training time to get the same benefits as I would running," says Janene Willer, a former national class racer. "I've recently heard some estimates that it should be four times as much." According to Dr. Kenneth Cooper, the person who coined the word *aerobics*, the equivalent energy expenditure of jogging two miles in twenty minutes is cycling five and a half miles in twenty minutes. It is estimated that you need at least forty minutes for a minimum workout on a bicycle to get the aerobic effect.

Unless you ride on level terrain, cycling develops both the aerobic and anaerobic systems. The anaerobics inevitably figure in when climbing hills. It is here that both the weight of the bicycle and the rider become important. If you were able to reduce total weight by one-half, which is unlikely, your speed would be twice as great. However, the heavier the rider, the weight saved by investing in a lightweight racing bike will be comparatively less important.

Hills and grades are the nemesis of both beginning and advanced cyclists. On a ten-speed bike, the tenth speed is the smallest, lowest gear. It gives the rider the greatest mechanical advantage over gravity. The ninth speed gives a little less, and so on. It is best to train to the point that you can keep the lowest gears in reserve for the steepest grades. A good way to do this is to master a stretch of road in the lowest gear, then switch to the next lowest gear, and so on, and keep at it until the hill is no longer that difficult in higher gears. You get the most results for your effort by pedaling in a gear that allows sixty-five to eighty-five revolutions per minute.[7] This is a fairly quick pace, and you should feel the tension in your legs throughout the entire revolution.

Bicycling lends itself to interval or fartlek training. High-intensity sections can be gauged to end where there are stop signs or other obstructions. Rest periods can correspond with the downhill portions of the course. Nevertheless, the training course must be on a secondary road or in a park or suburban area.

If you plan to take up touring, which is often the logical consequence of bicycling for fitness, how hard you should work on hills depends upon what kind of country you intend to tour. Don't assume that if you commute to work and shopping you're prepared for an extended tour. Long-distance touring, according to one woman, is to commuting as walking to the post office is to backpacking.[8]

When are you ready for touring? Day outings can be done comfortably when your workout sessions reach thirty minutes, your pace is ten miles per hour, you can cycle continuously for fifteen miles, and you average no less than twenty-five miles weekly. Once you reach a peak pace of fifteen miles per hour, can ride thirty-five miles nonstop, and average no less than sixty miles a week riding, you're ready for touring. At this level of proficiency you can do trips planned in ten- to twenty-mile intervals. At the point when your workouts exceed ninety minutes, your peak pace is twenty or more miles per hour, you can ride fifty miles nonstop, and your weekly mileage is no less than eighty miles, you're ready for the world!

If your training ground does not include hills and your tour objective does, a good preparation is to run stairs—lots of them. And six to eight weeks before an actual tour, you should start carrying the same weight on your bike that you will during the tour. All this training could conceivably be done on a stationary cycle, especially if your ergometer can be adjusted to increase the force that is needed to imitate climbing hills. But that kind of high mileage would be deathly boring. It is better

Sally Desonia, a Salt Lake City cyclist, shows the intensity of mind and body needed to race. This was especially so of the Portneuf Valley Stage Race time trial, some eight to ten miles over a plain and up the side of a mountain. Photograph by the author.

to keep in shape during inclement weather by running, cross-country skiing, or even swimming.

Bicycling requires by far the largest investment of the triathlon of endurance sports—biking, running, and swimming. A ten-speed bicycle ranges in cost from $250 to several thousand dollars. Other necessities include a helmet ($40), pump ($18), tool kit ($28), riding shoes ($35), and toe clips ($10 to $15). Bicycle camping requires an even greater investment, with the necessary panniers (saddlebags), rack, handlebar pack, and so forth adding another $200. Of course the camper can recoup this money quickly by the savings on motels. Other camping gear, such as sleeping bags, tents, and stoves, of course make the initial cost considerably higher.

Dehydration, heat illness, and hypothermia are all hazards to consider during distance cycling, including training. Your bike should be equipped to carry adequate water supplies at all times. You should also carry the range of clothing to be prepared for changes in weather. A light, water-resistant poncho (not a slicker) is a must.

The majority of cycling accidents result in abrasions or road burns. They occur most frequently on the left side of the body because the cyclist will try to avoid falling from the right side of the bike, where the derailleur is located. The most frequently skinned areas are the hips, elbows, and knees. Among the most frequent causes of falls are road conditions, including the tailwind of semitrucks, and flat tires. The best protection from road burns is to cover the arms and legs. However, except on cool days, when heat buildup is not a problem, this isn't always practical. You could wear long pants and a long-sleeved top when road conditions are hazardous, then switch back to shorts as conditions (light traffic, smooth roads) allow.

A helmet is necessary if you ride at high speeds or on the open road. Many competitive cyclists prefer leather instead of hard-shell helmets. But one distance master racer feels that leather helmets are worthless. "They make the cyclist look like a gladiator, and some racers do approach cycling that way," he says. "But if you truly want to protect your head, you need a hard-shell helmet that won't cave in under impact." Factors to remember when choosing a helmet are ventilation, lightness, peripheral vision, hearing, a color that reflects the heat and makes you visible, and a sturdy chin strap that will keep the helmet on your head.

Saddle sores are common among distance cyclists. The most frequent cause is excess movement across the seat. This can't be helped, but a seat set too high or low grossly exaggerates this movement. The seat should be adjusted so that your knee is just barely bent when the leg is fully extended on the pedal. A saddle somewhat wider than that used for racing is designed to fit a woman's wider pelvic bone. It is recommended for distance cycling because it increases the area over which impact is absorbed.

Shorts with a smooth chamois or cotton lining help prevent saddle sores. Wearing two pairs of riding shorts or two pairs of underpants also reduces friction. Once underpants or shorts become damp from perspiration, the protection is lost. Frequent changes are necessary to avoid saddle sores and boils, or "road rash," as they're sometimes called. If a sore develops, carefully cleanse it with an antibacterial soap both at the beginning and at the end of the ride to lower the chance of infection. Use a sponge as a pad over the irritated area and apply ice to reduce pain. If a sore opens or becomes painful, take a day off to allow it some time to heal.

A bicycle that fits you will do much to reduce injuries. A bicycle the right height should give you at least an inch leeway between your crotch and the top bar when you straddle it while wearing your riding shoes. Riding shoes have almost no heel, so you're likely to be shorter than you are when wearing street shoes. The adjustable stem (the post on which the handlebars are mounted) must also be the right height to reduce stress on the upper back and shoulders. You should be able to touch your elbow to the tip of the saddle while your fingers just touch the back of the handlebars. Too much drop in the handlebars can also produce upper-body pain. You will have to hyperextend your neck to be able to see, and this in turn will cause neck pain. While you're bound to have some shoulder and neck pain the first few days of a tour and during difficult road and wind conditions, it should be only temporary if your bicycle is fitted well.

Handlebars should be covered with a thick padding to absorb shock. If you use a handlebar bag, you should also purchase a bracket to hold it away from the top of the handlebars; otherwise the bag takes up too much space. This seemingly minor point is important: Change the position of your hands every five minutes. The more space on the handlebars, the more places to put your hands. This frequent changing of position helps prevent the painful and possibly dangerous compression of the ulnar nerve in the hand. The nerve branches in two as it enters the palm. One branch extends across the palm and the other to the insides of the ring and little fingers. Constant weight upon it can compress the fibers and result in the inability to transmit impulses. Warning signs are a numbness or tingling in the ring or little finger and/ or weakness in the hand. These symptoms must not be ignored because, at worst, they can lead to permanent paralysis of the hand.

Cyclists and runners are often troubled by *chondromalacia patella,* in which the surface between the kneecap and the joint becomes cluttered with debris from the damaged joint. Among runners, incorrect foot placement is often thought to be the cause. Likewise, incorrect foot placement on the pedal may exacerbate the problem. Running shoes are not really good for bicycle touring. Touring shoes should have deep channels in the sole, which align the foot correctly on the pedal. On other cycling shoes, most often those for racing, cleats are added. If these are incorrectly placed, they force continual misalignment. Cleats should be put on new shoes when you have ridden far enough to leave the pedal's impression on the sole of the shoe. The thin pedals common on ten-speeds often leave little surface area for the bottom of the foot. This can result in localized pressure, which can cause severe pain. Good cycling shoes will have a rigid plate in the sole that distributes the force against the pedal more evenly and reduces or eliminates this source of pain. The pedal should be wide enough so that your foot doesn't extend beyond it.

Toe clips are important because they maximize the power of the pedal stroke. "They increase the efficiency of pedaling 100 percent," says Janene Willer. They harness the powerful calf and shin muscles, which contribute to power output during the upsweep of the pedal. But should you begin to lose control of the bike, remember to kick free or release your feet from the toe clips.

The following strength-training program for bicyclists can be adapted to whatever system is available to you. The numbers beside each exercise refer to the number of the muscle groups that are worked by the exercise.

1. Hips, lower back, buttocks (one exercise)
2. Chest, upper arms (two exercises)
3. Thighs, hamstrings (two exercises)
4. Calves, shins, ankles (two exercises)
5. Shoulders, triceps (two exercises)
6. Abdomen (one exercise)
7. Biceps (one exercise)
8. Forearms, wrists (one exercise)

Free Weights	*Universal or Nautilus*	*No Weights*
Bench fly (2,5,7)	Bench fly (2,5,7)	Bent-leg sit-up (1,6)
Bench press (2,5,7)	Bench press (2,5,7)	Dip (2,5,7)
Calf raise (4)	Bent-knee sit-up (6)	Lunge (1,3,4)
Clean and press	Calf raise (4)	Pushup (2,5,7)
(1,2,3,4,5,6,7,8)	Front pulldown (2,7,8)	Quarter-squat (1,3,4,6)
Lunge (1,3)	Leg curl (1,3,4)	Toe raise (1,4)
Quarter squat (1,3,4,6,7)	Leg press (1,3,4)	Squeeze tennis ball (8)

Distance bicycling is one endeavor in which the temptation to ignore stretching is less likely to occur. Stretching is not only a welcome relief, it's essential for relaxing the legs both before and after cycling. Knee pain is common during training increases in mileage, frequency, and intensity, and when climbing hills. Other areas that frequently register overuse strain are the calves and hamstrings. The stretches recommended for cyclists focus on these problem areas as well as relaxing other areas of the body that are strained by cycling: head/neck rotation, hyperextension, leg raise, lunge, squat, and toe touch.

Running

So much has been written about running that it's hard to add much to it. It is worth mentioning that the 1984 Olympic games will be notable in that women will be allowed to run the marathon for the first time and also to do distance biking.

Women are getting faster, of that there's no doubt. The present women's world marathon record, 2:25:28, is held by New Zealand's Allison Roe. It is 26 percent faster than the 1967 women's record. In contrast, Alberto Salazar's present 2:08:13 is only 1 percent faster than the men's 1967 record. This doesn't mean that men have been slacking off for the past fifteen years, but that women are finally using their potential.

Although women go on recreational outings with men, most would rather compete against other women. All-women's races such as those sponsored by Bonne Bell, Avon, and the YWCA draw proportionately three times as many women as mixed races. One "why" of this is simple: It's nice to be the one to break the ribbon, and the winners get more attention than they would in a mixed race. Witness the countless mixed races in which women's times are often overlooked entirely by sports reporters. Another reason women's races are preferred is that women can enjoy the support and camaraderie of other women as they begin to involve themselves in yet another traditionally male-dominated sport.

Cross-country running is a track event that has slowly begun to find practitioners among the general public. It is much more difficult than road running because of the uneven terrain and often extreme grades. The following excerpt from an article that appeared in the unfortunately defunct *Women in the Wilderness Quarterly,* written by Anne Ketchin, a former Women in the Wilderness regional contact in Boulder, Colorado, is a thoughtful soul-searching of the why of running, wilderness use, and heroism.

It has been seven months since I last "ran"—twenty-seven miles over three passes (the highest was 12,700') to cross the Continental Divide. The run was a culmination of an unspoken promise to myself, made in January 1974, after I was told I had a rare fungus meningitis and that the cure was a long, uncomfortable, and dangerous process. It was a little like worming the horse—the dose of poison being just under the threshold of the horse, and hopefully just over the threshold of the worms.

I pushed hard towards recovery. I forced myself to run, on mountain trails and roads. I could hardly stand, and failed consistently at interaction with other people, but I went running. How? I don't know. I was terrified. It wasn't smart, but I was compelled. Why? I don't know. I was filled with emotion and terror which I struggled to hide for the next five years. Each time I stepped onto my trails I tentatively put one set of stiff toes forward, encased in a running shoe, asking with the movement "Do you still love me?" The mountains would expand before me and I would feel like an orphan who had heard someone answer "Yes." Eventually I thought I was as ready as I would ever be. There was some despair in the thought: that THIS would be as strong as I could get.

The day dawned cold and grey—sleeting.

The trails were slippery, and the rocks were loose because of the moisture in the soil. Inside I was cursing in a helpless childlike fashion, feeling thwarted on this one day I NEEDED help. But the old bootstraps optimism took hold.

My friends gave me a wonderful send-off at 7 a.m. I did in fact have help from people, for they met me in a couple of places along the route with orange juice (a mistake. Don't ever try it), and big smiles. But for half the route there was no way they could reach me.

The weather took its toll, but I refused to stop. My knees were beginning to stiffen and the pain was occasionally nauseating. At the top of Arapaho Pass, the point of no return, one of them froze up on me temporarily, and still I refused to turn back.

The run was much more of a metaphor for my experience with illness than I had planned on. Much of what I might have learned from being sick had been put off because I had been unable to live through it at the time. I was not to be permitted to get away with this forever, however.

At about mile nine the metaphor began to emerge with uneasy clarity, taking me on a bobsled ride of confused, intermingled thoughts. I could no longer create for myself a nice division between the time of my illness and each moment of this run. A portion of my journal from after the run reflects this confusion.

The sound of my breathing was too heavy. It sounded like someone else was doing the breathing, so I checked my chest, taking a good long look. It was moving. There were footsteps which were becoming more and more audible, almost drowning out the heavy breathing. I glanced around, a little calmer now, but still hyper with anxiety. And I saw no one else. Fog was all I could see; dense white fog, dizzying and disorienting. Something was happening to my muscles which I could not understand; they seemed to twitch right out of control.

I strained my right arm a little, moving it from under the covers towards the button. There's something wrong. I need to call the nurse. I can't control these chills and jerks. It seemed like a century before I reached that button. The footsteps were in my room, but few words were spoken. Both were soon gone.

The fog cleared some, lifting a little. More of the tundra was visible and for the first time I had a sense of movement through time and space. The footsteps were my own; the breathing was my own; the rocks and grasses took on color. My aching knees were my own, and the cold moist air at 12'000' was real to me. I still could not see the deep glaciated valley below me, or the peaks ahead, but enough of the landscape showed itself to give me the confidence that I was really there, on the tundra, running very slowly along a rocky path towards Glacier Overlook.

At mile fourteen I plunged down from Glacier Overlook dropping 1,100' in under two miles. My left knee revolted in earnestness. In a helpless, childlike explosive fashion I cried to myself, HOW ARBI-TRARY! WHY TODAY? and said, TO HELL WITH YOU! The metaphor rushed over me, no matter how hard I tried to avoid it. What choice did I have really? When I had been ill I had felt the same way. The last miles of the run were extremely painful. Yet as I remember that final mile I could have run further, riding on the exhilaration of realizing I was coming in, coming to rest, seeing my friends there. What an incredible boost and undefinable strength human beings can give each other if only they will!

In writing this story it sounds worse than it really was, like many similar things. At the time it was just something I had to do, and I accepted it. The retelling gives it a glamour that I did not feel.

Now, looking back, I am happy with what I did . . . At the time I found myself in the midst of a strange depression, which began about halfway through the run. The key to why I felt this way lay in my disillusionment with the promises I felt had been made to me: If you really want it and can overcome your attitudes you can do anything.

Even as I took the final steps, filled with joy at seeing my friends, I knew I had not finished what I had set out to do. I had not achieved in one sweeping thrust the end of an era, erasing all remembered emotional pain. That block in time was still with me. I was arrogant to think I could put an end to the process of grieving and growing through sheer effort and symbolic statement.

Perhaps Anne's inability to put aside grieving in one fell swoop accounts for why people continue to go back to the wilds in spite of trips the recounting of which makes you wonder why they went. The need for renewal is constant.

On a more practical level, one woman compares cross-country running to an obstacle course in basic training. You can't daydream and dodge rocks, prairie dog holes, and sagebrush all at the same time. It can be the ultimate challenge for the runner because it demands agility, grace, and balance. A few precautions and considerations should be kept in mind when cross-country or trail running. Stick to lightly used trails on which the likelihood of colliding with a hiker or other user is small. Never run in bear, moose, or other big-game habitat for the dual reason that it's dangerous and incompatible with the "go lightly" approach of low-impact backcountry use. In a tragic incident, a woman was jogging a trail in Yellowstone National Park. She surprised a grizzly sow on the trail, and it attacked her. Fortunately she lived, but she had to be hospitalized for extensive reconstructive surgery.

Open hilly country is an ideal choice because it provides not only the challenge of getting off the pavement, but the reassurance of being able to see what lies ahead. A good place to run off-season is a ski resort. "My husband and I do the opposite of what most people would do at a ski resort. We run up the hill and take the lift back down," says one woman. This avoids the tremendous strain on the knees, ankles, and quads of running down a steep grade. "The catwalks make ideal trails, and you don't have much worry about running into other people."

Walking or running up and down stadium stairs is a good supplemental workout for the cross-country runner, hiker, skier, or mountaineer because it is good preparation for climbs and descents. Your calves won't be unpleasantly surprised if you have been descending long flights of stairs, and your hamstrings will be prepared for the uphill stretches.

Bob Anderson, author of *Stretching* and adviser to various professional football teams, who should certainly know about stadium stairs, provides some suggestions for running stairs. When you start, walk up them two at a time at a steady pace. The descent is done in a traverse rather than straight down to prevent undue stress on the knees and ankles. As you become accustomed to stairs, you can run them, and descents can be made to imitate the degree of slope or grade you would take down a mountain. But remember that most trails descend using a traverse.

The majority of running injuries occur among beginners who expect too much and among distance runners who put abnormal demands on their bodies. If you follow the general principles in this chapter, you should be able to avoid many stress/overuse injuries. The areas most commonly injured are the knees, Achilles tendon, shins, and

ankles. The most common minor injuries are blisters and bruised toenails. Blisters result from increased mileage or shoes that don't fit.
Covering the sensitive spot with masking tape or moleskin can help
avoid blisters. But do this before a blister develops or after it heals.
Tincture of benzoin can be applied daily to toughen the skin. You can
also grease your feet with Vaseline before putting on your socks.

Black toenails are contusions caused by short shoes or long toenails. To avoid them, keep your toenails clipped and make sure that
your shoes fit. The nail will eventually fall off, and you don't have to
stop running unless it is too painful. When buying running shoes, stand
with your feet pointing downhill on an incline. Your toes shouldn't
touch the end of the shoe. If they do, they will bump against the end
of your shoe when you run downhill and possibly cause black toenails.
An application of Vaseline on the inner thighs helps prevent chafing,
or "chub thigh," a problem more common in women.

Uterine cramps, which can be induced by exercise, may be caused
by reduced blood flow to the uterus, and this may cause the release of
inflammatory, pain-producing prostaglandins. Cramps often afflict beginning joggers and more experienced women who push themselves
hard. Aspirin inhibits the release of prostaglandins. Try taking two
aspirin half an hour before running. If aspirin doesn't work, try a
stronger antiprostaglandin such as the prescription drug Motrin.

Suggested strength-training exercises for the runner are given according to the various training systems available. The numbers beside
each exercise refer to the muscle groups that are worked by the exercise.

1. Hips, lower back, buttocks (two
   exercises)
2. Chest, upper arms (two exercises)
3. Thighs, hamstrings (two exercises)

4. Calves, shins, ankles (two exercises)
5. Shoulders, triceps (one exercise)
6. Abdomen (two exercises)
7. Biceps (one exercise)

Free Weights	*Universal or Nautilus*	*No Weights*
Bench fly (2,5,7)	Bench press (2,5,7)	Bent-leg sit-up (1,6)
Bent-leg sit-up (6)	Calf raise (4)	Dip (2,5,7)
Clean and press	Front pulldown (2,7)	Lunge (1,3,4)
(1,2,3,4,5,6,7)	Leg curl (1,4)	Pushup (2,5,7)
Dead lift (1,4,5)	Leg extension (1,4)	Quarter-squat (1,3,4,6)
Quarter-squat (1,3,4,6)	Pullover (1,5,6,7)	
Roman chair (6)	Roman chair (6)	
	Toe raise (4)	

The stretches suggested for runners are the calf stretch, lunge,
hyperextension (standing), raised leg, standing V, and toe touch.

Strength Training

The image of ideal female beauty has changed in the last twenty years. The *Playboy* centerfold of 1963 is positively Rubenesque compared to the contemporary siren, who looks like she'd be almost as at home on a belay as a bearskin. The *Vogue* model was as thin then as she is now, but she also has acquired identifiable muscles in at least her calves and thighs. Gone forever, we hope, are the gravity-defying hairdos of the 1960s and the equally rigid girdles.

A major breakthrough for the acceptance of woman as athlete, in addition to Title IX of the Education Acts of 1972, was a study published in 1974, which seemed to prove that women and girls could acquire similar percentages of strength as men and boys without masculinizing muscle enlargement.[9] Gone was that barrier to the weight room, not an insignificant development because strength and power are most quickly acquired with weight training.

The benefits of weight training, whether the weight is imposed by a barbell, Nautilus machine, or your own body, are not confined to strength alone. Weight training can increase endurance, speed, and flexibility. Inflexibility comes not so much with the acquisition of strength, but with massive enlargement of certain muscles while the antagonistic muscles are neglected. Muscular strength and endurance are not proportionate to muscle mass. In women particularly, there can be a high level of strength without a great deal of mass. That flexibility improves following a proper weight-training program is reason enough to consider the term "muscle bound" a misnomer, writes Edward L. Fox in *Sports Physiology*. So women can look like women yet be strong enough to be anthracite coal miners. And men can look like men and have the grace and flexibility of a Bolshoi Ballet dancer.

There are four basic methods of strength training. The cheapest is using your own body as the resisting force by doing pushups, pullups, sit-ups, and dips. This method has its limitations, and its benefits are confined almost entirely to the upper body, since there are no equivalent lower-body exercises. Most women are not strong enough to lift their own weight, so this method can be discouraging, since the gains can seem so few and hard won. It has been shown that people tend to improve more quickly if they have immediate external feedback.

If you use this system and cannot do complete pushups, pullups and dips, there are intermediate measures. A modified pushup, in which you rest on your bent knees, not your toes, can be done until you can do full pushups. Dips and pullups can be done at first by starting at the top of the position and lowering your body, then starting over at the top. Eventually you will be able to do a full up-and-down pushup or dip. In the meantime it's nice to know that the most strength is gained during that portion of the exercise in which you lower your body (or other resistance). (See page 203 for instructions about how to do dips.)

When you first begin a strength-training program, you can substitute jugs filled with water or sand for genuine barbells and dumbbells or the Universal or Nautilus system. But you will quickly get to the point that these won't be heavy enough. Now you will have to consider the expense of either joining a gym or club or acquiring weights to use at home. A home system can cost between $500 and $600, not including the weights. Of necessity, they are hardly as complete as what you will find at a club, high school, or college. Most home sets are limited in the amount of weight (plates) they're designed to handle, unless you purchase professional-quality weights, which cost $1.00 per pound. Before making a financial commitment, find out how much weight you can reasonably expect to handle. Unless you are exceptional or very dedicated, you won't need more than two-thirds of your own body weight. The only exceptions to this are leg presses and front pulldowns, which usually can't be done on a home system anyway. The cost of a club can start at about $300 for those such as the YMCA. Universities and high schools, if they allow public access, can be considerably cheaper. However, you won't necessarily get an instructor, as you should with a club.

If you have the option of choosing a system similar to Olympian, Nautilus, or Universal, there are a few points to consider. The Nautilus is based on a system of weights and gears (cams) designed to distribute the weight evenly throughout the range of motion of any given exercise. Of the three, it appears to do the most to promote flexibility. The Universal system is a simpler version of the Nautilus and is based on weights and pulleys. Free weights, usually Olympian, were the first to be developed, and they allow the greatest diversity. Many professional and varsity athletes use them in combination with either the Universal or Nautilus system. You can't cheat on them by allowing one side of your body to carry more of the load than the other because you *must* balance them evenly to lift them. They promote strength in the hands, which is important for certain outdoor sports. It takes less actual exercise to accomplish the same goals with free weights because you can do blockbuster exercises like the clean and press. The main drawback of free weights is that to be safe lifting a big load, you need a strong, experienced person present as a spotter.

The sample weight-training chart in this chapter includes the major exercises and the muscle groups they strengthen. The application to specific weight-lifting systems is noted. Although the names of the specific exercises and machines may be slightly different on the system you use, you can figure out which is which by analyzing the movement. The exercises that require no weights have no notations beside them. Some, such as the lunge, which is normally done with weights, can be done without weights. An experienced friend or teacher or a book can explain the basic moves. Included here are some basic principles that many books overlook. Most books and articles written for women suggest exercises that are just too easy to build appreciable amounts of strength. They stress numerous repetitions with light weights. This is fine for the "firm and trim" approach of yore, but it's a waste of time if you plan to power your own body plus canoe, pack, and ropes against water, snow, and gravity. Consider how much you weigh, then think about how much good it will do you to monkey around with ten-pound barbells.

As with an aerobics program, your immediate improvement will be the most dramatic. A healthy young sedentary adult can improve her strength by up to 30 percent in just two weeks. If you are already using your upper-body muscles, it will take about six weeks to see significant strength gains. To reach a pinnacle of strength, beauty, and performance, it usually takes several years of intensive training. If you have gained strength and are wondering why you cannot see the muscles, the sheath of body fat is hiding them. Female body builders generally have only 5 or 6 percent body fat! You should work out at least twice a week to see any improvement in strength. If you work out three times a week, you can make the greatest gains without risking chronic fatigue. Allow at least forty-eight hours for recovery between bouts.

Muscle groups should be exercised using the largest first and the smallest last. No exercise involving the same muscle group should follow another. The following list, which emphasizes building overall strength, shows the order in which muscle groups should be exercised. Each session should consist of approximately twelve exercises.

1. Hips, lower back, buttocks (two exercises)
2. Chest and upper arms (two exercises)
3. Thighs and hamstrings (two exercises)
4. Calves, shins, ankles (one exercise)
5. Shoulders and triceps (two exercises)
6. Abdomen (one exercise)
7. Biceps (one exercise)
8. Forearms and wrists (one exercise)

Traditionally it has been assumed that lifting light weights and doing a large number of repetitions would increase endurance, and that lifting heavy weights and doing a small number of repetitions would increase strength. Actually, various studies suggest that the two types of training produce almost identical results.[10] If you want to keep your time in the weight room to a minimum, the general rule is to lift the maximum amount of weight you can for eight repetitions. Once you can lift this amount in good form for twelve repetitions, drop back to eight reps and increase the load.

You are at your limit when the muscle begins to "burn." Burns could indicate the beginning of small tears in the muscle. Some body builders subscribe to the theory of "no pain, no gain," but their objective is to build mass. Women body builders rarely come close to the hypertrophy of their male counterparts. The principal struggle of female body builders is to keep thin enough so the muscles will show. Burns, if they *are* a factor in mass, may partially account for the muscle size in female body builders. It *is* known that muscle size is not necessarily related to muscle strength!

Whether you should lift the weight quickly or slowly depends on the energy system you want to develop. In most outdoor sports the intermediate (lactic-acid) system is used most often, so it is suggested that you do the exercises slowly. The timing of the movement should be as uniform as possible. If you follow the short method, your weight-lifting sessions should last between twenty and forty-five minutes. Be sure to rest for at least one minute between each exercise. If you are tired, don't force repetitions. Most injuries occur during the final set. There are potential day-to-day variations of muscular strength of between 10 and 20 percent, so don't worry if you can't complete your normal number of repetitions on a given day.

Attire for weight lifting should be loose enough to allow maximum flexibility, light enough not to be too hot once you have warmed up, and designed so that you won't feel self-conscious. Sexy, lowcut leotards and the like are fine if you want to attract that much attention. Shorts should have a liner for the sake of privacy. A good, solid tennis shoe is recommended for balance and bearing heavy weights. Gloves with leather palms, such as those worn by cyclists and batters, will prevent calluses and blisters on the palms. An inexpensive, fairly tight pair of work or gardening gloves with the fingers lopped off also works.

Weight training should be most concentrated during periods when you are not active in the outdoors. While you are very active, one session a week in the weight room should be enough to maintain strength. The stretches recommended for weight lifting are the back hyperextension (standing), lunge, pulldown behind neck, raised leg, squat, and toe touch.

SAMPLE WEIGHT-TRAINING CHART

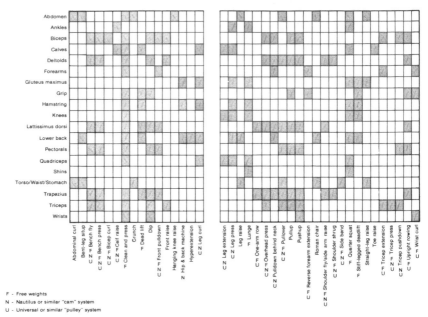

F - Free weights
N - Nautilus or similar "cam" system
U - Universal or similar "pulley" system

Warm-Ups

The trend toward warming up and stretching was no doubt inspired by pain. For those who looked on stretching as some kind of arcane ritual to dramatize the undertaking, it was a waste of time. Later, they found out that it is now advocated as a primary means of preventing injuries. So even if you think, like many, that it's boring and a little smugly exhibitionistic, never mind. It's good for you.

Warm-ups are a good idea before any strenuous undertaking, including and especially weight lifting. A warm-up raises the body and muscle temperature. This speeds oxygen to the muscles and helps enzyme activity, which in turn increases muscle metabolism. A higher temperature also increases muscle contraction and reflex times. Warm-ups also may decrease the danger of inadequate blood flow to the heart, which could occur with abrupt, strenuous exercise, and they lower the incidence of injuries to muscles and joints.

A person who doesn't warm down may feel abused, like a horse that has been "rode hard and put away wet." Besides giving you a chance to change gears, a warm-down clears lactic acid from the bloodstream and thus prevents both general and localized fatigue. Lactic acid is a fatigue-causing substance that results from the incomplete use of muscle sugar during the nonoxygen anaerobic process. Both warm-ups and warm-downs should consist of a stretching period and a period in which you do your planned activity at a moderate pace. The stretching period can last from ten to twenty minutes depending upon how strenuous your planned activity and how long it takes you to feel ready and your muscles primed at the beginning of a workout or relaxed at the end of one.

Stretches

Stretches should be done slowly and held in the final position for twenty to thirty seconds. Think about what you're doing. Feel it. It feels good, sensuous, like a cat when she stretches after sunning on a windowsill. You shouldn't bounce during the exercise because it can tear the muscle. During a routine, all the major muscle groups should be stretched, with the most emphasis upon the muscles that will be used and their antagonistic muscles. An example is the thigh muscle (quadriceps) and its antagonist, the hamstring.

The following stretches are the simplest of a seemingly endless array as old, vast, and graceful as yoga, K'ai Men, and gymnastics. Since it is often uncomfortable to sit or lie down at poolside, trailhead, roadside, or boat launch, for practicality only exercises that can be done standing are used. Many of these stretches were adapted from running and exercise lore, but it was Bob and Jean Anderson, in their book *Stretching,* who put stretching into its proper place in the sports world. These exercises are adapted in part from Bob and Jean.

Calf stretch: Lean forward with your hands against the wall. Put one toe forward, almost touching the wall. The other foot, held flat on the ground, should be extended behind you. You should feel the stretch in the calf of this extended leg. If you don't, put your body at a sharper angle.

Hyperextension (standing): Stand with your feet slightly apart and your hands on your hips. Bend backward until you feel the pull in the abdominal muscles. Hold for twenty seconds.

Head/neck rotation: Rotate your head slowly around in a full circle. Repeat in the reverse direction.

Lunge: This is similar to the lunge used in weight training. Step

Calf stretch. Photograph courtesy of Kathryn Collins, M.D.

Hyperextension. Photograph courtesy of Kathryn Collins, M.D.

Head/neck rotation. Photograph courtesy of Kathryn Collins, M.D.

Lunge. Photograph courtesy of Kathryn Collins, M.D.

Pulldown behind neck. Photograph courtesy of Kathryn Collins, M.D.

Raised leg. Photograph courtesy of Kathryn Collins, M.D.

Squat. Photograph courtesy of Kathryn Collins, M.D.

forward as far as you can with your right foot. Gently lower your body until your left knee almost touches the floor. The knee of your right leg should be directly over your right ankle. Hold for twenty seconds. Repeat with left foot forward.

Pulldown behind neck: This is also similar to a weight-training exercise of the same name. Hold a towel rigid between your hands in front of you. Raise your arms over your head and extend them as far down behind your neck and back as possible. Hold for ten seconds.

Raised leg: Elevate your heel on something fixed so that it will be level with or slightly higher than your hip. Hold on to your elevated ankle and bend forward as far as possible. Hold for twenty seconds.

Squat: This is *not* the weight-lifting squat. People use it all the time as custom in Nepal, where the floors are too dirty to sit on. Squat with your feet flat, knees spread, and toes pointed slightly outward. Your arms should be between your knees and your shoulders slightly bent. Hold for twenty or thirty seconds.

Standing V. Photograph courtesy of Kathryn Collins, M.D.

Standing V: Find something you can hold onto, like a ladder. Hold onto it at about level with your chest. Put your toes against the wall. Now push your rear end out as far as possible. Hold for twenty seconds.

Toe touch: Place your feet even with your shoulders. Bend knees slightly. Bend as far down as you can, touching toes/floor with finger-tips/palms. Hold for twenty seconds.

Treating Muscle and Joint Injuries

The initial self-treatment of most minor muscle and joint injuries is the same: Rest, Ice, Compression, Elevation (RICE).

Applying ice is the first step. It eases the pain by slowing the conduction of nerve impulses and preventing muscle spasms. It reduces swelling by constricting blood vessels in the injured area. Swelling itself is painful, and the degree of swelling is one measure of the severity of the injury. An ice pack should be applied for ten to twenty minutes every two hours at first until the swelling stabilizes; thereafter, apply it four times a day for the next two or three days, depending on how badly you're injured. If ice is not available, snow is an alternative. If necessary, immerse the entire limb in a cool lake or stream.

Heat application is not recommended because it increases swelling and may actually be harmful. It can prolong the recovery period if applied within the first one to three days. If your problem is stiffness, not an injury, heat may be useful, but stretching is probably better. Heat is also used to help restore motion in a joint after the swelling has subsided. However, its use for injury recovery is controversial, and some therapists and trainers don't recommend it at all.

Compression is a mechanical means of restricting swelling. When bandages are applied, they should be rolled rather than stretched on so as not to restrict circulation. The tape or Ace bandage should be the right size for the injured area. Bandages on knees, arms, and hands are difficult to keep on anyway, and the wrong size tape will make it harder. A two- or three-inch bandage is needed for the hand and wrist, a three- or four-inch bandage for the elbow or ankle, and a four- to six-inch bandage for the knee or thigh. The injured area should be taped until the swelling subsides.

Elevation also helps reduce swelling because it drains the blood and other fluids away from the injury. Elevate the injured area above the heart, especially the first day or two and as much as possible or convenient during the next few days.

Rest is important immediately after injury to encourage early healing of tissues and to avoid worsening the injury when the tissues are most vulnerable. Ideally, rest is continued until the pain largely subsides during rest *and* with movement. In practice, you will probably have to continue using the injured part, and nonelastic taping or a mechanical brace, if available, will help stabilize an injured joint.

Suspected dislocations and sprains should be immobilized, and medical treatment should be sought soon as possible. Sometimes this isn't possible in the field and a good first-aid book, such as a recent edition of *First Aid*, published by the American National Red Cross, or *Medicine for Mountaineering*, edited by James A. Wilkerson, is strongly recommended for any outing.

Chapter 2

Backpacking, Hiking, and Snowshoeing

Pathfinders

A voluminous stack of her correspondence, diary excerpts, and articles lies on my desk. It chronicles a woman who is one of the founders of trekking in its contemporary sense. Dr. Margaret "Jo" Prouty, now seventy-four, has led the kind of life many dream about yet never usher the chutzpah or dedication to put together. She is a mountaineer, but even with more than four hundred ascents in twenty-two countries, by her own account making the summit has been almost incidental to the adventure.

She began her mountaineering career in the Colorado Rockies while working at the resort town of Estes Park during summer vacations from the University of Nebraska. The Great Depression came when she was midway through studying for a premedical bachelor's degree. It was during her senior year that happenstance inspired a lifelong goal.

I walked downtown one noon to the largest department store, where on a strict budget I could get an individual chicken pie and glass of milk for 25¢. As I made my way to the elevator, I passed between tables of books being displayed on a publisher's sale. Liking books almost as well as food, I picked up the largest one, George Finch's *Making of a Mountaineer*. As I leafed through it, I was enthralled. Finding that I could have it for 25¢, I gave scant thought to my lost lunch. George was the first to use oxygen on Everest in 1922, and he established a new altitude record, although he did not reach the top. I became determined that I too would some day go look at Everest, although I had no thought of climbing it.

With practice and instruction, her mountaineering skills improved, and eventually she became a licensed guide in Rocky Mountain National Park. In the meantime she had entered medical school. The guiding gave summer employment during her medical training. "At last that, too, was accomplished, and I settled into the practice of pediatrics. Eventually my earned vacation times lengthened to six weeks yearly. I could get far afield in that time."

Far afield she definitely got through many adventures, often of her own organizing. In pursuit of mountains to climb, she says, she became an authority on the subject of primitive toilet facilities from the arctic to the equator, from sea level to 21,000 feet. While on a difficult, boggy approach to climb in the Ruwenzori Range (Mountains of the Moon) in Uganda in 1960, her party encountered jaguar tracks. "The trench dug for us [women] seemed close and unsheltered during daylight hours, but at night the journey was long and scary." As she left the primitive mountaineering hut that night to use this latrine, no more had the door closed than "the night cries of animals surrounded me." She worried that she would be pounced on the moment she put out her flashlight.

Mountaintops also presented problems. On a summit above 14,000 feet in Switzerland, she asked permission to remove the rope that joined her to her guide.

"Nein," he responded curtly and sat down resolutely, seemingly absorbed in the panorama of empty space surrounding us. It was in an era when methylene blue was thought to increase the oxygen-carrying capacity of the red cells. This chemical was eliminated in the expected way. Separating myself from the guide as much as my rope tether would permit, I watched the bright blue stain spread over the ice of the summit. Ineffectively I hacked at the marble-hard ice with my axe, hoping to cover the tattletale sign.[1]

A side trip to Lake Perron, during an attempt on the then unclimbed Mt. Yanapaccha (21,709 feet) in the Andes in 1958, when Jo was fifty, was hardly a promenade.

It was a day of frustration. We went high to avoid brush, only to return to escape the hazards of chasm and gorge. One gorge bisecting our way appeared to be uncrossable. Finding a herdswoman, Donato (the porter) learned that there was a path descending its face. At noon we ate our black bread, sausage and cheese beside the stream on its floor surrounded by semi-tropical vegetation; lush with trailing creepers and a few aerial flowers. We looked warily about when Donato reminded us that there were probably snakes as well.

By midafternoon we were in "jungle"; massive vines, interlacing branches, brush and thorns that caught and clung, tore and scratched. Often on hands and knees, faces torn by brush-like devil's club, we hacked our way.

The terrain was too rough for a campsite and our party split for easier search. Two made their way to the bank of a stream. At dusk, far above us, we saw their beacon fire. Through the "jungle" we again made our way until we reached our companions. They had found a tiny clearing. There being too little space to spread our bedrolls, we slept sitting up.

Our wakening prospect the next morning was more bushwacking, for the trail was on the other side of the river gorge. After several false starts in impenetrable brush and more belly-crawling through thorn thickets, we found a hazardous, frail, brush-work diversion dam. Hanging on to each other's ice axes for balance, we carefully snaked over the roaring river and reached the trail.

Once our troubles were over, we joyfully hid our packs and set out to explore the lake. It was good to sit on a boulder at the foot of the lake and quietly try to absorb all the beauty around me. The beautiful blue-green water laid in a great gorge which widened out above it with great snow spires flanking its upper reaches.

The lake presents a special danger in that it is naturally dammed by an enormous ice tongue and moraine. Remembering that only a few years before a similar lake burst and swept through Huras, killing several thousand people, including our porter's father, mother and brother, an inspector is kept at the lake to watch for high water, unusual amounts of rain or stresses on the ice tongue.

"Several years later," she adds, "an earthquake broke the ice tongue, the moraine washed out, and the resulting flood rushed down the canyon completely destroying the village of Yungay and killing all the people."

In 1964, eleven years after Mt. Everest's summit was first reached, Jo Prouty fulfilled her thirty-year ambition of seeing the earth's highest mountain. It was not the sort of trip casually arranged with a travel agent, she said, and she wondered how to arrange a trek half a world away that required thirty-five days of walking along a track so rough and precipitous that its length could be managed only on foot. No one that she knew of had arranged such a "tour" before. So she contacted a member of the British Embassy in Katmandu, Nepal, reasoning that if he could supply 909 porters for the 1963 U.S. Everest Expedition, surely he could find a few for her. She and two other women made the difficult trek to the isolated monastery of Thangboche at the base of the great mountain. They also made the world press as the "three elderly midwestern women trekkers aged 56, 62 and 64." The beauty of Jo Prouty and many accomplished women like her is that they have the healthy attitude of "you can do it too." This is exactly what she told the readers of *Summit* magazine in 1966 in her article about the adventure, "To the Foot of Everest."

Carol Alice Liska, who held the altitude record for U.S. women mountaineers until 1977 by reaching the summit of Noshaq (24,580 feet), has been on five expeditions and says that people who haven't done the same are more overwhelmed than those who have. "They don't realize that you work up to it in slow, slow steps. It takes awhile to realize that you can live through hiking fifteen miles a day with a pack on."

Says Virginia Nolan, who is thought to be the first woman to climb all of the 14,000-foot peaks in the continental United States, some sixty-nine peaks: "I have led many a climb and have seen individuals (many, many women) who got to the top through sheer determination. That is *so* important. If you are halfhearted about the whole thing, forget it. You have to want to do it and with that comes the willpower to do it and that is ninety percent of the whole game."

Of course not every woman who hikes, backpacks, or puts on a pair of snowshoes is interested in doing something of the magnitude of Alice Liska, Virginia Nolan, or Margaret Prouty. The point is that men have always had heroes and role models, from Davey Crockett to Sir Edmund Hillary, the first person to climb Mt. Everest. But the woman struggling up the trail with a burdensome pack has only recently been able to look to women for inspiration. The woman jogging a painfully boring track, round and round and round for eight or nine laps to log each mile, can think of Beverly Johnson, who in 1978 for ten days inched her way up the 3,600-foot vertical face of El Capitán in Yosemite National Park alone and with 100 pounds of gear in tow! The beginning jogger who counts each step can think of that woman on the wall of stone alone with her finger and toe holds who says she counted each day, each move, and each hold separately so that the magnitude of the undertaking wouldn't overwhelm her.

If jogging more than or even a mile or two seems an impossible and unlikely feat, consider Irene Ayres, who does three to four miles three times a week. "Not much, I guess, but what can one expect from a 68-year-old who is trying to run away from arthritis—and succeeding to some extent in some ways," she writes. Irene made a number of first ascents in Wyoming's Teton Mountains with her brother during the 1930s, and since then she has climbed mountains all over the country.

"My first backpacking trip was not fun," says one woman. "At least not at first. I spent all day wishing I could take the damn pack off and all night worrying I'd get eaten by a bear. It wasn't 'til the second day when we got up to a ridge line and I looked out over literally hundreds of miles of nothing but forest and mountains that I knew why I'd gone to all the trouble." She adds that while backpacking is still difficult it's no longer Herculean, and the key is to keep in shape.

Many women say that it's cultural conditioning that keeps women from expecting to be strong physically and competent in the outdoors, the implication being that such barriers are a load of historical baggage that can be dropped once you realize you have been dragging it around. Would that it were this easy. "I told one woman she had beautiful biceps and it hurt her feelings," says Janene Willer, an accomplished bicyclist. "It was a sensitive issue. Apparently she'd been made to feel strange about looking strong. Of course, I meant it as a compliment."

There is similar ambivalence among women as to how capable they can become and still be attractive to men. Can a man interact closely with a woman whose skills are equal or superior to his own? Anne LaBastille, in her book *Woodswoman*, which is about living alone in a cabin she built in the Adirondack wilderness, writes:

> The process of learning how to cope as a woman alone had backfired to an extent. I had noticed that the more competent I became, the more insecure certain men acted, or the more aggressive others behaved toward me . . . I was constantly faced with a choice. To go ahead and act competently and independently, as I had been doing, thereby alienating the man I cared for. Then I was forced to handle the situation in a most careful and diplomatic manner. Or, to act like a "dumb blonde" or "helpless female" to build my man's ego. Then I compromised my integrity.[2]

Even more difficult to handle and interpret are the mixed signals that can come from a male peer. He may take pride in your accomplishments so long as they are never quite equal to his. If he's been your teacher, he may become so accustomed to you in the role of student that it is difficult for him to see you in any other light. Often the only solution is outside validation. Once you lead a few of your own trips, or someone else gives you good reviews, the man will be more likely to accept you as an equal. Of course skilled women may have the same barriers to acknowledging accomplishments of those in their charge. But since most women know what it feels like to be patronized, they should be more likely to recognize when they themselves behave this way.

Training and Preparation

The physical demands of backpacking, hiking, and snowshoeing are similar, which is why they're grouped together in terms of training. Hiking and snowshoeing are about 95 percent aerobic and backpacking about 85 percent. They're also similar because as modes of travel they are easy to master.

Snowshoeing is best in the East, where the terrain has more brush and trees. It may be the answer, however, for anyone who wants to get out during the winter but doesn't have the inclination to master skiing. "I hate skiing with a pack on," says one woman. "It's too hard to keep your balance. Snowshoeing is much easier." However, if you think that snowshoeing is merely the klutz's answer to winter travel, consider that the record for the mile on snowshoes in Canada, where the sport is more popular, is four and a half minutes.[3] "Snowshoeing is such a sensible and even necessary way to walk in winter that it seems odd that women did not do it much until recently," writes Anne LaBastille. "In fact, the first reference I have found, other than frontier women in strictly survival situations, was in 1912. A Mrs. Shirley C. Hulse wrote about the sport in *Field and Stream*—a then unknown subject and market for a female writer! Apparently, the first time she put on snowshoes, Shirley walked fifteen miles and climbed over a 3,000-foot mountain."

In snowshoeing you must walk with your feet farther apart to make room for the snowshoes. You lift your foot up and forward without trying to lift the snowshoe. Let it drag along as you move forward. On loose snow the energy cost of walking on snowshoes is somewhat higher than it would be if you were skiing.

Although it's obvious that going uphill is harder than walking or snowshoeing on level ground, it might not occur to you that it can take more energy and is harder on the knee joints and leg muscles to go downhill. This is so on steep declines, which require a haltingly slow speed. It's possible to become adept at covering steep downhill grades quickly as you learn to let gravity do the work for you while you offer little resistance. But this works only on trails. It is also very hard on the knees, shins, and calves unless you're used to it or have been doing

Snowshoeing in the Adirondack Mountains. Photograph courtesy of Anne LaBastille, Ph.D., West of the Winds Publications.

conditioning, which includes strength training or running down stairs and hills.

If you hike or snowshoe without a backpack, the sum of your conditioning program can be long, slow aerobic workouts. If you want to cover steep hills, mountains, or canyons, include mild interval or fartlek workouts and running down hills or stairs. The picture changes drastically when you include a backpack. Backpacks do not bring to mind ecstatic flight. The soundtrack for *Chariots of Fire* would have been more difficult to write if the movie had been about backpackers. A woman who likes to run in the mountains compares backpackers to diesel trucks and runners to Porsches. But of course it's the pack that allows you to get far into the wilds, and the more you can carry, the farther you can go.

A backpacker's aerobic training needs to be more rigorous than a hiker's to accommodate the stress put on the heart and lungs by the weight of the pack. Running is the best aerobic exercise for backpackers (see chapter 1). In general, you should run about one-fourth to one-third of the distance you plan to cover daily while backpacking. Remember that each elevation gain of 500 feet on the trail is equal in effort to one linear mile. It's best to have a running course on which you can do hills or stairs. If such a course is not available, do about one-quarter of your run in intervals.

Jo Prouty says that before she retired, to keep in shape she ran each morning from the basement to the seventh floor of the hospital where she worked. She often used the treadmill in the early morning before the clinic opened. At home she used a stationary bicycle. On weekends she hiked or snowshoed. Since retiring, she takes brisk one-and-a-half-mile walks in the morning up a steep hill and often spends a couple of days each week on six- to nine-mile hikes.

Strength Training

Strength training exercises are important not only to develop the specific muscle groups used in backpacking and to prevent injuries, but to help produce bursts of anaerobic energy. The following exercise program for backpackers can be adapted to whatever facilities are available to you. You can add or substitute different exercises for those recommended by referring to the chart on page 38. Adjust the program to put emphasis on those parts of your body that you know are weakest. The muscle groups are assigned numbers. The numbers beside each exercise refer to the number of the muscle groups that are worked by the exercise.

Backpacking in the Grand Canyon. Photograph courtesy of Ralph B. Maughan, Ph.D.

1. Hips, lower back, buttocks (two exercises)
2. Chest, upper arms (one exercise)
3. Thighs, hamstrings (two exercises)
4. Calves, shins, ankles (two exercises)
5. Shoulders, triceps (two exercises)
6. Abdomen (one exercise)
7. Biceps (one exercise)
8. Forearms, wrists (one exercise)

Free Weights	Universal or Nautilus	No Weights
Clean and press (1,2,3,4,5,6,7,8)	Bench fly (2,5)	Pullup (2,5,7,8)
Quarter squat (1,3,4,6)	Pulldown behind neck (1,2,7,8)	Pushup (2,5,7)
Upright rowing (2,5,7)	Overhead press (5)	Quarter deep-knee bend (1,3,4)
Bench fly (2,5)	Leg curl (1,3,4)	Lunge (1,3)
Calf raise (4)	Leg press (1,3)	Bent-knee sit-ups (1,6)
Toe raise (4)	Leg extension (3)	Calf raise (4)
	Calf raise (4)	Toe raise (4)
	Toe raise (4)	Squeeze tennis ball (8)
	Bent-leg sit-ups (1,6)	

Extra emphasis is placed on strengthening the knees, calves, and shins because they take so much abuse. One woman diligently weight-trained and ran four miles several times weekly in preparation for backpacking into the Grand Canyon. The morning after the 5,000-foot descent, she awoke with calf muscles so severely strained that she could hardly walk. This affliction is known as the "canyon shuffle," and it can be prevented or lessened in several ways. The first is to stretch fully before hiking, and during a demanding hike do stretches along the way. At night in camp, stretch even more. The other way to prevent it is to do calf and toe raises in strength training. To do calf raises, stand on the edge of a stair or on something thick, like the New York City telephone book, so that your heels hang over the edge. Slowly rise to your tiptoes, then lower yourself back down, extending your heels as far below your ankles as possible. Repeat ten times or until you get tired. This exercise can be done on the Universal or free-weight system with weights added to make it harder. To do toe raises, sit on a chair and place your feet on the floor. Hook your feet under a low-slung chair or coffee table. Keeping your heels on the floor, lift the table with your feet. Repeat eight to twelve times. You can add weight by loading books on the table or chair.

Shoulders and upper- and lower-back muscles should be strengthened because this is where much of the weight of the pack will be. An otherwise strong woman will be miserable trying to carry a heavy pack unless she has some strength in her shoulders. Rather than being forced to keep your pack weight down to the one-fourth of your body weight, as is recommended for the average woman, it seems better to increase it to one-third and not have to worry about what you had to leave at home.

Snowshoers should include lying-side leg raises in the exercise and stretching regimen. These help prevent strains on the inner thighs and crotch, which often result from snowshoeing. To do these, lie on your left side with your legs straight and your head propped up on your left hand. Raise your left leg as high as you can. Do twenty-five times, and repeat on the right side. This exercise can also be done on the Universal system with an ankle attachment.

The butterfly is another good exercise for snowshoers. Many women already know how to do this because it's a popular warm-up for modern dance. Sit on the floor with the soles of your feet together. Bring your feet as close to your body as possible. While holding onto your ankles, use your elbows to push your knees gently toward the floor. But don't push so hard that it hurts. Hold for ten seconds, and repeat five times.

At first glance, it might not seem that the backpacker, hiker, or snowshoer would need any more than the average degree of balance. However, the need for good balance will be obvious the minute you must cross a slippery log, steep snowfield, scree slope, or boulder field. One woman resorted to the ignominy of crossing a wide but slippery log on her hands and knees. Practice walking on downed logs or on curbs. A walking stick can also help. In the beginning, snowshoers sometimes use ski poles for balance.

The peculiarity of the area you enter may dictate certain training programs. Frank C. Craighead, Jr., his brother John, and those who worked with them on the innovative and controversial study of grizzly bears in Yellowstone National Park in the 1960s, were able to get close enough to track the animals partly because they could climb lodgepole pine trees. The park is a virtual monoculture of these tall, skinny trees, which have few or no branches on the lower ten feet of their trunks. Those tracking the bears became adept first at rope climbing. Consequently, if a bear seemed dangerous, they could shimmy up a lodgepole, which they often did. Although one woman who was treed by a bear for more than eight hours says that you're so full of adrenalin that you can shoot right up any tree, the Craigheads didn't take any chances. This works only with grizzlies. Most black bears can climb trees.

By some estimates, as much as 60 percent of all sports-related injuries could be prevented by a simple ten-minute warm-up. The stretches recommended for backpackers, hikers, and snowshoers are the calf stretch, hyperextension, lunge, raised leg, squat, and toe touch. These are excellent at the beginning and end of the day. Stretching and light exercise are highly recommended after a day of hard work. Done during the day at trailside, they may help relieve and prevent cramps and stiffness. The butterfly, lying-side leg raises, and the lunge are musts for snowshoers. If you don't have a convenient place to lie down, do the leg raises while standing.

Although, technically, lying down with your feet propped high against a rock isn't stretching, it sure feels good and helps to reduce the throbbing in your feet and legs. To unkink the muscles in your neck and shoulders, grab an overhanging branch and bend over with your arms (and the branch) over your head. But watch out for sap.

Environmental Injuries and Ailments

Major injuries are not common among backpackers, hikers, and snowshoers. However, minor mishaps and inconveniences such as scratches, insect bites, and pulled and strained muscles are so common that you will be lucky to finish a trip without a few of them. Many women share the viewpoint of a former Girl Scout camp director who says that women's groups are far more safety conscious than coeducational groups. She says that she has seen far more men than women overdoing it with negative results.

Scratches, lacerations, insect bites, sunburn, and windburn are best avoided by keeping your body covered. However, many people will put up with these troubles to wear shorts and a T-shirt. A scarf or hat will protect your head from sunburn and overhanging branches.

Eye Injuries

Photosensitive sunglasses are suggested to prevent eye injuries and reduce direct and reflected sunlight. A strap to hold the glasses securely in place so that they won't slip off your nose when you sweat is distributed under the trade name Croakies. It is available at most backpacking and sporting goods stores.

Eye injuries, such as scratching the cornea, can be painful. However, unless the object that caused the scratch remains in the eye, the injury can be treated by securing a sterile pad over the eye for twenty-four hours. During this time, the cornea can heal because the normal repetitious blinking of the eyelid no longer irritates it. For more serious or questionable eye injuries, seek medical attention. To check if foreign matter is lodged under the lid, place a pencil or finger at the base and pull the lid outward over it. This will expose the underside of the lid.

Heat stress, heatstroke, and heat/salt cramps, which are thought to be caused by high water losses when you sweat, occur with some frequency among backpackers and hikers. Snowshoers shouldn't rule them out either if the day is warm, the sun bright, and a lot of body heat has been worked up. To treat these ailments, see chapter 9. If possible, arrange your trip so that you don't travel during the hottest part of the day if overheating is a danger. Wear a light hat and light-colored clothing, which reflects rather than absorbs sunlight.

Sunburn

While a deep suntan is considered attractive, the wrinkles and possible skin cancer that can result from constant exposure aren't. Light-skinned persons should use a sunscreen with a maximum protective factor of fifteen. Those with darker skins can use a sunscreen with a lower protective factor. While black people have a great deal of built-in protection from the sun, they also can burn, and excessive exposure can take its toll. Children are more susceptible to sunburn than adults.

When applying sunscreen, don't forget obscure parts of your body such as the tops of your ears and the part in your hair. One windsurfer burned his feet so badly that he couldn't stand to put on his shoes. The rest of his body had been protected by a wetsuit. Sunscreen should be applied liberally and often. Lips and the undersurfaces of the nose and chin should not be overlooked. Lipstick is not good protection, and some kinds actually increase sensitivity to sunlight. Certain agents in drugs, cosmetics, soaps, and first-aid creams also increase sensitivity to sunlight. Among the more common of these are antibiotics such as tetracycline, diuretics, and barbituates. One treatment for sunburn is to apply a paste of aspirin and sodium bicarbonate. The tannic acid in tea can soothe a sunburn if you apply cool, wet teabags to the skin. A cool compress also helps relieve the pain, as do various commercial sunburn preparations.

Hypothermia and Frostbite

Hypothermia and frostbite are also discussed in chapter 9. While snowshoers are more prone to these problems, any trip that involves a dramatic change in altitude most likely will also involve a dramatic change in weather. Take the woman and her husband who visited the Grand Canyon in March. When they hiked in, the weather on the rim was chilly. At the bottom it was in the high 60s. While they were hiking back out, a blizzard hit. During the last 1,000 feet to the top, the wind was fierce and the snow fell heavily. Since he was faster, her husband hiked ahead. When she got to the rim, it was bitter cold, and the blasts of wind almost knocked her to the ground. She could not remember where the car was parked. After dumping her pack at the lodge and shedding her soaked mittens for dry ones, she went out to look for her husband. It was fortunate that she did. When she found him, he was back at the trailhead preparing to descend to look for *her*. Had they been at a more remote trailhead, where a warm lodge and car weren't nearby, they might have been in danger of hypothermia. Back at the lodge, the person who seemed best prepared was a man who happily strode by carrying an umbrella. He may have looked silly, but he was dry.

Insect Bites

Insects and their bites must be taken seriously because they can make you miserable and ruin a trip if you are not prepared. Always carry insect repellent. The kind in pressurized containers can be sprayed on clothing to keep insects from biting through to your skin. (The risks of long-term and heavy use of insect repellent are not known.) In heavily infested areas, wear protective clothing. Take a tent with tightly woven netting, and drape mosquito netting over your head and neck. Wear a bandanna over your nose and neck to prevent inhaling flying insects when they are in thick swarms.

In addition to insect repellent, sulfur, available as a powder from drugstores, is an effective chigger deterrent. You can sprinkle it around your ankles, shoes, pants legs, and shirt cuffs when in chigger country. Chiggers are hard to get rid of. Mosquitoes, black flies, ticks, and chiggers each have their favorite season and habitat. You should determine the chances of their presence while planning a trip. Check with experienced acquaintances or public officials who manage the land you intend to visit. Cold water, calamine lotion, cool mud, and ice help provide relief from insect bites. Some veteran hikers say that a paste of Adolph's meat tenderizer works too.

If you are in tick country, check for them periodically. They show up easier on light-colored clothes. Do a strip search before you go to bed, and change into different clothes. Ticks are most likely to head for your bra and panty lines, scalp, pubic and underarm areas, and behind your ears. Should they become embedded, soak them in gasoline, kerosene, or Vaseline to make them detach. A light touch with alcohol or a warm match may also encourage them to back out. If a tick dies without disengaging (a common problem!), grasp it with tweezers as close as possible to the point of attachment and pull slowly and steadily. Some advise a counterclockwise rotation. Wash the bite with soap and water and rinse with antiseptic. If bare hands touch the tick, wash them thoroughly with soap; tick secretions can be infective.

Symptoms of the various kinds of tick fever manifest themselves in three to fourteen days. Chills, fever, headache, and muscle aches are most common. Some tick fevers, such as Colorado Tick Fever, are caused by viruses and are treated with rest, fluids, and aspirin. Rocky Mountain Spotted Fever is caused by a different organism and is characterized by a rash that appears several days after the onset of the disease. In 60 percent of cases, the rash occurs on the palms and soles. The most serious of all tick fevers, it can even cause death unless treated early with the antibiotics tetracycline and chloramphenicol. It is most usual in the Rocky Mountain states and in North Carolina, Virginia, and Maryland. Tick fever occurs most often in western states during spring and early summer.

Poisonous Plants

Poison ivy, oak, and sumac can be beastly uncomfortable. Every first-aid, scouting, and backwoods book talks about them, and for good reason. The usual upshot of contact is swelling, sores, and localized itching, which can spread. Some people react with violent rashes, pus, and dangerously high fevers. Even though you have been around these plants in the past and have had no trouble, one day you could find yourself with an itching rash. When these plants are burned, they release the poisonous chemical urushoil, which can cover all exposed parts of your body, especially your eyes. It can also be inhaled and coat your throat. If you come in contact with burned plants, wash off the urushoil with water and soap as soon as possible. If only a small area is exposed, you may not need to use medicine to treat it. Calamine lotion, cool mud, or a cool, mild solution of saltwater helps stop itching. A difficult case requires application of a steroid ointment. Disabling doses may require steroid tablets or injections.

The berries of these plants are white. Poison ivy and oak always have three leaflets. Poison ivy grows everywhere in the United States except California. Its leaves are glossy and it can appear as a small plant, vine, or shrub. Poison oak grows in California and adjacent states. It appears mostly in shrub form, but it can also be a vine. Poison sumac is endemic to the East. It is a woody shrub or small tree. All three plants turn delightful shades of red in the fall.

Cuts and Lacerations

Bleeding from a cut or laceration can usually be stopped by direct pressure with a clean dressing. Using pressure points on main arteries is of little value (unless they themselves have been lacerated), and it impedes blood flow to the rest of the limb. A cut should be washed gently with a mild, preferably nonperfumed soap. If it is bad enough to require stitches and such treatment is not available, close it by pulling the edges together with "butterfly" tapes or Band-Aids. Avoid an excessively tight closure, which can cause the wound to fester. Wounds are often closed in this manner to reduce bleeding. But enough bleeding to expel foreign material should be allowed. Wounds that require a tourniquet are uncommon among backpackers, hikers and snowshoers. Tourniquets are justified only when the danger of bleeding to death warrants the risk of the loss of a limb.

Blisters

Blisters are extremely common with new hikers or with new boots and hiking shoes. One woman accompanied her boyfriend on her first backpacking trip to Idaho's rugged (and crowded) Sawtooth Mountains. He insisted that she not take along her thongs because "they take too much room." She sneaked them along anyway—luckily. After the first day in new boots, her feet were so blistered that she could hardly walk. She finished her four-day hike in her thongs.

Blisters are best avoided rather than treated. Make sure your shoes are comfortable. Wearing two pairs of socks, an inner light pair and a heavier outer sock, reduces friction between boot and skin. Should a hot spot develop, cover it with moleskin to prevent a blister.

There's some disagreement as to how to treat a blister. On one hand, if you break it, you expose the sterile insides to contamination and invite infection. Some physicians recommend leaving blisters intact and surrounding them with a piece of moleskin into which a hole has been cut to the size of the blister. On the other hand, if you break a blister and it doesn't get infected, it heals faster. If you do this, break it with a sterile needle to allow the fluid to drain. Then cut away the dead skin and cover it with a sterile pad. At night, uncover it for awhile to let air in and dry it out. Recover it before you go to bed.

Contaminated Water

The chance of getting sick from drinking biologically contaminated water unfortunately is high. The common *E. coli* bacteria is usually the cause if the water is contaminated by human waste. The incubation period is six to forty-eight hours, and you may be sick for two to five days. In general, the faster the symptoms develop and the greater their severity, the shorter the duration of the illness.

Giardiasis, caused by the one-celled protozoa *giardia lamblia,* is not confined to areas of human use. It can be carried by most warm-blooded animals and is most common in the western United States. Alpine streams, fast-moving cold water, and other traditionally safe water sources may not be so if tiny particles of animal feces have been washed into the water by snowmelt or rain. Because the giardia goes through a cyst stage, symptoms take longer to develop. You may not become ill until you return home because the incubation period is a week or more. The main difference between the symptoms of giardia and simple *E. coli* diarrhea is severity. Another culprit in causing water-borne illness in the mountains is *campylobacter* (campy), a bacterial organism that has recently been isolated in various mountain streams. The symptoms are diarrhea (often bloody), abdominal pain, and fever. It may appear to be more severe than giardiasis, but its course is more often self-limited if the antibiotic erythromycin cannot be obtained.[4]

The best way to prevent illness from contaminated water is to boil it for ten minutes at altitudes below 10,000 feet and for twenty minutes at higher elevations. This should kill the majority of infectious organisms.

The debate over whether chlorine or iodine is better for treating water instead of boiling continues. Chlorine, such as that in laundry bleach or Halazone tablets, is an effective chemical means of purification if there is little organic material in the water. Chlorine tablets have a six-month shelf life and lose potency with air contact. A new, unopened bottle should be purchased for every trip. Water that is slightly alkaline (high in salts and minerals) also reduces the effectiveness of chlorine. If you use laundry bleach, add ten drops per quart of clear water and twenty drops per quart of cloudy water. Let it stand for thirty minutes to let the chlorine take action; a slight chlorine odor should be detectable. Cold or cloudy water should be allowed to stand for several hours or overnight.

The main drawbacks to chlorine tablets are their short shelf life and their ineffectiveness in alkaline, cold, and heavily contaminated water. For these reasons, some recommend using iodine instead. Liquid iodine can be used in concentrations of four drops per quart, or six drops in heavily contaminated water. Iodine crystals may be simpler if you must disinfect water for large groups. Put four to eight grams of USP-grade iodine crystals in a clear medicine-sized (one-ounce) bottle. Add water and shake the bottle for thirty to sixty seconds. Then pour it into a quart of water. The crystals are poisonous, so be sure not to get any into your drinking water.

Some researchers have stated that iodine will kill giardia cysts. Others say they will not. Still others say to use both chlorine and iodine. However, this tastes so awful that you may not want to drink water at all. Neither iodine nor chlorine has been found to be reliable in killing giardia cysts, although both effectively eliminate *E. coli* and campy. Recently, straws with filters have appeared on the market. They have not proven to be 100 percent effective for filtering out giardia cysts, but they definitely help. They will *not,* however, get rid of *E. coli* or campy; these organisms pass right through the filters. The name and address of one of these straw manufacturers is Pocket Purifier, Calco Ltd. (7011 Barry Avenue, Rosemont, Illinois 60018).

The treatment of gastrointestinal diseases caused by polluted water is fluid replacement and a bland diet. Whether or not you should rest depends on how you feel. Codeine may be given every four hours to relieve severe diarrheal cramps. Bacterial diseases are treated with antibiotics, while giardiasis is treated with quinacrine (Atabrine) or metronidazole (Flagyl). While long-term use of Atabrine can turn your skin yellow, repeated use of Flagyl may be cancer-causing.

Foot Fungus

If you are constantly in wet conditions, you may develop an annoying foot fungus. This is where numerous changes of socks become invaluable. High-topped hunting boots and mountaineering boots with the tongue sewn down all the way to the collar are good for wet conditions because they help keep your feet dry. A foot powder, scrupulous cleansing, and thorough drying are also preventive measures. If an infection develops, apply a fungicide.

Muscle, Joint, and Connective-Tissue Injuries

Numbness in the shoulders, arms, and hands from the weight of a backpack is not unusual. It can result from the weight of the pack resting too far forward on the collarbone area instead of where it should be, on the trapezius, that large set of muscles in your upper back and neck. Occasionally this can result in "backpacker's palsy," which is a paralysis or tremors of this nerve area. It is usually temporary. Just take the pack off and readjust it. A pack that fits properly and is loaded with a woman's physique in mind will help avoid the problem. Instructions that tell you to put the heaviest objects at the top, medium-weight items in the middle, and lightweight ones at the bottom of your pack were not designed for women. Most women find that they do better with heavy objects loaded at the bottom, medium ones in the middle, and lightweight ones on top. Elevating your hands over your head from time to time will help alleviate the numbness. And remember to adjust the shoulder straps so that the weight does not rest on the collarbone. Leaning forward with the pack at a forty-five-degree angle will temporarily shift the weight and relieve some of the stress. Shifting the load and tightening or loosening the straps at intervals may also help. The best solution, if possible, is not to carry more than you can handle for long distances. To prevent chafing, apply moleskin or tape to the places where the pack rubs.

Almost every backcountry user experiences muscle strains and cramps. They are more likely to occur if your body is subjected to unusual demands. Karen Swafford, who has backpacked for about a decade and was one of the original board members of the Idaho Conservation League, was hiking up Mt. Borah in Idaho, which involves an elevation gain of 5,200 feet. The walk-up included four or five scrambles. "Scrambles" means climbing with good feet and hand holds, but climbing nevertheless. If she slipped, it would mean a fall of several hundred feet. Until then, she had thought a scramble was maybe a crawl over a boulder field. She hadn't counted on actual climbing with significant amounts of exposure. With the help of a reassuring friend, who talked her through the hard spots by telling her where to put her hands and feet, she made it to the top of the peak. Midway to the top, her legs cramped up, first one entire leg and then the other. Stretching didn't help. But she continued to hike and the cramps eventually went away. "I wanted to get to the top so bad, the cramps didn't stop me," she says.

Her cramps could have been caused by loss of salt, potassium, and magnesium through heavy sweating, or possibly because of the depletion of muscle glycogen, since the stretching didn't work. They could also have been caused by a lack of proportional strength between her back and front calf and thigh muscles. In the first case, a drink of water or Kool-Aid might help. If these didn't work, she could have tried an electrolyte-replacement fluid, such as Gatorade. If it was glycogen depletion, eating carbohydrates, such as sugar or crackers, or drinking Kool-Aid would help. In the third case, prior strength training may have prevented the cramps. A final, possibly immediate cure could have been to stop, sit down, and do a leg press against a heavy stone or log and/or calf and toe raises. These would get the nerves to fire in another direction, thereby stopping the pain impulse.

The frequency of ankle injuries and sprains among women backpackers and snowshoers is one reason why calf and toe raises are advocated. Women are more likely to incur sprains by stumbling against their own body weight. This is because of that old bugaboo, lack of strength. Men are more likely to sustain ankle injuries and the like in contact sports. If you are susceptible to sprains, because of pregnancy, an old injury, or just plain weak ankles, try a high-topped boot such as the hunting boots made by Red Wing. The recent trend toward extremely lightweight boots has its advantages, but one of them is not ankle protection.

Groin and hamstring strains and pulls occur fairly often among snowshoers because you must walk with your feet farther apart, which puts more strain on the inside of the legs. Side-lying leg lifts and butterflies, both before and after, help prevent and relieve this kind of strain. A modified lunge done sideways also helps. If stretching doesn't do the trick, apply an ice or cold-water compress to the area. If the pain lingers and is severe, try to keep your weight off of it. At worst, although the likelihood of a pull this severe or a tear is not great, you may need to see a doctor and be put on crutches.

Be forewarned that occasionally a pain in the crotch is actually a fracture of the bottom of the pelvic bone. The pain starts high on the inner thigh. After several days it will shift to directly under the crotch. This injury appears to be more frequent among women, and you should see an orthopedist if you have these symptoms.[5]

Overload/Stress Injuries

Women who have backpacking ranger and guiding jobs find that over the years the hard work can take its toll on the knees, shins, and back. One woman who had just such a job finds that she can no longer backpack for a long period without severe pain in her shins and knees. The constant pounding up and down in the mountains led to chronic overuse syndrome. Although many women suffer no lasting physical effects after years of hard outdoor labor, the possibility exists, especially when the woman carries at the highest levels of her physical capacity over a long period.

It's important to pay attention to overload/stress injuries because they can become chronic. If you are a recreational rather than professional backcountry user, there's no reason to push yourself into constantly going too far, too fast, and carrying too much weight. As a professional, you may find that you have little choice. Overload injuries are more likely to occur when carrying a heavy pack. Force torquing on your muscles, bones, joints, and connective tissue occurs when you increase the load by one-fourth or one-third. Snowshoers are not so susceptible to stress injuries because the snow is soft and helps absorb some of the impact of each footfall.

The potential for injury is greater as you grow older. Regardless of your age, it's wise to set aside every third day for rest or lighter activity to allow the body to recoup energy stores and heal minor insults and injuries. This is one of the most important ways to prevent injuries, including major traumas that can result from poor judgment when you're overly fatigued. Strength training is another major method of preventing chronic problems. Although it may seem redundant to keep emphasizing these points, it's better to be redundant than injured.

Although no boot or walking shoe made will take all the stress out of hiking and backpacking, well-fitted and well-designed boots are important if you do high mileages under heavy loads. If you are hard to fit, you may have to have your boots custom made.

Shin Splints

Shin splints, a stress injury, is one of the more descriptive terms in the sports medicine vocabulary. One doctor speculates that the term originates from the fact that your front lower-leg muscles act as a splint to restrict and absorb the jolts of hard and uneven surfaces. Shin splints are not a specific injury but refer generally to pain that occurs in the front of the leg between the ankle and knee.

The muscles of the shin are fairly easy to overstress because they normally don't get as much exercise as your calves. Deliberate strength training, such as toe raises, develops these muscles. Good padding, stiff soles, and a solid heel cup in your boots or shoes act as shock absorbers and stabilizers and help prevent injuries. Boots that are too long or wide force the toes to provide stability. This extra work is transferred to the shins. A crest pad from a drugstore can be placed under the three middle toes to add stability. A roll of moleskin placed under the three middle toes is also serviceable. If good boots/shoes, strength training, or padding don't do the trick, you may have structural problems, such as one leg being shorter than the other, a duck-foot gait (pronation), pigeon toes (supination), flat feet, or fallen arches. In these cases, you may need a professionally made orthotic.

Shin splints develop gradually and are characterized by pain and stiffness. You will most likely notice them at the beginning of the season on the morning after covering a long distance on rough terrain. The usual short-term treatment is ice and an antiinflammatory drug such as aspirin or Motrin, accompanied by a day of rest, reduced mileage, or a lighter load. It is not a good idea to walk during this injury because you can make it worse. *Worse* means possible multiple hairline fractures up and down the shin bone. This can, at the extreme, translate into "chronic" if proper medical treatment is not sought. Hairline fractures often don't show up in an X-ray right after they have occurred. It takes about two weeks for scar tissue to form along the fracture line and be seen on the X-ray. These fractures will mean that the weight must be taken off the bone and you may be on crutches. Backpacking and hiking are definitely out for at least four weeks. If the fractures are bad enough, you may need a cast.

Knee Injuries

The knees are the most vulnerable joint in the body and account for the majority of athletic injuries. Many backcountry activities, including backpacking and skiing, put a great deal of pressure on this architecturally weak joint. A slight misalignment of the body, such as a shorter leg, being knock-kneed, or pronation, may not bother you until you try covering seventeen miles in a rainstorm on a muddy trail with a heavy pack. One woman found that her right knee started to slip slightly out of joint in this situation. The sensation was not painful, but it was unpleasant and slightly alarming—alarming enough that she has since maintained a strengthening program for her knees. She has had no further problems. Women are more likely than men to suffer dislocation of the kneecaps (patella) and have knee-joint instability because of lack of strength and greater extensibility of the ligaments themselves.

Lower-Back Problems

The lower back, like the knees, is structurally vulnerable to injury. Lower-back problems are basically of two kinds: those caused by a sudden traumatic incident, such as wrenching, twisting, and lifting, and those resulting from chronic stress. Like most stress injuries, those of the lower back may show up on a backcountry trip simply because of unaccustomed stress. The cause may be weak back and abdominal muscles, an improperly loaded or fitted pack, the jolting of descending a rocky trail or cross-country section, lack of padding and stiffness in the soles of the boots, lifting a heavy object (such as a pack), trauma from a fall, or an inherent misalignment of the body itself. The extra loading on the spine by the weight of the pack, especially if you are fat or out-of-shape, can compress the spine over several days. The result is that you can hurt your back in what feels like one traumatic incident.

Actual trauma to the lower back is not frequent among backpackers, snowshoers, and hikers because these activities usually don't involve wrenching, twisting movements. If you decide to reengineer a stream crossing by moving heavy logs to form a bridge, you most definitely can wrench your back. You can do the same by improperly hoisting your pack to your back. Just as the OSHA (Occupational Safety and Health Administration) signs admonish in the workplace, you should lift heavy objects in the backcountry by kneeling, then straightening your legs—not by bending over from the waist. The same holds true for the weight room.

Contrary to popular belief, lower-back problems do occur in persons under thirty. These are primarily the result of bad posture, and they can become more pronounced while backpacking. In older persons, lack of strength in the back and antagonistic abdominal muscles is often cited as the cause. High heels are bad for the back because they throw the spine into misalignment and can aggravate back problems or create new ones. It's entirely possible, in fact not uncommon, to have lower-back problems brought on by your fitness program. These problems in runners are legion, and weight lifters have their share too. Lower-back pain also can be caused or aggravated by constipation and menstrual cramps.

Chronic lower-back pain can result from a lack of strength to support your body and pack. This is why bent-knee sit-ups are recommended for backpackers, snowshoers, and hikers. Sit-ups performed with the legs straight are believed to aggravate lower-back problems. But some people feel that even bent-knee sit-ups put too much stress on the back. Instead, they recommend abdominal curls.

Stress, as opposed to traumatic, lower-back problems is fairly common among high-distance backpackers. If you have these problems, look first to your legs. It is not unusual for one leg to be somewhat shorter than the other. This might pose no problems until you start backpacking or running. The shorter leg is frequently accompanied by a slightly smaller foot, and it is often weaker than the other. Dr. Murray Weisenfeld, in *The Runner's Repair Manual,* suggests testing your legs with a carpenter's level. Place the level on the ground. If the bubble aligns exactly in the middle, the floor is level. If the bubble tilts, find a place on the floor where it doesn't. Take a straight-backed chair and check to make sure that it is level too. Then sit on it with your knees together and place the level on your knees. Does the bubble float in the middle? If not, one leg is shorter than the other from the knee.

Next check to see if your hips are even, since the discrepancy may be from the knee up. Are your hipbones even? Are those two dimples above each buttock even? If you can't tell, get a friend to use a felt-tipped pen to mark the dimples and hipbones. Place the carpenter's level horizonally across them. Is the bubble level? If not, you may have identified a cause of your lower-back problems. You can buy heel pads at the drugstore in varying thickness from about 3/16 inch to 3/4 inch. If the discrepancy is greater than 3/4 inch, Weisenfeld suggests seeing a podiatrist, since padding under the heel alone won't be sufficient to correct the problem and you may need padding in other places along the foot as well.

If your back starts to bother you on the trail, try the recommended stretches. Then try shifting your load. If you have one of the new high-tech internal-frame packs, such as those made by Lowe, you can shift the weight via straps. If this doesn't work, you may simply be tired or out of fuel. The back pain should go away with rest, some carbs, an aspirin or Motrin, and massage.

If you wrench your back, you cannot always tell whether a disc or a small muscle or ligament is hurt. In this case, the best first aid is also the most conservative. Take aspirin or Motrin, apply a cold compress, then rest and hope it goes away. If it doesn't and you're deep in the woods, canyons, or mountains, you may have to shift your burden to a partner or hide your pack and retrieve it later. This is a drastic measure, but you shouldn't put additional weight on an injury, particularly if a delicate disc is involved. This kind of severe, disabling pain requires medical evaluation. Take heart that more than 90 percent of all people recover from lower-back pain with sufficient time and rest.

Equipment

"When I first came to Colorado from Cleveland, Ohio, in 1946, I was about as green as any novice could be," says Virginia Nolan. "First of all I joined the Colorado Mountain Club. Shortly after that I was invited by a long-time member of the CMC to join him for a hike one Sunday afternoon. I was new and quite flattered that he would ask me. I showed up in silk slacks, silk shirt, etc. What a well-dressed mountaineer should wear—as I said, I was *green*."

"Believe me, I get green-eyed when I see the freeze-dried food, and light weight backpacks and sleeping bags of the 'now' generation," says Eleanor Bartlett, now eighty-five, who between 1916 and the 1930s made some fourscore ascents, some the first, of rugged mountains in the Rockies and Sierras. A person she frequently climbed with had also climbed in Switzerland, and he brought back advanced equipment—like a 100-foot rope and an ice axe! "This was all we ever had. Not having an auto, we took trains to get as near the peaks as possible. Then we hiked in with our heavy loads and climbed with heavy, hobnailed boots."

The revolution in gear is occurring so quickly today that books about it are dated almost before they get off the press. There's a vast range in quality and price of what you can get in department and sporting goods stores and in specialized mountaineering and backpacking shops. For essentials like boots, packs, sleeping bags, and snowshoes, quality matters a great deal. Other items, such as durable clothing, can be picked out of the bottom drawer of your dresser or purchased at an Army/Navy surplus store.

Two of the largest mail-order equipment distributors are Recreational Equipment (Box C–88125, Seattle, Washington 98188) and Eastern Mountain Sports (Two Vose Farm Road, Peterborough, New Hampshire 03458). Both carry large lines of most of the equipment you will need to outfit yourself for the outdoors. Both have free, comprehensive catalogues.

Backpacker magazine (c/o Ziff-Davis Publishing Company, One Park Avenue, New York, New York 10016) and *Outside* magazine (3401 Division Street, Chicago, Illinois 60651) frequently review outdoor gear. *Sierra,* the monthly magazine of the Sierra Club, not only has articles about equipment, but many about how and where to enjoy the backcountry, as well as how to take care of and preserve it. A subscription to *Sierra* costs $30 a year. (The address is 530 Bush Street, San Francisco, California 94108).

Shoes and Boots

Hiking is the cheapest way to go, although it is also the most limited. The only investment a hiker needs to make is in a good pair of shoes, a daypack, and a water-resistant poncho or jacket. Athletic shoes, such as those used for running or racquetball, are fine if you don't mind wearing them out in a hurry. Shoes designed for the court or road won't hold up well on a muddy, rocky trail. They're OK for your first few times out, but it's just as well to purchase a pair of hiking shoes, which cost the same or less than a brand-name pair of running shoes.

Although a boot or shoe made on a women's last is not essential for all women, our feet are usually narrower at the heel than a man's.

A man's or unisex shoe generally won't fill the bill. When buying hiking shoes, wear the same medium-weight wool socks you would on the trail. For boots, wear two pairs of socks (a light liner and a heavy wool outer). Check to see if there's slippage in the heel area. Stand on your toes. Does the shoe slip off your heel? If it's a boot, stand with your feet pointing downhill. If your toes touch the end, the boot is too short. Walk around the store for ten or fifteen minutes to make sure the arch is compatible with your own, that no seams rub, and that the boot is not too tight or too loose. Shoes and boots should feel absolutely comfortable. After you have walked for same distance, particularly if you are wearing a pack, your feet will often swell, and a too-tight boot or shoe will hurt.

The traditional Oxford walking shoe, known to Girl Scouts the world over, ranges in price from $45 to $70 and is a good shoe for a hiker. The more expensive ones are often water-repellent and have a corrugated tread and a steel shank in the arch for support. Most come in women's sizes. Boots for backpacking vary in price from expensive to expensive. The heavy (five-pound) lugged sole, high-collared, double-tongued mountaineering boots range in price from $80 to $275. What's the difference? The least expensive are designed for good trails in dry weather. Many do not hold up well if you splash through streams, posthole through snowdrifts, or knock about cross-country.

Do you backpack only a couple of times a year? Do you stay mostly on trails? Do you hike mostly in dry conditions? If so, the lighter, less expensive boot should serve you well. The lighter the boot, the shorter the break in time. But the lighter the boot, the less protection from the elements. For your first pair of boots, go with the lighter, cheaper models. Make sure you like backpacking well enough to justify a larger investment. It's still somewhat problematic for women to be fitted in mountaineering boots, especially the heavy-duty models.

It's absurd for the average backpacker or snowshoer to buy a $200 mountaineering boot. Don't assume that the best boot for you is the one that's the most expensive. One man did exactly this and wound up carrying his six-pound boots rather than vice versa. Technical mountain boots are designed to accommodate crampons. (Crampons are a steel-toothed bridge that is strapped onto the boot for walking on ice and snow.) These boots must withstand cold, ice, snow, and rock.

At the other extreme are the $35 waffle-stompers you can buy in department stores. These are a good choice for beginners, but they won't last long in the great outdoors. The soles are glued on and tend to peel away at the toe upon contact with water, dirt, and rocks. Comes your first high mountain snowdrift, and you'll want better boots.

Do you have weak ankles (such as during pregnancy), cover a lot of brushy terrain, or like a boot with a raised heel? Companies such as Red Wing, White, and Danner make high-topped "hunter's" boots in women's sizes. These boots have been tested by women who work for the U.S. Forest Service and have been found to be great in the field. Smokejumpers like the higher heel because it helps absorb the impact of landing when you parachute from a plane to fight a back-country wildfire. These boots average in price from about $70 for the less expensive Red Wing models to $100 for those made by Danner and White. The difference is the weight of the boot, the heaviness of the leather, the strength and weight of the steel shank, the type of soles, and the height of the hightop. The cheaper models are good for desert and other dry conditions, but not for areas of high rain or snowfall. All three companies will custom-make boots. Sharon Bradley, a forester on the Challis National Forest, likes the Danners because they have lower heels than the Whites (if you have flat feet, take note) and are more durable than the Red Wings. She says the break-in time is minimal, and the cost to have them custom made is not great. (The addresses of these companies are: Danner Shoe Manufacturing Company, Box 22204, Portland, Oregon 97222; Red Wing, 419 Bush Street, Red Wing, Minnesota 55066; and White's Shoe Shop, North 6116 Frey Street, Spokane, Washington 99207.) The high-pack/hunting boot is the one recommended for snowshoeing because it gives stability to the ankles and helps keep out snow. Gaiters are recommended if you don't have a high-pack boot. Gaiters, sort of like leggings or spats, attach to the arch of your boot and extend from about mid-calf to the knee. They cost about $20. Be sure they fit over your boots because some are designed to fit only a streamlined cross-country ski boot. Gaiters are also nice because they keep your pant legs clean and dry when you have to travel through mud and other guck.

The New Balance Rainier Hiker is the state-of-the-art entry of the running shoe companies into the backcountry market. This and others like it are strongly recommended by some hikers. Those who do a lot of scrambles love the Rainier, calling it the closest thing to a dry-land crampon. These shoe/boots cost between $60 and $125. One of the main advantages is their light weight (three pounds or less) and non-existent break-in time. Look for such features as a high or snug collar around the ankles to keep out the rocks, snow, and other debris, removable cushioned insoles, light weight, water resistance, and lug soles. The more expensive ones combine all of these features and are generally made of Gore-Tex, which is how you can have a light fabric shoe yet still keep relatively dry, although most users are far from convinced of the waterproofing abilities of Gore-Tex. None of these, however, will keep you warm. The principal disadvantages of these shoes is that many do not come in women's sizes, they don't support and protect the ankles, and they won't last long in rough conditions. Among those that do come in women's sizes are Spritzer ($75), Danner Lights ($105), New Age Hiker ($75), and DMC Gore-Tex ($71).

Backpacks

Although sleeping bags and packs are of equal importance, it takes more time and thought to find an agreeable pack. Daypacks cost between $15 and $40. Cheaper versions are adequate for carrying your lunch, a light jacket, camera, and other small items. If you plan to buy a small pack for overnighters, make sure that it has leather patches at the bottom for attaching a sleeping bag. Dayhikers, backpackers, and snowshoers should always carry a water-resistant jacket or poncho. A backpacker's poncho costs about $40, while a Gore-Tex jacket costs about $125. Even the plastic versions bought at the five and-dime are better than getting soaked, but they don't "breathe," and you will get wet if you're working hard.

Good backpacks for women are very new to the market and usually are not among the rental items you can find at a mountaineering or sporting goods store or university equipment center. The waist straps of most rental packs hit the average woman at about her crotch. You will have to put up with these unless you're lucky. If you are small, consider borrowing a child's pack. It may also be serendipitously possible to borrow a pack that fits from a woman friend. Good luck. In the meantime, ask your rental center to get some packs designed for people under 7'6".

Until the last few years, only backpacks with rigid outer frames were available. These were found to be inconvenient for off-trail rambles because the frames could snag on branches or rocks. The load, set apart from the body, would also tend to shift, and balance is essential. In addition, most frame packs put the lion's share of weight on the shoulders, not a good situation for women. Recently, frame-pack manufacturers have come up with any number of systems to remedy some of these problems. Camp Trails now makes a pack with a frame that adjusts to fit persons from 5'4" to 6'4". Jansport makes several frame packs, such as the D5, Cascade 2, and Framesack 2, for persons 5'2" to 5'9". The D5, with its companion D3 pack for taller people, has a removable hip extension that puts much of the weight on the hips. Alpenlite also makes a pack with a permanent extension bar that puts most of the weight on the hips. Most adult packs are not built to fit people under 5'3", and a small pack frame is built for a small man, not a small woman. Women are shorter-waisted, so even a frame pack that should fit may still be too long. So far, there are no frame packs built specifically to fit women.

Taller women don't have such a problem with fit. They can also take advantage of the North Face Black Magic and Jansport Alpine Phantom, both of which have an articulated joint that allows the pack frame to bend at the waist. The Black Magic comes in small, medium, and large sizes. The Phantom fits only those 5'8" and taller. Women who are shorter than 5'2" may have to purchase a child's pack. EMS has two such packs, and although the carrying capacity is limited (1,500 to 2,000 cubic inches), these packs are only about $50. Frame packs range in cost from $90 to $175. The advantages of frame packs are greater carrying capacity and ventilation. Because they aren't compressed against your back like the soft internal-frame rucksacks, they allow the air to circulate and are cooler.

Lowe has recently come out with a series of rucksacks designed for women and those with small backs and short torsos. The Lowe Nanda Devi series is named after the Hindu goddess of the Himalayas. They are highly recommended by many experienced women who are so grateful finally to find a pack that fits that they'll pay the higher price. The cheapest Nanda Devi, the North Twin costs about $135 and has a carrying capacity of 2,400 cubic inches. The Nanda Devi Expedition pack, at 4,800 cubic inches, costs $170. These Lowe packs do manage to transfer most of the weight to the hips.

Rucksacks are an important innovation, but just like a good camera, you have to know how to use them or you will defeat their purpose. The harness should be adjusted to fit the length of your body from shoulders to waist, and with most models the internal frame will have to be bent to match the contours of your back. Instructions for adjustment should come with the pack. A snowshoer should look for a pack that will carry snowshoes without too much hassle. Look for patches on the back through which you can loop straps to carry the snowshoes.

Snowshoes

Snowshoes come in four basic shapes. The widest are bearpaws and are used for terrain that has a lot of undergrowth and brush. At the other extreme is the long, skinny Alaska Yukon snowshoe designed for open country and deep powder. In between are models such as the

Green Mountain Bearpaw and Modified Beaver Tail, which cost about $65. The Green Mountain is recommended for beginners. It seems to be the most versatile and is good for carrying heavy weights. The size of the mesh on a snowshoe should vary according to the kind of snow. For wet, sticky snow, such as that in the East, look for a large mesh to help prevent sticking. In the West and North, where snow falls at low temperatures and is either fluffy or granular, a small mesh is best. Neoprene lacing in the web is more functional than leather lacing because it resists snow build-up, stretching, and damage. Rawhide is still preferred by many snowshoers, probably out of nostalgia, but it is no cheaper than neoprene. The best snowshoe bindings are made by Sherpa for about $30. These are hinged under the foot and give much better traction when you're going uphill. The Howe style at $10 is a second choice. Crampons, which cost about $10, can be added to snowshoes to give bite.

A do-it-yourself Green Mountain snowshoe kit costs about $50. The best all-purpose snowshoe is the Sherpa Snow-Claw. The webbing is a solid piece of neoprene, which gives more flotation than the ordinary shoe. The binding system holds the boot in place securely and is easy to take on and off. The built-in crampons give additional traction. The Sherpas cost $160. Vermont Tubbs has a similar model, the Alum-A-Shoe, for $120. (Some snowshoe manufacturers and their addresses are: Safesport Manufacturing Company, 1100 West 45th Avenue, Denver, Colorado 80211; Sherpa Inc., 2222 Diversey, Chicago, Illinois 60647; and Vermont Tubbs Inc., Forest Dale, Vermont 05745.)

Sleeping Bags and Tents

Sleeping bags for backpacking range in price from $90 to $260. They vary in weight, insulation, and material. Look for a bag with a temperature range suited to your needs. There's no reason to buy a $260 expedition bag if you hike in the desert; it will be too hot. Although down was once considered the only fiber worthy for most backcountry use because of its light weight and warmth, this is no longer true. Many new fills, such as PolarGuard and Hollofil, are just as good, and they are cheaper and easier to take care of. Even when wet, they retain some of their insulating abilities, which down does not. For this reason, experienced people use down bags only for high-altitude summit attempts in which wetness is not a problem and weight is. Another negative of down is that it takes an exceedingly long time to dry—not a situation you would want if your life depended on the bag.

Good lightweight, waterproof, two-person tents cost between $140 and $300. Weight and durability are the two primary factors affecting price. Two-person tents weigh from two to six pounds. The weight can be split between you and a companion, with one person carrying the fly and poles and the other the tent. A rainfly, whether separate or attached, is essential to keep out the wet weather. Ground cloths should never be put under a tent because they trap moisture and will cause the floor of the tent to leak. Because of the weight and expense of tents, many people prefer using a tarp. Tarps cost about $50 and weigh one or two pounds. It takes some skill to be able to erect a tarp so that it will really protect you in a storm. They also don't provide much of an escape from an onslaught of flying insects.

Bivouac sacks are another alternative to tents. They range in cost from $30 to $170 and weigh one or two pounds. The cheaper ones are simply tubes for your sleeping bag and to protect you from the weather, and many don't even do that. The more expensive ones are like small tunnel tents. You may want to get one made of Gore-Tex so that it will breathe and you won't get wet inside. The waterproofing abilities of Gore-Tex, especially in a steady downpour, are highly debatable.

Stoves

At one time stoves were not an essential item for the backpacker or hiker. Today, particularly in areas of heavy use, you can't get by without one. In many areas, because of overuse and seasonal fire hazards, fires are prohibited. The most popular backpacker's stoves are still the Svea and its cheaper imitation, the Optimus. The Svea costs about $40. If you buy a Svea or similar stove that you load with fuel yourself, be sure to buy a fuel bottle, which costs about $7. Cartridge stoves, such as the MSR X–G/K Multi-Fuel model, are good but more expensive alternatives for severe conditions. You don't have to pour the fuel into the stove and prime it, so they're easier to start. Because they start reliably in the cold, they are good for winter camping, and since there's no contact with the fuel, you don't have to worry about spilling it. In addition, you can sleep with the cartridge to keep it warm and make the stove easier to start. Naturally, you pay for this state of the art. The MSR with such necessary accessories as the cartridge costs about $90.

Becoming Proficient

The time needed to master the basics of hiking, snowshoeing, and backpacking is about as long as it takes to break in your boots. However, to learn to navigate, do first aid, read weather, and maneuver over difficult terrain can take several years. The measure of your competence is how safe you would feel if you were alone and well away from help. You can learn quickly or not at all. If you remain under someone's protection and guidance, you may never acquire the skills you may need one day.

Although not all women learn under the tutelage of a husband, father, or boyfriend, most do. Karen Swafford comments that only recently has she learned to navigate cross-country by herself or dare to go on trips alone. "My husband and I learned together," she says. "He wasn't pulling me along. But we often went into country he'd known since boyhood, so he navigated and I followed. If he had dropped dead, I would have been in trouble."

When Karen and her husband were divorced, she found herself in the position familiar to many women. If there wasn't a man around to go backpacking with, she didn't go.

> One time during a float trip on the Snake River, I wanted to go hiking when everyone else wanted to sunbathe. I went ahead alone. That gave me confidence. Later I started to dayhike just around the area where I live. Then I did my first solo on a mountain near my home. It was a little scary. There was one cross-country section in which I had to beat the brush to get downhill to the trail I was looking for. I found it alright, but I worried all the time until I did.

Karen says that the main reward of going alone was seeing all the wildlife, because as a loner she was quiet. She also likes the freedom and independence of being able to travel, wake, sleep, and think at her own will. Although you may never want to go backpacking alone, you should be skilled enough to be able to!

Most experienced women at one time or another have been lost, close to hypothermic, or otherwise come in harm's way. But most found that the experience increased their confidence and deepened their appreciation of the wilds. A woman who walked to the top of Mt. Whitney (14,494 feet), the highest mountain in the continental United States, and back in one day was overcome by exhaustion and cold. Nearly at the summit, she wedged herself in a crack in a rock. It was then that she understood why Indians used to go to the mountains to die.

The wilderness can provide the kind of emotional and intellectual complexity required of all deep relationships—excitement, boredom, fear, courage, pride, anger, peace, ecstasy, pain, pleasure. And for almost all backcountry users, one of the benefits of working long and hard to reach an objective is the satisfaction of having done it yourself. Women like Jo Prouty and Virginia Nolan are excellent examples of the benefits of a lifetime of physical fitness. Both are strong physically, intellectually alert, and have a rich tapestry of accomplishments and unusual adventures. Jo Prouty is especially encouraging because so many of her adventures were done after she had reached middle age. She takes the punch right out of the youth culture and all its negative ramifications for women who have been taught that aging is limiting. Women who *do* things with their lives know that their value as human beings is not based solely on what they look like.

The difficulty of getting into the backcountry is one of the reasons often cited for not protecting certain public lands as official "wilderness." If everyone can't or won't put out the effort to get there, then it's of no public value. This is much like contending that because not everyone can paint, we should close art museums. The day that local chambers of commerce start putting smog, junk yards, and high wall strip mines on the covers of their promotional brochures instead of snow-capped mountains, trout streams, and waterfalls, will be the day that the public will have truly forsaken the value of wilderness.

The difficulty of access does restrict use. And not sticking a roadhead and developed campground every five miles is one way of reducing use and protecting the environment. We accept the fact that 300 people can't use a tennis court at the same time, as Roderick Nash, author of *Wilderness and an American Mind*, pointed out a decade ago. The same holds true for the wilds. No, access isn't easy. But it shouldn't be. If it were easy, there'd be no wildlife, no fishing, no privacy, no adventure, and in essence, no wilderness.

Chapter 3

Climbing and Mountaineering

—When you get to the top of the hill . . . keep climbing.

A Woman's Movement

Across the table sipping tea in a noisy Boulder, Colorado, restaurant sits Coral Bowman, a petite, vivacious, feminine woman. She speaks excitedly but thoughtfully about women and rock climbing, and her school, which connects both. It's pleasant to find her so far removed from the stereotyped "lady jock." She insists that women don't have to abandon their femininity as they ascend into the exciting world of rock climbing. "I love the juxtaposition of power and femininity," she says about the counterpoint of elegant beauty against the theater of harsh rock.

Coral's early introduction to rock climbing was, as is often the case, being sandbagged by an aggressive male who expected her to do a climb that was much too advanced for most beginners. But she had the good fortune to catch an awed glimpse of an expert woman climber on an adjacent climb, who provided the rare role model and its attendant inspiration.

I'd been climbing maybe a couple of times at most, and this guy was taking me up the first pitch of the Bastille Crack.. . .When I finally did it years later as a competent climber, I thought, how did I ever get up it? Fear and loathing, much of it; or being so furious with my partner for taking me there, that I was damn well going to get up it. And not more than ten to fifteen feet away was Diana Hunter. She was leading the first free ascent of "Wide Country," an extremely difficult 5.11 climb. Here she was with this group of about ten men. And when I found out what had happened (that she had *led* the climb), I thought, "Wait a minute! You mean it's possible for women to be among some of the best climbers in the country and do well, lead?" And there was some part of me that wanted that for me.

Six years later, having achieved similar proficiency, Coral realized a closely related personal goal: to encourage women to enjoy and master the intricacies and beauty of this artful and demanding sport. Her rock climbing school, Great Horizons (Box 1811 Boulder, Colorado 80306), now in its third year, is geared to a supportive environment in which women (and men in her coed classes) can learn to climb—each according to her own inclinations and abilities, with emphasis to identify and supersede culturally imposed limitations and fears. Involvement in womens' groups and growth workshops brought Coral to a double realization: that women can learn to climb more easily the more they learn about themselves; and that rock climbing is an interesting way to learn: "I don't look at it as a counseling service, but an attempt to integrate rock climbing as introspection. I think a lot of programs try to do that, but a lot of them still come from a very male model."

Her courses typically last two to five days and are held during the spring, summer, and early fall around Boulder and the Rocky Mountain region. She also sponsors ice-climbing seminars in the winter. While her classes can be competitive, she encourages that competition to take place within the student herself and not expect to enter climbing at the same level of everyone else in the group. This approach underlines her philosophy that, in rock climbing, there should be "more room for people to be there in whatever way they want to be." Yet she also enjoys being an encouraging role model, to inspire her students to proficiency and excellence: "They see me do something, and even though they know I'm a talented rock climber, they think they can do it. 'There's a woman, look at her! She's not that big. If she can do it, I can,' and they spur themselves on."

Climbing is acknowledged to be a graceful, personal sport, requiring a blend of high-level physical fitness and mental and emotional strength. As much as it demands, so it also gives. It is a means to

Coral Bowman leading a 5.11 climb "Dead on Arrival." Photograph courtesy of Sue Giller.

become awesomely and sometimes painfully aware of oneself. For women in particular, self can be terra incognita: What do *I* want for myself? Where do *I* want to go? How can I get there under my own power? Climbing may be the hardest and most objective answer you will ever get. "I really believe that women are on the cutting edge of the frontier, that things are going to change because women are going to make them change in terms of culture. And I want to be a part of that," says Coral.

The Basics of Climbing

There are three types of climbing—rock, ice, and mountain. The emphasis in this chapter is on rock because it leads to the others. Sure, you can bag peaks without knowing a quark about ropes, ice axes, belays or crampons, but you will never be a true mountaineer unless you pass muster on rock and ice.

The pure sport of rock climbing begins on the smaller, more accessible crags. As you gain experience, techniques learned here can be applied to higher goals: the great walls of California's Yosemite Valley or the alpine granite of the Wind River Range in Wyoming.

Getting hauled up a mountain via ropes, pitons, pulleys, and what-not is not considered mountaineering. In the early years, whatever means got you to the top did not necessarily diminish the fact of getting there. This is no longer true. Since all of the world's highest peaks, except a few in China, have already been climbed, the art now lies in the *form* of the climb, the most aesthetic route. This has come to mean that the most respected climbs on the highest peaks are done without oxygen and on lower walls without artificial aids. There are some who hypothesize that such oxygen deprivation can lead to brain damage. At any rate, climbers love their rocks, and altering them with pitons and other junk is tantamount to defacing a Picasso or a da Vinci.

To understand free (unaided) climbing requires an understanding of the climbing rating system. Three basic ratings make up the system: Grade, Class, and Decimal.

Grades describe the amount of time it takes for the experienced, physically fit male to do the route. It does not describe the *technical* difficulty of the climb, although Grades IV and above are bound to be hard.

Grade	Time	Number of Pitches
I	1 hour	1–2
II	1–4 hours	2–4
III	4–7 hours	3–8
IV	7–10 hours	6–12
V	1–2 days	10–18
VI	2 days or more	15 or more

The Grades rating is used widely in the United States. The Europeans also rate climbs by Grades I to VI, but these describe technical difficulty and the type of equipment needed. European grades are equivalent to the U.S. system of classes, which was developed by Sierra Club climbers.[1]

Class	Equipment and Technique
1	Walking. No special equipment or technique.
2	Scrambling. Proper shoes advised. Hands may be needed for balance.
3	Climbing. Inexperienced climbers will need a rope.
4	Exposed climbing (a fall could be fatal). A rope and belays are advisable. Belay anchors may be needed.
5	Difficult free climbing. Protection anchors for the leader are advised.
6	Aided climbing. Rope and anchors are used to assist in moving up.

In recent years, Class 6 has been replaced by the letter *A* to indicate that aids are used. Class 6 climbs are no longer necessarily more difficult than the others, since many have been done without aids, and it is obvious that a climb done without aids is harder than the same one done with them.

Class 5 (free climbing) demands that nothing artificial intervene to aid your upward progress or rest stops. The only elements involved are the rock and the ingenuity of the climber to divine a sympathetic hold on a reluctant pitch.

The decimal rating is the most confusing and ill-defined; consequently, it is an arbitrary rating system. Not yet standardized, it is almost always used in combination with the class system, and you will see climbs described as 5.4., 5.8, and so forth. In general, climbs are rated from .1 to .10. A few, suicidal climbs are rated .11, .12, and even .13. Climbing 5.8 is advanced. The decimal system is further refined with the addition of lower-case letters *a, b, c, d,* and so forth. A guidebook to climbing may look something like a course in library science. Nevertheless, the letters generally refer to the most advanced pitch (section) within the route.

Bouldering, or climbing close to the ground without a rope for protection, is an important training aid as well as a sport in itself. As you venture higher, the nasty consequences of a fall are unnerving and the security of a rope appreciated. It is now time for your partner to assume her role as the *belayer,* who will check your fall should this be necessary. Assuming easy access to the top of the cliff, your belayer stations herself securely above and drops to you the end of the rope, which you tie yourself into. As you begin to climb, she pulls up the slack. This is one of the methods of *top roping.* Another method is to set up an anchor at the top of the pitch, loop a rope through it, and belay the climber from the ground. Climbing without rope protection is Class 3. Two persons roped together without intermediate protection points are climbing in Class 4. Their climb involves exposure (a fall could be fatal), which is why they have roped up.

At some point above her belayer, the leader may choose to place protection and attach the rope to the rock. This upgrades the climb to Class 5. She can continue to place protection at any comfortable interval. The rope runs freely through carabiners, or C-links, attached to each protection point. For instance, if the leader then climbs four feet above her last protection and falls, her plunge, assuming no complications, is arrested four feet below her protection, for a total of eight feet plus. The climbing rope stretches, and under the force of a falling climber, it absorbs much of the energy generated by the fall. (This is a good reason not to buy used ropes.) A leader fall of ten feet on steep terrain can be a gentle experience, but the rush of adrenaline usually shocks the system.

When the leader runs her rope out from one belay station and establishes a new one above, this distance climbed is called a *pitch*. Now the leader becomes the belayer, and the second climbs up to her under the safety of a top rope. This sequence may be repeated, or the pair may leapfrog.

Many a backpacker has scrambled (Class 3) to the top of some enticing peak. But the flanks of countless other mountains are so steep that their summits remain inaccessible to all but those alpinists qualified for the crags of the world beyond the cloud-filled valleys. Not only does alpine mountaineering require rock climbing techniques, but it can also demand a variety of unique snow and ice climbing skills, all of which may one day be called upon under extreme conditions. On colder, snowy mountains, glacier travel presents special problems, such as hidden crevasses. You need not journey to the great ranges to experience ice climbing. Glittering columns of frozen water suspend in quiet blue-white beauty to wait longingly until spring frees their journey to the sea. Many frozen waterfalls are accessible from highways that follow a river's course. Waterfall climbing, like bouldering or crag climbing, is a sport in its own right and also gives training for the most severe alpine ice routes. The protection system used in ice climbing is essentially the same as that for rock. Most ice climbers, including the alpinist, regard the ice as an extension of the rock.

The Demands of Climbing

Perhaps more than any other self-propelled sport, including kayaking, climbing breaks with the traditional feminine behavior set. This is perhaps why some women see it as inherently liberating. The first and probably most important break comes with the risk of getting hurt, even dying. It has been acceptable, even encouraged, for women to make personal sacrifices and take risks for some altruistic purpose such as birthing or protecting offspring, but risk-taking for personal glory, adventure, or pleasure has not been traditional for women. And few women do it. Women have been the conservatives of our species, and some sociobiologists believe that this life-protecting behavior is biologically based. If both men and women were out climbing mountains, wrestling alligators, and warring with their neighbors, who would take care of the babies?

Following this essential fact, the risk of death, come the others—

Ice climbing is a total body exercise, putting endurance demands on the arms as well as the legs. Photograph courtesy of Richard Collins.

strength, discipline, concentration, ambition, mechanical ability, mathematical ability (geometry, trigonometry, and physics), then freedom, exhilaration, and accomplishment. None of these abilities and rewards has a great deal to do with the way the majority of women in our culture have been reared or taught to excel. This is why there is only a handful of accomplished female rock climbers and hardly a thimbleful of accomplished female ice climbers.

It is doubtful that women will change the ego-oriented nature of the sport of rock climbing. As Coral Bowman notes, it is not a gentle sport. Nor is there any fundamental way to make it gentle without negating or diminishing its essence. What women like Coral seem to hope to bring to climbing is a benign and supportive teaching method—not mollycoddling, but also not sandbagging or terrorism. Climbing is hard. But the idea of teaching it is to make the first few sessions so easy and enjoyable that the novice becomes addicted enough to put up with the hardships.

Although she gets angry at herself for this, Coral allows the women to push themselves more when she teaches a class that includes men.

> I tend to back off a little bit with just women in terms of the difficulty of the top rope that I set up. A part of me so wants them not to have a bad experience because so many women start with it being so hard and awful that I'm protective of them. Yet when I get a mixed class, I naturally assume that I have to set up some things that are more strenuous for the men. And the women will try it. And I don't find them discouraged by it.

Men have the penchant for adventure pretty much engrained in them. It's part of their mental makeup, and some evidence says that it is biologically/hormonally based. So to excel at climbing, a woman may have to put in a lot of mental overtime to reach the state that a male partner may already have. So much of success in climbing depends on this mental state. And as Richard Bach writes in *Illusions,* "Argue for your limitations and sure enough they're yours."

To get past climbing 5.8 routes and particularly leading beyond 5.8 takes total confidence, says Lynn Hill, probably one of the world's best women climbers. "It's a turning point. If you have a lapse of confidence, you'll blow it. To lead beyond 5.8. means you must have complete control and not let it lapse," she says. The way to get mental control and confidence is to boulder. Mental control makes the difference between being able to lead and being the second on the rope (seconding). Leading is a way of acquiring mental control and improving performance. When you lead, you *must* be in control. You generally climb better when you're leading because you must. You can't let your mind wander as you can when you're seconding.

Of course sometimes you have to kick your own rear psychologically to get going. Sometimes someone else will have to do it for you. Coral says that when she teaches she has to learn who needs what. "There are times when I know that what someone needs is a kick in the ass. I'll hold back and hold back from doing that and then some part of me will just let go because I'll know a woman is using that, 'Watch out for me. I'm a delicate female. Be careful,' and I'll say, 'There's no way. You have to do it, and you *can* do it.' For some women it works. They need that. I need it too."

Becoming too success-oriented can make climbing very grim. Along with overconfidence, it can lead to mistakes and accidents. "I've done rappels on harder pitches," says Coral about an accident. Usually climbers will clip two carabiners to belay anchors as insurance in case one snaps loose. But distracted, Coral failed to do this. When she backed off to rappel, there was nothing holding her. Luckily she and her partner, Sue Giller, had a haul rope set up to bring up their gear. She grabbed this and ended up with third-degree rope burns on her forefingers, and the other parts of her fingers and palms were burned to the second degree. Within three weeks she was taping her fingers and took off on some climbing trips. It took several years for her hands and fingers to heal completely.

Why didn't Coral check her carabiners and belay better? "I was in perfect physical shape," she says. "We'd trained all summer for that climb. But I had no place being on the rock because of what was happening in my personal life. I just insisted that I would turn off the mental static. I'd been doing that for a couple of years and I was good at it. But some part of me that day just said, 'This is it. You aren't going to do that anymore.'"

Climbing is safer if you're at peace with yourself. Coral contends that you cannot obtain this mental clarity by following the male model and blocking out emotion. Consequently, it may be more pleasant and safer to climb with a female partner because women are more likely to recognize and allow for emotional or personal turmoil. Being less goal-oriented, they won't push when they or a partner is having a bad day. "When I climb with women, I feel I have every option available," she says. "We can go down. We can go up. She'll understand. She may be angry, and that's healthy, but she'll probably be willing to change plans without blaming me. When I climb with men, I immediately cut off some of my options because I assume from experience that the man will be disappointed if the day doesn't go according to *his* plan. And if I back off, he's going to be angry."

As illustrated by Coral's accident, climbing takes a good deal of concentration, particularly if you lead. One way to clear the mental decks for the task at hand is to be utterly in control of your equipment. What good is a safety system if you don't know how to use it? You have to know how your equipment is functioning and how to identify when a rope, for example, is worn to the point of danger. You have to become accustomed to checking your ropes and other gear before you depend on them. Letting the man take care of equipment can one day get you in trouble if he becomes injured or is out of earshot to give advice.

Training and Preparation

Climbing usually consists of segments up to 150 to 165 feet each, the distance being limited by the length of the rope. As such, it is generally 70 percent anaerobic. It *can* be 70 percent aerobic if you climb quickly, for example, on easy terrain. But despite the relatively low aerobic demands, climbers should go through an aerobic conditioning program. First, unless you enter at easy access spots, you will need as much and more aerobic energy as a backpacker for the walk-in because you're not only carrying backpacking gear, but ropes, carabiners, and other hardware. Second, the better aerobically conditioned you are, the less you will fatigue. This is true regardless of whether or not you breathe hard during a climb. The anaerobic energy system depends upon the aerobic system to refuel. The climber who has great muscle strength but little aerobic endurance had better hope that hard pitches come early in the climb.

Aerobic power is extremely important in mountaineering. Often you must put in predawn to postdusk days to get on and off the mountain before sunset or bad weather traps you. You must have the reliable endurance strength to cross avalanche chutes quickly. Mountaineering is 99 percent hard work and the repetition of trudging up, up, and up. To compound the aerobic demands is the fact that all this hard work is often done at high altitudes. Aerobic power is less essential for those who do short, technical climbs. But bouldering, like Class 5 climbing, often requires a walk-in. You won't climb well if you're exhausted by the time you get there.

The choice of an aerobic program for climbers is not as straightforward as for other self-propelled sports. You use every imaginable muscle and then some. Swimming has its merits for the woman climber because it develops upper-body strength. But a woman does not *have* to mimic the male technique of powering up a pitch with her shoulder, chest, and arm muscles. In fact, the proper climbing technique uses the arms more for balance than power. Out of necessity, a woman may learn good technique because she cannot rely on her upper body to carry her upward. Although upper-body strength is not nearly so crucial as some might imagine, many women are so weak in this part of their bodies that endurance-strength development, the kind that comes from swimming or rowing, is crucial. Nevertheless, most of your weight usually is borne by your lower body. So an aerobic training program that develops the lower body is also a good choice.

Running is probably the most popular form of aerobic conditioning among climbers, but bicycling is also a good choice because it develops the quadriceps and calf muscles. The recommended mileage is about the same as it is for backpackers—two to four miles running or six to twelve miles biking, depending on the nature of your excursions. As in backpacking, it is important to run or bicycle hills to develop the intermediate energy system.

Another factor in training is age. Many young climbers, especially men, can get away with no aerobic training at all. Some, when asked how they get in condition, have answered unhelpfully, "horizontal training—drinking beer, eating pizza, sleeping late, conserving energy for the expedition."[2]

For the women who climbed Annapurna I (26,540 feet) in 1978, the aerobic training recommended by advisers at the Institute of Environmental Stress at the University of Santa Barbara was at least a half hour daily. But most mountaineers do much more than this. Some with the time to do it will prepare for a major mountaineering venture by hiking six to eight hours several times a week with a loaded pack. Arlene Blum, the expedition leader and author of *Annapurna: A Woman's Place,* hiked in the hills near her home with sixty pounds of bricks in her pack or ran five to ten hilly miles. Especially encouraging about the fitness tests the women made before the climb is that although they ranged in age from twenty to forty-nine, there was no apparent decrease in fitness with age: "testimony to the value of regular exercise in maintaining fitness," Blum wrote. As Michael Loughman says in *Learning to Rock Climb:* "Running does shorten and stiffen the muscles in the back of the leg, and climbing requires these muscles to be loose and supple. If you run, be sure to keep up daily stretching exercises. Climbing itself is one of the best stretching exercises."[3]

Interval training can be a real boon to the serious climber. In fact, intervals may be your best method of aerobic conditioning because the rest-activity sequence is so much like climbing itself. Intervals that develop the lactic-acid system may be the most valuable (see chapter 1).

Michael Loughman says that the main physical handicap for women is not lack of strength, but height, because handholds may be out of reach. While there may be some merit to this in some situations, in others being small is an advantage. For example, Polly Prescott, who, with Marguerite Schnellbacher, was the first woman alone to climb Mt. Louis in Canada and traverse Mt. Edith Cavell, comments that Mt. Louis is "continuously good, rather exposed climbing with a large chock stone in the final chimney to surmount spread-eagle. Some have trouble fitting into the chimney. It can be tight."[4] Some of the best climbers, like Lynn Hill and Yvon Chouinard, are barely more than five feet tall. A more important factor than height is a high ratio of strength to body weight, and this can be acquired. While some women, such as the late Diana Hunter, who led 5.11 climbs and could barely do one pullup, can still be good and have little upper-body strength, you're at a decided advantage if you do have it.

The kind of strength needed for climbing is not the same as what you will need for other sports. While the arms, legs, and shoulders are important, strength is also needed in the forearms, wrists, hands, and fingers. This spectrum, especially that in the lower arms, is unique to climbing. Among the more specialized ways of developing this unique spectrum is to climb with a pack that is slightly heavier than you're accustomed to wearing. Another is to climb ropes while wearing a pack.

A favorite training method among climbers is pullups. "It took me about a month to do a pullup. I had to start with a lower bar," says Coral. "Shortly after I could do three. Now, maximum, I can do 13." Lynn Hill, who does pyramid sets of 100 pullups, says that when you get to the point that you're leading climbs of difficulty above 5.10, you should be able to do five to seven pullups. Pyramid sets are done by first doing one pullup, resting for a few seconds, then two pullups and resting, then three, and so on until you get to ten. Then you go back down, doing nine, eight, and so forth. All told, it amounts to 100 pullups.

Pullups are especially important if you are a lead climber, since you will spend so much of your time "hanging out." This means that you are poised on the rock in likely difficult positions while you put in chocks for friends and then attach the carabiners and rope. Naturally you need a free hand to do this, and it's nice to have plenty of strength in the other arm.

Some climbers recommend doing pullups in which the palms face away from the body. This is because you usually climb with your palms facing away from you. Others recommend also doing chinups with palms facing toward you, possibly for variety and more balanced strength development. A mixture of both, with emphasis on the palms-away position, is probably best.

Fingertip pullups done while hanging from a doorjam are also helpful. If you can't pull yourself up, you can straddle/shimmy up with your feet, then let yourself down slowly. This method is nice because it requires no special equipment.

Considerable shoulder strength is important in ice climbing because of the heavy packs and the repetitive insertion and extraction of the ax into the ice, often with every step. This takes a lot of hand and arm strength and coordination. Your arms are usually held over your head as you sink the ax into place. Pullups done slowly and methodically are a great help to the ice climber, both for strength and coordination. (When gripping the ice ax, don't strangle it, since this will cause unnecessary fatigue.) On most extended alpine routes you do wear a pack. Even ten to fifteen pounds on your back can make an incredible difference in the time it will take you to burn out. The best method for developing this kind of endurance would be with aerobic upper-body training, such as swimming or rowing.

Dips are good for developing the kind of shoulder strength needed for mantling. This strenuous move requires pulling your body up with your arms until your head is above your hands. It is done when there is no way to "walk up" a move with your feet. The wrist curl is valuable to climbers because it builds strength in the forearms and wrists. It is generally done with professional weights, although you can improvise by loading buckets with sand. A variation of the wrist curl, the fingertip curl, can be done only on the Universal system or one similar to it. With this you let the bar you're holding roll slowly to the fingertips, then slowly roll it back into the palm. Fingers are extremely important to the climber. Loughman feels that a climber should take care of her fingers the way a concert pianist would. And, in fact, piano playing probably is good exercise for the climber. Another method of developing strength is to do fingertip pushups. Instead of resting on the palms of your hands, do the pushup on the tips of your fingers. Hard! Try doing one fingertip pushup for every set of regular pushups.

Lower-body strength is also important for the climber, especially for the mountaineer. Strength in the quads and calves is needed to cover downhill distances with minimal stress to the joints. The weight of your gear adds to this stress, so weight training is good preparation for it. Strength in the quads is also important for uphill stretches because these muscles propel your body upward against gravity.

The calf muscles are important to climbers in a unique way. Occasionally a climber's calves will "sewing machine," meaning they will shake uncontrollably when put under stress, such as when you're balanced precariously on a ledge or toehold. Although not entirely preventable, "sewing machines" may be avoided by developing strength in the calves. Good balance, good technique, and knowing how to relax may help more. For example, toeing in on a hold puts too much weight on the front of the foot, and this strain moves into the calves as they contract to hold the foot in this uncomfortable position. Relaxing can be hard when climbing, but doing lots of stretches before and after a climb helps. Of course shifting your weight on a hold helps relax the calves.

The calves can "burn" when you're climbing ice, especially steep ice such as that on a waterfall. This happens when you stand on the front points of your crampons. You can prevent this by using proper cramponing techniques when on the ice and by doing the recommended strength training and stretching. Chair/stair stepping (see chapter 1) and calf raises (see chapter 2) are especially good exercises. Weight-training exercises of special importance to climbers are the leg extension, leg curl, and leg press. (The leg extension is not recommended if you have chondromalacia because it can increase the damage.) Another good exercise for the leg is the wall sit, explained in chapter 7.

The exercise program for climbers is similar to the one for backpackers with the additions of the wrist curl, fingertip pushup and wall sit. It can be adapted to whatever facilities are available to you. You can add or substitute different exercises for those recommended by referring to the chart on page 38. Adjust the program to put emphasis on the weakest parts of your body, for example, your shoulders. The muscle groups are assigned numbers. Beside each muscle group is the minimum number of exercises you should do. The numbers beside each exercise refer to the number of the muscle group that is worked by the exercise.

1. Hips, lower back, buttocks (one exercise)
2. Chest, upper arms (two exercises)
3. Thighs, hamstrings (two exercises)
4. Calves, shins, ankles (two exercises)
5. Shoulders, triceps (two exercises)
6. Abdomen (one exercise)
7. Biceps (two exercises)
8. Forearms, wrists (two exercises)

Free Weights	*Universal or Nautilus*	*No Weights*
Bench fly (2,5)	Bench press (2,5)	Bent-leg sit-ups (1,6)
Calf raise (4)	Bent-leg sit-up (1,6)	Calf raise (4)
Clean and press	Calf raise (4)	Chinup (2,5,7,8)
(1,2,3,4,5,6,7,8)	Leg curl (1,3,4)	Pushup (2,5 7)

Quarter squat (1,3,4,6)   Leg press (1,3)   Fingertip pushup (2,5,7,8)
Toe raise (4)   Leg extension (3)   Quarter deep-knee bend
Upright rowing (2,5,7)   Overhead press (5)   (1,3,4)
Wrist curl (8)   Pulldown behind neck   Squeeze tennis ball (8)
                                (1,2,7,8)   Toe raise (4)
                             Toe raise (4)   Wall sit (3)
                             Wrist curl/fingertip (8)

Stretching and Flexibility

Very few other sports, outside of gymnastics, require as much flexibility and stretching as climbing does. A full-scale stretching program, such as yoga, is of great benefit to the climber. Muscle groups of special importance in a stretching program are the shoulders and neck, the hamstrings, calves, and forearms. Stretching thoroughly before climbs may help prevent such disasters as "sewing-machine" calves. Stretch between climbs and again at the end of the day. The best stretching exercises are the same as those explained in chapter 1—the calf stretch, forearm stretch, head/neck rotation, hyperextension, raised leg, squat, and toe touch. The one important addition to these is the forearm stretch. To do the forearm stretch, extend your arm straight out in front of you. Press the palm of your other hand against the extended fingers of the outstretched arm. Push/pull the fingers on the outstretched arm as far back toward the wrist as possible.

The climber's need for good balance is obvious, and it's not surprising that many top climbers have a background in gymnastics. Many exceptionally good climbers, including men, take ballet to improve their balance, agility, and grace. Speed sports, such as skateboarding, surfing, windsurfing, and alpine skiing also develop these attributes.

You can do several things to train specifically for balance. One of the easiest is to practice walking over skinny logs or walking on scree slopes. Some climbers even run over talus, the rubble of large rocks on a mountain. This is called, appropriately, talus running. Simply walking across talus, especially while wearing a heavy pack, takes getting used to. Running across it is demanding, tiring, and conducive to sprains. If you get good at it, congratulations. You won't have much company.

One interesting way to acquire good balance for climbing is to walk along a slack chain. It's not actually a chain in most cases, but a length of rope strung between two trees. Some of the more dedicated will set the system up indoors with bolts attached to the wood studs in the wall. Whether indoors or out, the slack chain can provide a challenge. Another method of acquiring balance is to practice climbing easier pitches without using your hands.

Injuries and Ailments

Serious accidents and fatalities are not uncommon among climbers. However, most climbers believe that rock climbing is much safer than mountaineering. There are few data to confirm or deny this. What studies do exist tend to lump rock climbing, ice climbing, and mountaineering together, so it's all but impossible to make an evaluation of the relative safety of the three. Although he doesn't document this, Michael Loughman says that the list of expert rock climbers killed on rock cliffs is impressively short, while the list of expert mountaineers killed during a climb is impressively long.

Contributing to the safety of rock climbing are guidebooks to most of the popular climbing areas. They rate the climb, so you can stay off routes beyond your skill level. Of course guidebooks are not the last word, and the criteria for rating climbs are not uniform. It's possible, even likely, that a climber will occasionally make a mistake and get off her chosen route onto one that is more difficult.

There's an element of choice in rock climbing over how safe your safety system will be and how trustworthy your climbing partners. Risk can be extraordinarily high if you free-solo exposed areas. This means climbing alone without safety equipment on pitches on which a fall could be fatal. Some free-solo climbers say the risk is not unlike Russian roulette. But then risks can be reduced substantially by such safety back-up systems as double-roping.

If there is one rule to climbing, it's to choose your partners and teachers carefully. Says Coral Bowman:

> I first started climbing with a man who spent a lot of time in the mountains. He was wild and willing to take many risks himself, although he knew how to make things safe, and I learned a lot about safety from him. But he would take chances that would put his partners in the same predicament. For awhile I chose to be his partner, that is, I chose to compromise my values. That was part of my rationale for setting up a climbing school. I wanted women to know that when you first learn to climb you do have choices over your own safety. You don't have to learn at the mercy of whoever you're with. Safety is one of the ways you judge a climbing partner.

In mountaineering there are "objective dangers," among them avalanches and that whole range of bad weather—cold, wet, storms, and lightning. Since these hazards cannot be eliminated from mountaineering, all you can do is to be well prepared, educated, skilled, and in good physical condition. Even so, in the most difficult mountaineering, climbing in the Himalayas, the fatality rate is one in ten. The fatality rate among mountain climbers in Teton National Park between 1976 and 1980 was 1 in 2,809.[5] This averages out to about 36 deaths per 100,000 persons, or about 3 a year out of about 7,165 climbers. For comparison, the fatality rate in motor vehicle accidents for 1978 was 25 in 100,000.

These data are not meant to scare you out of the mountains but to underline the importance of matching proficiency and safety equipment with the terrain you cover. In the Teton study, fatal accidents appeared to be associated most with climber error (57 percent). Among factors contributing most to climber error were inadequately placed protection, inadequate equipment (usually no ice ax), climbing off-route, inability to glissade, and inadequately placed anchor. The second characteristic that separated fatal from nonfatal accidents was travel on snow. Avalanches accounted for 20 percent, and 21 percent involved slipping on snow or a faulty glissading technique. There is no question among most climbers that leading is more hazardous than seconding, and the Teton study bears this out. Of all the climbers involved in accidents, 65 percent were leading a technical climb. Contrary to the belief among many climbers that most accidents occur on the descent (rappel), in the Teton study 51 percent occurred on the ascent and 34 percent on the descent.

According to Michael Loughman, the greatest hazard in rock climbing is to assume that equipment can substitute for skill. The modern emphasis on acquiring the skills to free-climb should logically make climbing less hazardous, since peer pressure requires that you be highly skilled before tackling difficult routes. The Teton study does seem to confirm this. The authors note that although the number of persons climbing in the Tetons has increased dramatically in the last ten years the accident rate has not.

"Mount Rundle draws the young men with their bright ropes and brighter hopes," writes Sid Marty in *Men for the Mountains*, about climbers in Banff National Park in Canada.

> The ones that go to it with no experience and no climbing partner, with nothing but shiny new equipment, are the ones it sometimes keeps, the ones it chews up and spits out. . . .
>
> Now another would-be climber of Mount Rundle surveys the summit. . . . I saw in him myself at seventeen, walking around theatrically with the same new rope slung over my shoulder, ignoring the advice of the local people to find an experienced partner or go to a rock climbing school to learn the basic skills of mountaineering.

So, the best prevention of climbing accidents is to develop and hone your skills. For example, most good climbers hate to rappel. Why? Because this makes them absolutely dependent on their equipment. Most don't care to trust their lives to an anchor that may or may not hold. They feel safer when the rock is under their control. They know to test a hold before putting their weight on it, especially when leading. They know how to treat gear. They don't stand on their ropes or grind dirt into them. They don't store the rope in the sun because this rots the fiber. They know how to tie knots correctly, and so on with the myriad details a climber needs to know if she intends to live to tell it to her grandchildren.

Rock climbing is risky, and this is part of its appeal, but you can make it less so. There's a new rope available, the Robbins Lifeline, which is half a millimeter thicker than the 11-millimeter rope used for lead climbing. Or there's double-roping, in which not one but two, ropes are set up for protection. Double-roping is admittedly more of a hassle. It takes longer and adds more weight to your load. But it's reassuring to have a backup, the more so if you have ever popped off the rock and dangled there in space calculating how long it will take the granite crystals to cut fatally into your lifeline.

One of the hazards of popular routes is getting hit by a rock dislodged by someone above you. If you topple a rock, you're supposed to yell "rock" as loud as you can. Everyone else is supposed to yell "rock" too. "I was almost killed climbing the Apron in Yosemite," says Kathryn Collins.

> I was seconding a pitch and we had about forty feet to go to this rock ledge that was at the top of four routes. Someone on the ledge knocked some rocks loose. There were three voices above me yelling "rock," and all of a sudden two rocks came careening out of the sky. I tucked in close to the rock I was on, and just in time. The first rock missed me. But the other struck hard on my back. My head had been in its path a few seconds earlier. . . . That whole side of my back turned into a massive bruise. Because I was seconding, I could have jumped out of the way. But I didn't think of that.

This woman questions the value of a helmet had she been hit on the head. "A helmet might protect you from small- to medium-sized rocks, but I still could have gotten a fractured neck or a concussion," she said. Although most climbers own helmets, many eschew them, maintaining that they're hot, heavy, and restrict your field of vision. Although you do need them in mountains like the Cascades in Washington, where there's a lot of loose rock, many climbers now feel that it's better to use your head than cover it.

To avoid getting hit by rocks, try to climb in uncrowded areas— in Yosemite there are often lines to popular routes—go on weekdays, and be first on the route. In the Alps, where some routes look like a mayfly hatch, people will bivouac at the bottom of a route to be first on it in the morning. If you must climb below someone, wait until they're completely off the route before you get on it. If you can't get out of the path of a rock, put your hands or your pack over your head if there's enough time. Often the first person down will put her pack over her head to protect herself from rocks knocked loose by those still descending.

If you climb, it's inevitable that you will fall. Consequently, it's important to learn how to do it. Because most boys and men participate in sports in which falling is assumed, they may be more adept at this than girls and women. Bouldering comes into play here, for it is while bouldering that you learn how to fall and land. "I think you can practice jumping off," says Coral. "You can get to the point that as soon as you're falling, you relax. One time I was trying a rock-climbing problem alone. There were stairs below me. My foot slipped. As soon as it did, I relaxed. My mind was trained well enough." Instead of hitting the stairs and tumbling down them, she sprang over them and lept to the ground. As you climb, keep a running tabulation of what you would do if you fell, says one climbing guide. Watch as you go by and judge what you would do. If you lead, think the same thing through to determine where to put your protection.

A safe attitude is one way in which many women are already attuned to the needs of climbing. But this is true only if it is backed up with knowledge. A course in rescue, including crevasse rescue and rope litters, is strongly recommended for mountaineers. Another way to increase your margin of safety is to be aware of your own limitations and act accordingly. For example, if you hit an off day, pay attention to this signal and avoid difficult undertakings. Many climbers and mountaineers have had accidents because they ignored such signals.

Graduating from backpacking to mountaineering does not necessarily occur after you have completed a climbing course. Once you enter terrain in which an ice ax is advisable for self-arrest, you are crossing over into mountaineering. This is a signal that you need to know more about technique than how to put one foot in front of the other. The purchase of an ice ax should be accompanied by competent instruction. Recall the study of accidents in the Tetons in which 21 percent of the fatalities were related to slipping on snow or a faulty glissading technique.

Although nutrition for mountaineering is discussed in chapter 8, it is worth mentioning that you should increase vitamin C intake at moderate to high altitudes. Vitamin C aids healing. Altitude slows healing probably because of decreased oxygen intake. This can extend the healing process to about twice as long as normal. Sometimes a wound won't heal until you come down from the mountain. Foods high in carbohydrates are also good for high-altitude endeavors because they seem to increase the oxygen content of the blood, increase tolerance to altitude, reduce the severity of mountain sickness, and reduce some of the loss of physical performance.

Major injuries such as severe bleeding and compound fractures or those that result in coma are beyond the scope of this book. It is in advanced first-aid and emergency medical technician courses that you will learn what you really should know to be a mountaineer. *Medicine for Mountaineering,* an excellent field manual, is also highly useful. Other problems frequently encountered in the mountains, such as hypothermia, altitude illness, and heatstroke are discussed in chapter 9. They do have one thing in common: They are eminently preventable and potentially lethal.

Burns and Lacerations

Rope burns can occur when you're holding a fall or rappelling. Most nerve endings are close to the skin surface, so these shallow burns can hurt. One way to avoid them is to descend a rappel slowly. If you *must* make repeated rappels, wear gloves.Burns or skinning the back of the hands commonly occurs when you climb cracks. This is a special liability if you're climbing difficult cracks with rough rock, such as the Needles in South Dakota. Protect the back of your hands by covering them from the knuckles to the wrist with one-and-a-half- or two-inch adhesive tape.

Lacerations, particularly those from crampons and ice axes, are fairly common among mountaineers. The treatment of burns and lacerations is the same: Clean, disinfect, and cover the wound, and take a painkiller (analgesic). Although taping gauze over a wound will keep it clean, even better is a new product called Op-Site wound dressing. Op-Site is transparent and allows the wound to breathe. This aids healing, and you can see how the healing progresses without removing the dressing. (Op-Site is available from Acme United Inc., Bridgeport,

Connecticut 06609.) Gaping wounds should be closed with a butterfly bandage, but not closed so tight as to prevent air from getting to the wound and discharge from escaping.

The prevention and treatment of sunburn and snow blindness should be emphasized. The combination of glare from snow and ice and the less dense atmosphere at high altitudes makes mountaineers vulnerable regardless of the color of their skin. Vera Komarkova, the fair-skinned leader of the women's expedition to Dhaulagiri in 1980, burned, or more accurately, *fried* her hands while carrying loads on a sunny day at high altitude. It took about five days for the blisters to disappear. Two Sherpas tanned to the point that their skin turned black, yet they were burned red beneath the pigment. Even sunscreens with PABA (para-amino-benzoic acid), zinc oxide, or Glacier Cream won't entirely protect the skin under extreme conditions. Although it's uncomfortable, the best protection is clothing. Thin gloves and a face mask are musts when the sun is out at altitude. The intensity of ultraviolet rays increases by 5 percent for every 1,000 feet above sea level. By the time you're at 17,000 feet, it will have increased by 85 percent!

As to snow blindness, mountaineers should purchase good mountaineering glasses that screen out 80 percent of the sun's ultraviolet rays. It's a good idea to take an extra pair on long expeditions.

Muscle Injuries

The best prevention of almost all muscle injuries is strength, endurance, flexibility, and warm-ups. This isn't to say that you won't get any muscle injuries if you're fit, but it will reduce your chances. A fatigued muscle tightens up and is more susceptible to injuries.[6]

Climbers may experience immediate and acute muscle soreness, particularly when the muscles are "pumped" or contracted hard under

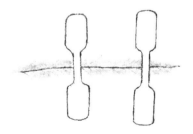

Butterfly bandage. Drawing by Janis Rockwell.

stress, such as when bouldering. The remedy for this is simple: Rest and stretching, which restores the circulation. Delayed soreness, which occurs from eight to thirty-six hours after exercise, is a little less certain both in diagnosis and treatment. What's the difference, for example, between soreness and an actual muscle strain? Assume that it's simple soreness. It is not certain what causes this, but some believe that the muscle fibers swell under stress if they are not used often. The muscle sheath or connective tissue may be irritated, or the muscle itself may go into spasm. Whatever the cause, you should be able to stretch without undue pain, and, in fact, stretching will help ease the pain. The other remedy is rest. Many find that an application of oil of wintergreen liniment feels good. It's not surprising that Ben-Gay is often sold out at the commissary at the Phantom Ranch at the bottom of the Bright Angel Trail in the Grand Canyon.

A muscle strain means that the fiber is torn. The greater the tear, the worse the strain. Minor tears are sometimes hard to distinguish from soreness. If stretching hurts, it's a muscle strain. Further stretching only aggravates the injury. A commonly torn muscle in climbers is in the shoulders. If many fibers are torn, localized, severe bruising may occur. Surgery is sometimes required to repair major strains. It may take three to six weeks for a major strain to heal, and you should not climb or backpack during that period. The treatment of all muscle strains is Rest, Ice, Compression, and Elevation (RICE). Although using heat is controversial, you may want to apply heat forty-eight hours after the injury.

A final muscle problem is cramps, which are usually caused by an electrolyte imbalance—a lack of salt, potassium, and magnesium. Some physicians believe that if you have a high salt intake (common in the United States) you are more likely to get "salt" cramps. It is thought that a body accustomed to large amounts of salt may waste or sweat away more of it during exercise, thereby leading to a salt imbalance and cramps. On the other hand, persons with an extremely low salt intake may have little on reserve and may also be more vulnerable to cramps. To identify, prevent, and treat muscle cramps, see chapters 9 and 2.

Tendinitis

Tendinitis, the classic overuse syndrome, occurs in rock climbers in the biceps, wrists, and forearms. It might occur in the biceps from repeated swinging of an ice ax or hammer. Among mountaineers, it can occur in the knees because of the repeated stress of carrying heavy gear over uneven or downhill terrain. It occurs when muscles, particularly tight ones, are used too much too quickly. Tendinitis is characterized by pain that sets in without any single traumatic incident. The tendons are fibrous tissue that connects the muscles to the bone. They are easily irritated and quick to swell and become inflamed. If you are doing a side traverse in which you must repeatedly "jump" from one handhold to the next, for example, you may notice a burning, shooting pain in your biceps some twelve to twenty-four hours later. This is tendinitis.

The treatment for tendinitis is rest and taking an antiinflammatory analgesic, referred to as NSAIDs (nonsteroidal antiinflammatory drugs). They reduce both pain (analgesic) and inflammation. Among NSAIDs are Motrin (ibuprofen), Zomax (zomepirac), Anaprox (naproxen sodium), and Ponstel (mefenamic acid). These are generally taken three times a day with meals. Different people respond better to different brands of these drugs, so some experimentation may be necessary. A short-range side effect of these drugs can be stomach irritation and upset, which is why they should be taken with meals. Another NSAID, aspirin, may be taken instead of these prescription drugs. However, many find that it is not so effective and that using it three times a day causes their ears to ring. This ringing is a sign that you're taking more aspirin than your body can tolerate. As with muscle strains, the use of heat to relieve tendinitis pain is controversial. Waiting about forty-eight hours after the onset of pain to apply heat should reduce the chances of it prolonging the injury.

Bursitis, like tendinitis, involves burning pain, and the pain worsens when you use the affected joint. It may be caused either by overuse or trauma. It occurs when the bursa, a small fluid-filled sac near the joint, becomes irritated. It can occur in any joint and in a number of locations around a specific joint. For example, there are fourteen bursae around the knee. The treatment of bursitis is the same as that for tendinitis.

Ankle Injuries

Most ankle injuries are sprains. Sprains are a stretching or tearing of the ligaments, the supporting tissue around the joint. Once a sprain occurs, it is more likely to recur. The pain and restricted motion resulting from an ankle sprain has been shown to linger in some people for as long as three to nine years.[7]

Because ankle sprains can become chronic, prevention is important. The main prevention is strength, particularly developed by calf and toe raises. Two other exercises, used both to prevent and to re-habilitate a sprained ankle, are the *alaphbet* and *tubing*. To do alphabet exercises, sit on a chair and write the letters of the alphabet on the floor with your big toe. Tubing exercises are more complicated but the basic idea is to bend the foot at the ankle forward, backward, and sideways against a resisting force. It was termed *tubing* because pre-viously a length of surgical tubing was looped around the ball of the foot. Resistance was provided by the person holding onto a length of nylon cord attached to the loop; or the cord was attached to a table leg or other stable object. The advantage of tubing is that it works the ankle through its entire range of motion and builds strength by adding resistance. This exercise is particularly good for weak ankles. Instead of a surgical tube, you can use a two-foot-long piece of heavy elastic, such as that used in skirt waistbands. Tie or sew the ends together, then attach a three- or four-foot-long piece of nylon cord. To do the backward and forward moves, sit on the floor and put the ball of your foot in the loop. Then point your toe away from your body, and provide the resistance by taking up the slack in the cord with your hands. To work the ankle in a backward position, attach the free end of the cord to a table leg. Loop the elastic around the ball of your foot, then scoot backward on the floor until the cord is taut. Bend your foot backward, with the toe pointing toward you as far as possible. Repeat the same procedure sideways on both sides of your ankles. Repeat the exercise in each position until your ankle gets tired.[8]

If you have weak ankles or old injuries be especially careful when you select shoes or boots. Some professional female foresters with weak ankles advocate high-topped boots such as those made by Red Wing and White (see chapter 2). Others prefer light hiking shoes, such as the Nike Approach and the New Balance Rainier Hiker. However, neither comes in women's sizes. If you prefer the light shoes, look for one with a heel counter to stabilize the heel and ankle. A new device called the Foot Doc Heel Counter Stabilizer can be attached to the outside of the shoe. This is good if you hike in your running shoes. They can be purchased from Power Soler, Inc. for about $7.50 (Box 618, Wetumpka, Alabama 36092).

Sprained ankles can be caused in numerous creative ways. One unique to rock climbers is bouldering on uneven ground, especially without benefit of a spotter. Another might be when you're leading a climb off a belay ledge, then fall back onto the ledge. A third way is catching your crampons on something unintended, like your pants, and tripping. This is all the more likely if you're not used to wearing crampons.

The immediate treatment is RICE and aspirin or Motrin to reduce

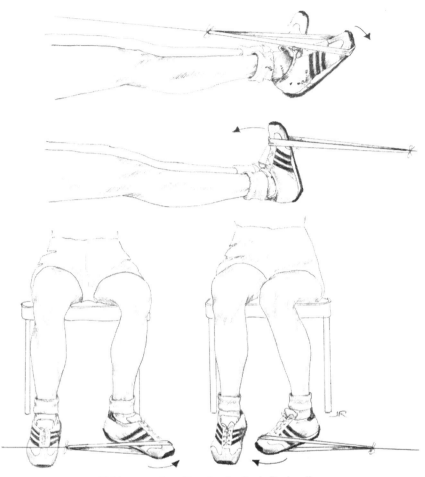

Tubing exercises. Drawing by Janis Rockwell.

pain and swelling. Do not apply heat because it increases swelling and retards healing. Taping a weak ankle with adhesive tape for stability is advocated for new and old injuries and weak ankles. However, adhesive tape can cause small blisters to form, is time-consuming to apply (requiring training or a professional), and painful to remove. Gratefully, now available is the Castiglia ankle wrap (or C-wrap), an innovative combination of Velcro and elastic that costs about $10 and can be applied by an amateur in a few seconds. (Casco/USA, 2455

Sunrise Blvd., Fort Lauderdale, Florida 33304. When ordering, state whether you want a right or left ankle wrap.)

Many people now feel that a sprained ankle should be rested only long enough for the swelling to abate. After swelling disappears (twenty-four to forty-eight hours), the sooner you start to exercise the ankle, the better. However, this can hurt. Another new invention, the Aircast ankle stirrup, gives stability and eliminates pain while allowing you to use your ankle. The air stirrup, which costs about $33, is a U-shaped plastic brace lined with inflatable air bags. Runners have run on sprained ankles with it and basketball players have played basketball wearing it. (It can be obtained from Aircast, Box T, Summit, New Jersey 07901.) The reason why you should exercise a sprained ankle a soon as possible is to prevent loss of muscle from disuse and loss of the range of motion in the joint.

You should be able to walk without a great deal of pain on an ankle that is moderately sprained. You should also be able to move your foot up and down with little pain. Tenderness and bruising should be only in the area right in front of the ankle bone. If you have swelling, bruising, and possibly pain on both sides of the ankle and cannot walk or move the foot up and down, you may have a severe sprain or possibly a fracture. If you have these symptoms, don't put any weight on the ankle and seek medical treatment. Stabilizing a sprain is important because otherwise you could further damage the ligaments. Sprains are usually caused by trauma. If the onset of pain is gradual, you probably have bursitis, or if it's the knee, chondromalacia.

If you have chronic ankle problems, definitely wear an air stirrup or C-wrap. Elastic tape and adhesive tape were shown in one study to lose 39 percent of their effectiveness after ten minutes of activity.[9] Of the two, adhesive tape provides more lateral stability. Blisters can be incapacitating for the mountaineer, especially at high altitudes, where they don't heal fast. See chapter 2 for how to treat them. But try to avoid them.

Knee Injuries

Among traumatic injuries, a dislocated kneecap is far more common than an actual dislocated knee. To determine if you have dislocated a kneecap, compare it to the one on the other leg. It will be obvious; a funny bump will appear in the wrong place. If you're in the field, you will have to put it back for comfort. This is not as hard to do as relocating a shoulder because the kneecap is not surrounded by a bunch of muscles. Gently apply traction in the direction of the deformity to loosen up the muscle, then ease the kneecap back into place by gentle pressure with your fingers. A dislocated kneecap will have to be splinted well because it is likely to pop back out. Fractured kneecaps are rare, but if you have one, you won't be able to walk. If the leg is splinted firmly behind the knee from ankle to the hip and bound firmly, you *may* be able to walk for short distances.

A sprained knee is treated like a sprained ankle. When a sprain occurs here, you may hear or feel a pop as the ligaments give. Knee sprains are usually caused by a twist or getting hit on the side of the knee, whereas a fracture is usually caused solely by a sudden force not accompanied by a twisting or catching motion. A sprained knee will usually swell.

A dislocated knee means that the ligaments have torn out, possibly completely. This injury requires extremely careful splinting. A dislocated knee may compress and block off the artery to the leg, and this is an orthopedic emergency. If you're in the field, you will have to relocate the knee to decompress the artery. Like emergency relocation of the kneecap, apply slow, steady traction in the direction of the deformity and slowly ease the knee back into position.

Fractured legs and other bones are possibilities you will have to accept as a mountaineer or climber. They can be serious and involve hemorrhages, neural damage, and infection and are characterized by pain and tenderness, swelling and bruising, deformity, and pain. A fracture must be immobilized. Relocation should not be attempted by the layperson unless you are days from help or circulation to the extremity is blocked. Relocating a fracture risks further damage and certain pain. Treatment for fractures often includes treatment for shock, hemorrhage, and soft-tissue injuries. As such, it is beyond the scope of this book to do it justice. See *Medicine for Mountaineering* or an advanced first-aid manual. Splinting and immobilization are the best things you can do for a fracture to prevent both further pain and damage.

Chondromalacia

Chondromalacia deserves its own heading under knee injuries because it is the most common overuse injury of the knee and appears to occur more often in women. Women with this problem outnumber men by two to one. However, among athletes the injury is more common in men.[10] This suggests two things: First, since women in general are less active than men, their chondromalacia is the result of weakness and can be remedied; second, since more male athletes play contact sports, they're more likely to pay the piper with chronic knee injuries.

From a medical standpoint, the benefits of recreational contact sports are dubious.

Simply put, chondromalacia is the roughening and deterioration of the undersurface of the kneecap. It can be caused by a single trauma, repeated dislocations, or overuse. Other contributing factors are inactivity, being overfat (putting too much weight on weak knees), and being born with knock-knees and "squinting kneecaps" (kneecaps that point inward toward each other like squinting eyebrows) or other misalignments of the legs that throw the knee off balance and put extra stress on the kneecap. The symptoms are pain when going downhill, swelling, weakness, and knees giving way and locking up. The "movie" sign is knee discomfort from sitting in a confined space, such as at the movies or in a car. If the pain goes away when you are able to stand up or otherwise extend your leg, you may have reason to suspect chondromalacia.

One doctor says that chondromalacia is one of the most frustrating knee problems to try to cure because strength training is the best remedy, but the exercises themselves usually cause further pain: "Thus, in some respects, the cure can be worse than the problem."[11] Because of this, chondromalacia is one of the few conditions for which isometric exercises are recommended.

Since chondromalacia is chronic and difficult to treat, it's best to prevent it. Get the strength and flexibility you need in your quads, hamstrings, ligaments, and tendons now, before you do demanding exercise on the rocks, ice, or in the mountains. If it's too late, this doesn't mean that you have to give up climbing. A number of things will ease the pain and progress of chondromalacia. If you're not addicted to running for its own sake, you can bicycle or swim for fitness and take the weight off your aching knees. You can also run on soft surfaces, such as wooden floors, grass, and tracks with a rubberized surface, and avoid running downhill stretches.

Isometric strength training is not as complicated as it sounds. Isometric means that you hold the leg rigid against a resisting weight. Dynamic weight resistance exercises, such as leg extensions, presses, and curls, can grind the kneecap into the groove between the thigh and shin bones and make things worse. Wall sits (see chapter 7) are good isometrics for the quads. One innovative method of isometrically strengthening the quads is called Daily Adjustable Progressive Resistive Exercise (DAPRE).[12] These are best done in the weight room on the machine for doing leg curls and extensions. It can also be done at home by using buckets filled with rock salt or sand. The advantage of the professional machine is that you can lift the weight into position with your hands. DAPREs are done one leg at a time. Sit on a chair/machine and extend your leg so that it points fifteen degrees down from straight forward. Hold it in this position for six seconds, then rest for four seconds. Repeat for four sets.

Strength gains are reported to come rapidly with DAPREs. Your initial weight might be as low as ten pounds, which can be disheartening. But the longer you have had chondromalacia, the weaker your quads probably have become. Don't be ashamed. It's natural to avoid pain, and you have probably been avoiding using your quads in hundreds of unconscious ways. If you have chondromalacia in only one knee, reduce the workouts to once a week when the strength in the weak leg is equal or near equal to that in the normal leg. The other indicator, of course, is when backpacking and other activities no longer produce aching knees. Once strength in both legs is nearly equal, you can start the next phase of rehabilitation. This includes walking up hills or up lots of long flights of stairs. If you have access to a high-rise building, walk up the stairs and take the elevator back down to avoid the downhill stress on the knees.

Treatment for chondromalacia, besides strength training, is rest, ice, bracing, and NSAIDs. Aspirin therapy of ten grains four times daily for six weeks has been shown to reduce inflammation, inhibit cartilage degeneration, and help in the regeneration of cartilage cells.[13] An infrapatellar strap, which is worn just under the kneecap, has been shown to relieve pain in 77 percent of the persons studied.[14] Also available is a neoprene "horseshoe brace" that holds the kneecap stable and allows activity such as running, as well as the knee brace made by Aircast. A woman who has used both prefers the Aircast because it is lighter, adjusts easier to fit the leg, and breathes well. She says that her neoprene cast by comparison is heavy and hot.

Back Problems

The main kinds of lower-back problems that are unique to climbers are those resulting from a fall. However, in the study of accidents in the Tetons, the incidence of them was not particularly high, only about 5 percent. Nevertheless, climbers should be aware of a few pearls of wisdom about back injuries. After a fall, if there is immediate back pain, it is more likely a severe bruise or fracture. Sometimes a broken rib can cause pain in the back. If you are short of breath, you could have a broken rib. Try taking a deep breath; if this causes pain in the ribs, your back injury may be a rib injury. This is generally good news,

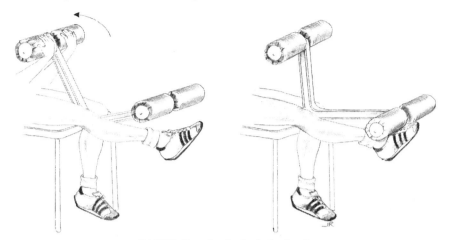

DAPRE. Drawing by Janis Rockwell.

because a rib injury (if it doesn't puncture the chest cavity) is usually much easier to treat and tolerate than a traumatic back injury.

If the onset of pain is delayed, the back muscles may have gone into spasm. Sometimes trauma won't result in long-lasting pain, but the muscles will be irritated. Even a minor movement, like twisting around slightly, may trigger a muscle spasm. Although this pain can be severe, it's usually not cause to worry about profound injury.

If you or a climbing partner has immediate back pain or tenderness after a fall and you have ruled out fractured ribs, it may be a fractured vertebra. A muscle spasm will often set in later and act as a sort of splint of rigid muscle around the injured bone. Traumatic back injuries may involve the spinal cord. Evidence of damage to the spinal cord can include pain that radiates to the front of the body or down the arms or legs. There may be numbness, tingling and/or paralysis. The awful possibility of permanent spinal-cord injury usually requires that the victim be evacuated by stretcher and the spine immobilized as much as possible during transport. Fortunately, vertebrae are often injured with no damage to the spinal cord. But such fractures should be handled cautiously to avoid spinal-cord damage.

Overload injuries often occur in the lower back. (See chapter 2 on diagnosis, treatment, and prevention.) Part of the problem for mountaineers in avoiding overloading the lower back is the heavy gear they often must carry. A tumpline, a long strap that loops around the bottom of the pack, then is placed slightly above the forehead, has begun to find favor among some mountaineers. This helps equalize the weight of the pack by placing more weight on the upper-neck muscles. Many canoeists are familiar with tumplines because this is how loads are traditionally carried over portages. (Tumplines adapted for modern backpacks are available from Chouinard Equipment, Box 150, Dept. BL, Ventura, California 93002.)

The treatment for most nontraumatic back pain is RICE, without the *E* for elevation. Usually it's best to lie on your back or side with your knees bent in a fetal position. Relaxants such as Valium are often used to ease muscle spasms. If a backache seems to be caused by a muscle spasm, massage or the more specialized acupressure may help relieve pain. Massage and acupressure can work for other muscle and joint injuries as well. Acupressure consists of a deep, localized massage at designated points on the body. One doctor tried it on her friend, who was disabled by a backache while they were climbing a peak. It worked and they were able to finish the climb. A good book about acupressure is *Acupressure's Way of Health: Jin Shin Do* by Iona Teeguarden.

Massage may aid rehabilitation of muscle or joint injuries by stimulating circulation, reducing edema, breaking up debris tissue, relaxing a muscle spasm, and relieving pain by a slight numbing.[15] It may also improve muscular performance because it warms the tissue. Apparently, muscles work longer and more efficiently after five minutes of massage. If you have a compatible partner, what better way to do your warm-up? For a warm-down, massage promotes relaxation, reduces muscle tension, relieves swelling, and helps prevent soreness. All this speaks well of this intimate and satisfying form of therapy.

Equipment

A modern free-climber, draped with a spectrum of brightly colored ropes, nylon, and ironmongery, ambles across the meadow toward a crag. All this gear beneath which she is buried is an elaborate and expensive "safety net." In some ways it can detract from the essence of climbing. An aspiring beginner can easily sample climbing on a boulder inches above the ground encumbered only by shorts and a T-shirt. As you venture higher, though, you will appreciate that net. Your teacher should have all the equipment necessary for your first rock climbs. Remember, it is wise to start under the supervision of a competent climber.

Clothing for rock climbing in dry conditions need not be sophisticated. It must, however, be expendable and unrestrictive. Many women like to climb in loose cutoffs, running shorts with attached liner underpants (for privacy), or sweat pants. If you can't borrow a harness, one can be fashioned inexpensively from nylon webbing. On some rock, such as smooth granite, your bare feet can be a successful way to begin an intimate relationship with rock. If not, an old pair of smooth, solid athletic shoes will work.

If you find that you like rock climbing, your first purchase should be friction climbing shoes. These look a bit like high-topped tennis shoes. However, the resemblance certainly stops at the $90 price tag. The majority of rock climbers in the United States use the French-made EBs (climbing shoes). French shoes tend to be narrower; consequently, the unisex EBs fit women fine. Friction climbing shoes are worn tight for control, and they are fragile. You won't want to wear them for the approach. Despite their drawbacks, mainly price, they make staying on the rock a lot easier.

The safety and comfort afforded by a custom climbing harness will probably make this your next purchase. When choosing a harness, take time to hang in it while in the shop to ensure a proper, supportive fit. An important setup for women to look for is a harness that can be loosened enough to allow you to shimmy your pants over your rump to urinate. One harness that allows this is the Chouinard sit harness, which retails for about $33. With it, you won't have to get out of your safety system to answer nature's call.

As you continue your apprenticeship, you will want to begin leading. As you spend more time on the "sharp" end of the rope, it's time to consider buying one. A leader rope (11 millimeters thick) costs between $100 and $140. This is when you will also begin to accumulate the necessary protection paraphernalia to keep from hitting the deck should you fall. Together, the sling, carabiners, chocks, and friends are referred to as a rack. The cost of a rack is extremely variable, from about $50 to $500. Some advanced but impoverished climbers have a minimal rack and combine equipment with their partners to get by with less expense and less gear. Before buying, do some research—especially regarding the ropes. You will be surprised at the number of options. Never buy a used rope. *Climbing* magazine (Box E, Aspen, Colorado 81611) lists mountaineering equipment suppliers. Companies that offer retail and mail-order service advertise in *Climbing*. Chouinard Equipment (Box 150, Dept. BL, Ventura, California 93002) publishes an excellent catalogue with detailed commentary on product use and performance, along with guidance on what you need to get started.

Decisions about clothing and equipment are more grave for the mountaineer. The layered principle, in which several layers of clothing are better than one heavy, less versatile layer, aids ventilation and decreases the chances of clothing becoming wet from body sweat. Cotton and down, standards for backpacking, have no insulating value once they are wet. Down sleeping bags, for example, are rarely used by mountaineers except on high-altitude summits where the snow is dry. A wet down bag can be a death sentence. A hooded coat is better protection than a hat because it keeps your neck warm and prevents cold air from leaking in. The next best alternative (or addition) is a turtleneck shirt. As yet, there's no really good raingear for the serious mountaineer. Consequently, you need clothing made of fabrics that stay warm when wet, such as pile. While wool also retains insulation when wet, it weighs twice as much for equal warmth. Pile absorbs about one percent of its weight in moisture, while wool absorbs much more.

Another example of the crucial role proper equipment can play is in the prevention of frostbite, a constant hazard for the mountaineer. A neoprene or waterproof nylon sock sets up a vapor barrier between the sweating foot and the inside of the boot. The heated moisture stays next to the skin and adds insulation. Because it doesn't escape through the sock, the inside of your boots stays dry and prevents cold from being conducted inward to your feet.

The Therm-A-Rest mattress, another innovation, is more comfortable than a thin foam pad and warmer than an air mattress, and therefore better for sleeping on cold ground. Even contact lenses have become more convenient. Recently available are extended-wear contacts, which can be worn for two weeks at a time.

Once you decide to make the step from rock climbing to alpine mountaineering, the matter of equipment becomes more complex. Some believe strongly that the alpinist, like any other climber, owes it to herself to rely only on the best gear available. Climbing is a sport in defiance of gravity, and any extra weight impedes progress as well as enjoyment. In the alpine situation, a speedier climb is almost always a safer climb—less time spent at the mercy of the mountain, less chance of an unplanned bivouac. The selection of each item of equipment must be exacting, for any failure or omission can quickly become critical. Your decisions will become more informed with experience—your own and what you learn from the trials of others.

One mountaineering guide feels that there is no such thing as finally having "everything I need." Technology is advancing so rapidly that the hot new item you bought two years ago may already be obsolete, he says. The properties of space-age materials such as polypropylene, Texoiite, Thinsulate, Quollofil, fiberpile, and Gore-Tex must be under-

Leading a climb on Haystack Mountain, Wind River Range, Wyoming. Photograph courtesy of Richard Collins.

stood to combine them successfully into systems that provide protection for a variety of weather conditions.

Boots become necessarily bulkier to provide warmth and stiffer to allow negotiation of snow and ice. A different technique must be applied to rock climbing in these boots, which are available in both leather and plastic. Most rock hardware is applicable in the alpine world, but you will want some more ropes. Experiment with ice gear. It is not unusual for a dedicated alpinist to own six ice tools. An ice ax can cost between $40 and $100. An ice hammer, a specialized tool for waterfall climbing, costs about $70. Crampons add another $50 or so to the bill.

Few sports provide the acquisitive with more opportunity to amass so much equipment. And doing so may put you ahead; for, as the saying goes, "She who dies with the most toys wins."

Becoming Proficient: Bouldering and Leading

Rock climbing is at the base of the climbing pyramid, with ice climbing in the middle and mountaineering at the top. The higher you go up the pyramid, the fewer participants you find, but the more literature. It's amazing how much is written about expedition mountaineering when you consider how few people actually do it. Of course there are precious few women who have dipped either their crampons or their ink pens into this rarefied medium.

One of the first steps in climbing is bouldering, which means climbing close to the ground without a rope for protection. Bouldering is the best strength and technical training of all. With it a climber can learn moves and solve problems with little risk of major injury from falling. It is often done with a spotter, on the same principle as spotting in gymnastics. The spotter stands ready with her hands about level with the climber's shoulder blades, waist, or rear end to break the climber's fall. If the climber gets high enough that her feet are above your head, hope that she's competent enough not to fall. When breaking a fall by spotting, it's important for the spotter to slightly push the climber forward during a fall so that she won't knock both of you over backwards into a heap on the ground. If you don't have a spotter—and this is good practice even if you do have one—choose a place to boulder in which there is a smooth, flat landing.

Most good climbers love to boulder—or they wouldn't become good climbers. Beginning climbers, particularly women, don't like it. It takes nerve, even at a few feet off the ground, to do something in which the climax is usually falling. "Initially I hated bouldering," says

Coral. But she wanted to become a good climber. In 1975, when she was in Australia teaching elementary school, she met the man she later married (and still later divorced). "He was one of the better climbers in Australia and one of the first to become a 'climbing bum.' Full-time climbing was new in Australia at the time, and I wanted to be part of it. I knew that to get as good as I wanted to be, to have the intensity of experience I wanted, I would have to climb all the time."

It was her husband who told her (1) she would never get good unless she got strong, and to get strong she had to learn to do chin-ups, and (2) she would have to boulder. "And I became a fanatic at it," she says. When she came back to the States, she says that most of the women who were climbing well, at comparable standards, didn't boulder very much. "There were a few things that I could do that resulted from bouldering. For example, I was used to incredibly tiny holds and overhangs."

The second essential to proficient climbing is leading. Leading is at once physically hard, mentally demanding, dangerous, stimulating, and satisfying. "Very early I realized that . . . the person who invariably climbs behind a good leader . . . may never really learn mountaineering at all and in any case enjoys only a part of all the varied delights and rewards of climbing," wrote Miriam O'Brien Underhill, one of the most famous and talented female climbers in the early 1900s, in her book *Give Me the Hills*.

I saw no reason why women, ipso facto, should be incapable of leading a good climb. They had, as matter of fact, already done so, on some few scattered occasions. But why not make it a regular thing, on the usual climbs of the day? Henry de Ségogne went to some pains to explain to me why a woman should never lead a climb. There is a lot more to leading, said Henry, than first meets the eye, a lot that must be learned, and that is best learned by watching competent leaders attentively and coming to understand their decisions. Women, however, never bother to do this. Since they know that they will never be allowed to lead anyway, they just come walking along behind, looking at the scenery. Therefore, even if they were given an opportunity to lead, they would be completely unprepared. I didn't find this argument too convincing, but I did realize that if women were really to lead, that is, to take the entire responsibility for the climb, there couldn't be any man at all in the party. For back in the 1920s women were perhaps a bit more sheltered than they are today. And in any emergency, particularly in an outdoor sport like mountaineering, what man wouldn't spring to the front and take over? I decided to try some climbs not only guideless but manless. The first step along this path was to learn to lead the rope, with a competent man behind.[16]

In the same book, she records the reaction of a male contemporary when she and another woman, in 1929, did the first manless climb of the Grépon, then considered to be one of the finest rock climbs in the Alps. " 'The Grépon has disappeared,' said Etienne Bruhl sadly that evening in Chamonix. 'Of course,' he admitted 'there are still some rocks standing there, but as a climb it no longer exists. Now that it has been done by two women alone, no self-respecting man can undertake it. A pity, too, because it used to be such a very good climb.' " And she records a comment by A. F. Mummery, who made the first ascent of the Grépon in 1881: " 'It has frequently been noticed that all mountains appear doomed to pass through three stages: an inaccessible peak—the most difficult ascent in the Alps—an easy day for a lady.' "

Although you may have to look far and wide, it's now possible to find women mountaineering instructors like Coral and schools that teach mountaineering, such as the National Outdoor Leadership School and Colorado Outward Bound, which have women instructors. As yet, mountaineering guiding is not regulated in the United States. There is a move among a few elite male alpinists, such as Yvon Chouinard, Jeff Lowe, and Royal Robbins, to set standards and regulate who can and cannot do this as a living. The name of the organization is American Professional Mountain Guides Association. (For information on applications or a list of accredited guides, contact APMGA, Los Yridises, Rancho San Julian, Star Route, Lompoc, California 93436.) This organization has been accused of being elitist—demanding more of those they certify than is necessary for most endeavors except winter ascents of Mt. McKinley. If this is true, there probably are few, if any, women in their membership. But this, too, will change.

She stretches on tiptoes, wedging her fist into the flared crack, but it's just a little too small. The clenched hand doesn't quite stick—not quite solid enough to move on up. The first thirty seconds pass and her calves begin to tire. A little more torque. The muscles of her forearm contract with effort. Her biceps twinge in protest of the contemplated movement. A toe finds its way into the crack at waist height, knee cranked outward, and her quadriceps rally to support her failing arm. Her breathing becomes labored—a forced exhalation, and the other foot leaves the ground. Her free arm dives into the widening crack above—in up to the shoulder. Her elbow presses against one side of the crack, her hand against the other. The muscles of her back, shoulder, arm, and hand strain together in a harmonious effort to hold her upper body in the crack. Her legs respond to the challenge. As they begin to extend, one foot twists, the heel now contacting the rock, transferring stress. Struggling, panting, sweating, she cheats gravity of another inch. Her entire body is now quivering with the effort of an intricate pattern of isometric balance. Both hands now grasp the narrow ledge and entirely new sets of muscles are called upon to pull her to the first resting place, eight feet off the ground. Just six hundred more to go. Not six hundred reps on a Nautilus in some stifling concrete sweat house, but six hundred magical feet of beautiful exposed rock and fresh air, high above the petty problems of everyday life.

Not all rock climbs will push you to your physical limits. Just as there are rewards for obstacles overcome on a difficult pitch, the uninterrupted rhythm of freely moving up a great sweeping slab in the sky can be equally exhilarating. But whether it's the static anaerobic stress of a precise boulder problem or a long, upward amble over easy terrain (and you will often incorporate both into your climbing experience), your physical benefits will be considerable. In fact, few athletic endeavors boast the totality of the workout your body gets when rock climbing. It is not too surprising that, for the third consecutive year, the leading woman rock climber, Lynn Hill, won the Survival of the Fittest competition put on by ABC sports.

As climbs increase in length, so do the conditioning benefits. A serious runner might consider a three-hour, twenty-four-mile workout to be a major accomplishment. But for an alpine mountaineer, a sixteen-hour day of near-continuous exertion is not unusual. Find a bigger mountain and put five of these exhausting days back to back with added weight for food and fuel and we're talking about a true endurance athlete!

"I wasn't thinking up or down . . . it was an in-the-moment experience," says Coral about one of her more satisfying climbs. "And there are plenty of times when I'm out of my life. I'm not in the moment. I'm thinking of something else. I think it's a good lesson. A lot of rock climbers are aware that climbing allows them to exist in that space, and they keep going back to rock climbing as a way to have that experience."

Chapter 4

Paddle Sports: Canoeing, Kayaking, and Rafting

Adventure: The Hanbury-Thelon Women's River Expedition

The boat chugged away, a receding echo of civilization, one noon in July 1980. Now, finally, the seven young women and their three canoes were ready to embark on an expedition covering 610 miles over fifty days, an expedition that took four years from inception to planning. But paddles weren't put expectantly to water on this Northwest Territories tundra river system. First there was a portage: three and a half miles to be done four times by Kathy Swift and two others, and three by the rest of the women. "I hiked/portaged twenty-eight miles," Kathy scrawled wearily in her journal after stumbling back to camp at 2 A.M.

The next day was one of more portages and false starts on "little squirty lakes" as they sought the main route to Artillery Lake and the Thelon River beyond. They were only ten degrees south of the Arctic Circle. The Royal Canadian Mounted Police back in Yellowknife had told them that they were crazy. They would die—unarmed women behaving as if the terrain of the barren-ground grizzly was a playground. In camp they were absolutely vulnerable: There were no trees to climb. "If a bear had come within ten feet, I wouldn't have been able to make it out. Tonight, I honestly couldn't see through my headnet," Kathy wrote on journal pages splotched with the remains of mosquitoes and black flies. "Black flies by day. Mosquitoes by night. Out on the open water, if we keep paddling, we lose the bugs unless we get close to land, then we get swarmed."

But the trip wasn't just one constant threat of being eaten slowly by bugs or quickly by bears. Everpresent in the background was a silence so profound that at first it shocked Kathy. There was a deep, binding tranquillity to the river, the undulating land, and the soaring, swooping Artic terns. "I'm feeling chilled but very much at peace," she wrote on day eight while floating near a point on the northern end of Artillery Lake. "The clouds reflecting off the water today were beautiful. The lake was so calm it was mirrorlike. This morning the clouds again seemed to surround but not cover the lake, as if it were special. But finally it clouded over in the afternoon. Now some ducks are wailing at us to stay off their waters."

Five of the women who did the trip were experienced. Kathy is a canoe racer, and her parents own a canoe-trip outfitting business in Ontario. Most of the others were present or former employees of a canoe-tripping camp that ran trips along the Thelon River. All told, each woman spent only $1,000. This included the purchase of two used canoes, food, boat ferry, the van in which they drove to Canada, gas, and airfare for the return trip to Yellowknife. Yellowknife is a story in itself (perhaps an example)—an outpost of incongruous high-rise engineering set like an exclamation point against the arctic frontier. Their costs were kept low because they had the connections to purchase the canoes and bulk food, and they chose an area that they could get to by boat rather than plane. The initial portage was a moneysaver.

That it would be an all-women's trip was an objective in the planning. "We're asked that question a lot, that is *why* an all-women's trip," Kathy says. "It wasn't to prove a point, although we were the first women's group to do this variation of this particular route. We kept it to women because we felt there'd be less conflicts, it'd be easier to express emotions, that we wouldn't have to try to keep up with men constantly, and that there'd be no roles."

Rarely does Kathy record in her journal interactions with people. Most of her accounts are of the perils and beauty of the land and water, an obsession with the unavailability of "civilized" food, the feeling of strength and contentment, and much about wildlife. She was out walking at dusk:

> I glanced up at a ridge to see something whitish, moving, and with a tail. The first thought that streaked through my mind was a person; but, my

God, it was an animal. For one small instant a silly conclusion was, "it's a dog." But I immediately recalled where I was and realized I was seeing an amazing thing. Something I had dreamed of seeing for years. Something I never thought I'd see, and there it was. The wolf ran a few paces. It must have been sitting there watching us. But when it saw me heading its way, it started, then stopped. It was within 200 yards of me. We both just stared at each other for what seemed like an eternity but perhaps was only thirty seconds; the wolf, unsure of what to do, as if drawn by me but mistrusting, disappeared on the other side of the sand ridge. I turned to see our tents lazily flapping in the slightest of breeze. I bolted to a higher point so that I could see. Once there, I immediately sighted the wolf. She sensed I was there. She was trotting, but in no big hurry, not overly concerned but definitely keeping an eye on me. She'd trot twenty feet, then stop and glance back. She did that for the next couple of minutes, while I watched intently. I watched until she disappeared over some slightly higher ground, then I never saw her again, although I stared until my eyes hurt.

This took place on the eighth day of the trip. By day twenty-six, after Kathy's fourth wolf sighting, she was wondering if she could possibily have begun to take them for granted. But then wolf four was gray and dirty, nothing to compare with wolf one or wolf three. Wolf three was the most spectacular, with a black face, muzzle, ears, and legs and a white underbody. This wolf leaped in the air and bounded along as if inviting chase. Kathy was drawn and followed her tracks. Then the expedition left to yet another portage. But this portage was easy, on solid ground rather than the usual stumble over the jello sponge of tundra.

It happened that the hardest part of the trip was first—the small lakes, portages, brush, and tundra. The second portion, although longer in miles, was expected to be easier because they had come to the river and large lakes. Kathy worried about the water being low, that they would end up portaging more rapids in the second section than they ran. On hitting the first rapids, she was pleased at the water level and exhilarated at the run. Still, the days were going too quickly.

They saw a few uncommon musk-oxen, then foxes, raptors, and numerous caribou, including a herd of two-hundred. Early in the trip, Kathy found a beautiful caribou rack with a bullet hole put neatly in the skull. She carried the impressive, stinking rack for the entire journey, at times feeling like a caribou herself as she balanced it on the back of an equipment pack over the portages.

But the women had fallen into a potentially threatening habit, one that could sink the unwary boater—rock collecting. Whenever they pulled in to make camp, they would immediately scuttle over the ground looking for rocks, rocks, and more rocks. This obsession seems to afflict many river travelers. During white-water jet-boat trips to Hells Canyon in Idaho, so many of H. W. W. "Blue Moose" Johnson's guests collected rocks that he became concerned. They would cart them back to port, intended as talismans of the river. But Blue Moose invariably found tons of them abandoned in the boat and he would dump them in the river. He calculated that if this happened often enough, the elevation of the port in Lewiston, Idaho, would become so great that it would reverse the flow of the Snake River, which would back up to its headwaters, thereby making Yellowstone National Park a swamp. (Stranger things have happened. Look at the Army Corps of Engineers.)

The Thelon River is protected, being part of the Thelon Game Sanctuary. But as Kathy notes, such protection requires vigilance. Chop off a piece here for oil and gas exploration, a piece there for phosphate development, sell mineral rights to enterprises with unreassuring names like Gigantisorus Resources, Piranha, Brass Ring, and Earth Pig, and you have lost the sanctuary. Seismic crews cannot coexist with musk-oxen, wolves, thirty-six-inch mackinau, and grizzlies.

The thirty-fourth day of the trip: The water was getting bigger, fed by tributaries that would soon merge with the three massive lakes the women needed to cross to get to journey's end. Their luck was about to change.

> I could hear the whitewater and could see it, but I saw the first canoe bounce down, so I thought it would be okay. I threw my camera in my camera bag, thank God, and we headed down. We bounced on standing waves that must have been five feet tall. A huge one filled us up, then we hit a second wave and we were under. The instant before we went under, we were suspended, frantically paddling the air. The roar of the whitewater drowned out words, but I'm sure I yelled something like, "Okay, Sandy, we're fine, hold tight," but I can't remember clearly. Then I was swimming in surprisingly warm water, watching the packs and the rest of the stuff swimming right along with me. My camera bag and two packs were bobbing along, and I grabbed them. The minute we went over, I started talking away to Sandy. I thought she might be stunned because she wasn't saying anything. It turned out that she had the maps in her mouth!

In minutes the current quieted, and the women could kick over to shore with all the packs and other gear in tow. Kathy saw her pants drifting by but didn't have a free hand so had to let them go. The women pulled up on the rocky shore, relieved, and wonder of wonders, the caribou rack was safe. It had snagged on one of the pack tumplines.

The other canoes had taken on a great deal of water, although no one else dumped. Most of the snack food was lost. Three cameras were ruined. Three women lost their boots—good thing the portages were over. One fishing pole was gone, curtailing that food source. The two weeks remaining started to look like a long time.

On hitting the big lakes, the women started to hurry. Time was short. With 130 miles left, they were now logging 20 miles a day. They canoed straight across one lake, where land was not in reach for four miles. Perhaps made aware of her own mortality, Kathy wondered if her grandchildren would want to hear about her adventures. She re-solved to spend a week with her grandmother.

On day forty-four they were beached. Strong winds whipped the lake into high waves. Smoke from a brushfire hovered like an ocean fog. "We're running low on food. Although we have enough, we don't have an extra two days," she wrote. "How frustrating, only ninety miles left, much on fast-moving river but a windy lake holding us back," Kathy wrote. The wind finally calmed enough to let them go on, but the rest of the trip was dreary with cold drizzle.

They got off the lakes and hit the river and the final miles to the tiny town of Baker Lake. On the morning of the final day on the river they woke up early and ate the last of the remaining food in a huge breakfast. This would be the one big push to go the final forty miles in one day. Kathy hoped that the wind wouldn't stop them. It didn't. They reached the day's halfway point with time to spare.

The closer they came to the end, the quieter they got. And then it was over. They were on shore—gorging themselves in the restaurant, calling home via radio telephone; washing clothes, making arrange-ments to sell the canoes. They parted at the airfield, some going south by train, others southwest by plane to Yellowknife, where they would pick up the van. Kathy was amazed when they landed in Yellowknife: only two hours by plane to cover the distance it had taken fifty days to canoe. It was over.

Training and Preparation

All three of the major wilderness paddle sports—canoeing, kay-aking, and rafting—require a good deal of upper-body strength, not just plain muscle power, but endurance/aerobic strength. Although easy paddling on short trips doesn't take much endurance, trips longer than five miles do.

A woman with little upper-body strength has a distinct disadvantage, but once she begins to increase it, some factors work in her favor. Her greater fat content will help keep her warm when she spills. Her lower center of gravity makes her less likely to capsize in a kayak or decked canoe. Her better hearing should help her detect changes in the water flow before she sees them. And women are in demand as guides and boatpersons among professional outfitters.

Canoeing, if done in a decked canoe, or C1 as it's called, is the most demanding of all three sports. Unlike the long, double-bladed kayak paddle, which can be maneuvered on either side, the C1 is maneuvered by a short, single-bladed paddle generally on one side only. The C1 boater must be fast, adroit, flexible, and master of numerous strokes to handle this craft well. Most women will choose a kayak over a C1 because it requires slightly less strength to handle. (But there is a whitewater canoe organization for women with the motto, "Half the paddle, twice the woman." To get in touch, contact CaNews, 1167 Millstone River Road, Hillsborough, New Jersey 08876; 201–874–6524.) Open canoes are usually used on lakes and smaller, more shallow rivers. Naturally there are exceptions. In the spring of 1982, Cataract Canyon in Canyonlands National Park in Utah, termed by some "the graveyard of the Colorado," was run in an open canoe. But canoeing is often called "tripping," which denotes the basic approach à la Longfellow's *Song of Hiawatha*.

The best aerobic conditioning for canoeing is swimming. Canoeing is about 70 percent aerobic. If you are a racer or planning a trip of the nature of the Hanbury-Thelon expedition, intervals of about 30 percent of your swim are suggested. If you run rapids or wind up in standing waves, intervals can be important. If you're prepared for the quick reactions and surges of strength needed for fast sections, you will tire more slowly through the day. Another option for canoeists is weight lifting. Boating itself, if done often enough, will add inches to the pectoral muscles while taking them off your waist. Poling a canoe, in which the boater stands in the craft and uses a long pole to pull and push through the water, necessitates good balance.

Next to the C1, a kayak is the hardest to master and requires the most physical strength. One estimate places it above skiing. Swimming is recommended for kayakers too; kayaking is about 80 percent aerobic. Interval training can provide a real edge for the serious or competitive kayaker and should comprise at least 20 percent of your swimming. Of course this depends on the kind of water you're running. The more difficult it is, the more you will need intervals. If you're a beginning or beginning-intermediate kayaker your training can be similar to that recommended for the average canoer. When you get to intermediate and advanced rapids, interval training is more important.

How you should aerobically train for rafting depends on whether you row or paddle. Rafts operated by one person are usually equipped with a set of oars. They are used principally by professional outfitters on big western rivers. Eastern rivers are generally too narrow to accommodate the long oars. If you row a raft, you should use a rowing machine for aerobic workouts. If this isn't possible, swimming is the next best choice. If you use paddles instead of oars, swimming is the first choice.

Rafting is about 60 percent aerobic and is the least physically demanding of the three sports. But before rafters take umbrage with this statement, let's qualify it. It is the least *aerobically* demanding, but you better have plenty of muscle once you hit wild rivers. If your river is a wild one, and particularly if you're the oarswoman, consider doing some intervals to develop adequate responsive strength. Unless you intend to race, 40 percent interval training is probably a bit much, and 10 to 20 percent is perfectly adequate. If your water is easier, you don't need intervals at all.

Strength training is important for boaters, especially for female boaters early in the season. Although swimming and rowing will develop the necessary upper-body strength, these are primarily endurance/stamina workouts. A woman should prepare by weight training. The demands put on the body vary somewhat according to which paddle sport you do. If you canoe or paddle a raft, the arms are worked the most. Next comes the back, abdomen, chest, and shoulders, in that order. When kneeling in an open canoe or C1, your thighs and hamstrings will get a workout too. In kayaking the demands are greatest on the arms and shoulders, then the shoulders and back, and finally the thigh and leg muscles. Rowing a raft puts stress first on the arms, then on the shoulders and back, and then on the thigh and calf muscles.

The strength-training program for boaters is essentially the same as that for swimmers, with a few important exceptions. Rowers are susceptible to boater's elbow, a stress injury similar to tennis elbow. To help avoid this, add tricep extensions to your list of exercises. These can be done on either free weights or the Universal system. If you don't have access to weights, pullups are an excellent (although difficult) alternative. Advance kayakers are susceptible to shoulder dislocations, especially female kayakers, because of one move—the bow draw, or Duffeck stroke. In this stroke the arms are bent up and back as a brace against the force of the water. It's easy for the arms to be pushed right out of their sockets against this tremendous force. Tucking in your elbows when bracing helps avoid this injury. Good weight-training exercises to strengthen the arms and upper-back muscles for this position are the overhead press (free weights, Nautilus, Universal), the pulldown behind neck (Nautilus, Universal), and pullups. The wrists, lower back, and hamstrings can also be injured or overstressed in paddling or rowing. Exercises for these are included in the overall program.

1. Hips, lower back, buttocks (two exercises)
2. Chest, upper arms (two exercises)
3. Thighs, hamstrings (two exercises)
4. Calves, shins, ankles (one exercise)
5. Shoulders, triceps (two exercises)
6. Abdomen (one exercise)
7. Biceps (two exercises)
8. Forearms, wrists (one exercise)

Free Weights	*Universal or Nautilus*	*No Weights*
Clean and press (1,2,3,4,5,6,7,8)	Bench press (2,5,7)	Bent-leg sit-up (1,6)
Hyperextension (1)	Bent-leg sit-up (1,6)	Calf raise (4)
Leg raise (16)	Leg curl (1,3,4)	Dip (2,5,7)
Pullover (2,5,6)	Leg press (3)	Leg raise (1,6)
Quarter-squat (1,3,4,6)	Overhead press (5,7)	Lunge (1,3)
Shoulder fly/side-arm raise (2,5)	Pulldown behind neck (1,5,7)	Pullup (2,5,7,8)
Upright rowing (2,5,7)	Shoulder shrug (5)	Pushup (2,5,7)
Wrist curl (8)	Wrist curl (8)	Quarter deep-knee bend (1,3,4)
		Squeeze tennis ball (8)

Boaters must do a lot of lifting, so strength in the lower-back muscles and the antagonistic abdominal muscles is important. It is essential to lift things correctly, bending from the knees rather than bending over at the waist. Sheila Mills, who with her husband runs Rocky Mountain River Tours out of Hailey, Idaho, emphasizes that you be in good shape when you start the season. She hurt her back while lifting heavy equipment and knows of another woman who did the same. "I wish someone (another woman) had warned me and recommended that I lift weights and get into shape before starting to row," she says. She adds that rowing strengthens the thigh and calf muscles and the arms and back. "You even get a lot of pull on the stomach. As a woman, you need to learn to use your legs more than a man might because that is where most women have most of their strength."

Boating is an excellent sport for those who are handicapped in the lower body. Since women who must use a wheelchair or crutches will already have a great deal of upper-body strength, they are well adapted to paddle sports. Tom Whittaker, founder of C.W. HOG (Cooperative Wilderness Handicapped Outdoor Group) at Idaho State University, comments that the slimmer and stronger a handicapped person is, the better she or he will adapt to a wilderness situation. "The lighter you are, the easier it is for able-bodied people to tote you around, and the stronger you are, the better you can maneuver on your own," he says. This isn't meant to imply that there aren't logistical problems in adapting a boating trip to handicapped persons, but they aren't such to deny access to many rivers and lakes. The Snake River Kayak School (Box 2098, Jackson, Wyoming 83001) and the Nantahala Outdoor Center (Star Route, Box 68, Bryson City, North Carolina 28713) have run trips with handicapped people. *Options: Spinal Cord Injuries and the Future*, edited by Barry Corbet, explores the means of expanding opportunities of those with spinal-cord and similar handicaps. (Available from the National Spinal Cord Injury Foundation, 369 Elliot Street, Newton Upper Falls, Massachusetts 02164.)

Warm-Ups and Warm-Downs

Warm-ups help relieve and avoid problems such as boater's elbow. "Most recreational paddlers give little thought to warm-up exercises, but they are helpful. One should concentrate on stretching the shoulders, lower/back, and hamstrings through the complete range of motion. These muscles are the most frequently injured or susceptible to fatigue," write Chara and Robert Burrell, in a recent issue of *The Physican and Sports Medicine*.[1] In addition to the warm-up and warm-down stretches—hyperextension (standing), lunge, pulldown behind neck, shoulder fly, and toe touch—get your muscles primed on easy water before taking on the harder stuff.

Injuries and Ailments

The most frequent cause of fatalities is attempting to run a river that is beyond your skill, and doing it in bad weather, high water conditions, or without adequate safety equipment. The faster and bigger the water, the harder it is to perform a rescue. In some cases, it's impossible. Almost 50 percent of all canoeing accidents occur early in the season, when temperatures are low, the water high, the weather more unpredictable, and the boater less in shape mentally and physically.[2]

Being able to swim is an absolute necessity for all boaters, including passengers. Be sure that you can pass the swimming proficiency test in chapter 1. If you can, even when wearing a Personal Flotation Device (PFD), you will be calmer in the water and more able to take care of yourself or others.

Drownproofing is a method of keeping afloat in slack water as opposed to rapids. To do it, keep the body in a jellyfish float position. It would look something like the letter *f*. Bend your head and shoulders slightly forward. Don't try to keep your head above water; relax and let the residual air in your lungs do the work for you. As you start to go under (you won't completely sink unless your body-fat content is low), do a slow, rhythmic scissors kick and slowly push your arms down to your sides. This will give the slight momentum needed to raise your head out of the water for a breath of air. Then let your head resubmerge slowly and resume the *f* position. Slowly repeat the sequence every three to ten seconds.[3]

If you are dumped out of your boat on a river, stay with it if possible but immediately get on the upstream end so as not to get crushed between the boat and a rock. Kick the boat into a position so that the nose is downstream, then try to get to slack water. If you are separated from your boat, put yourself into a sitting position with your legs pointed downstream to help fend off rocks. Don't try to stand in fast, deep water because your feet can get caught on the bottom.

Boaters should know how to right a capsized boat. The techniques for kayaks and canoes are given in *Canoeing*, by the American National Red Cross (Doubleday, 1977). Practice and perfect the techniques in a pool or safe slack water before you venture onto a lake or river. Righting an overturned raft is a considerably different procedure. Good instructions are given of this and for rescuing people in *Whitewater Rafting* by William McGinnis. If there is dangerous water directly in front of you, forget the boat and swim for shore—fast!

Drowning is the greatest danger associated with boating. Of the thirty-eight fatalities involving paddlers in California in 1973–74, only three were wearing PFDs. "Those who refuse to wear life jackets, please pay in advance," was one of "Blue Moose" Johnson's river rules. Good PFDs are rated by a classification system of the U.S. Coast Guard. The Type I, or Mae West, keeps your head above water even if you are unconscious. Most boaters find it too cumbersome for paddling, although it's fine for passengers. The Type II, or horse-collar life jacket, is ok for flat water, but it can slip off in turbulent water. The most popular PFD among kayakers and canoers is the Type III, which has a lot of bouyancy yet allows freedom of movement. The Type IV, which is approved for commercial whitewater use, is the most popular among rafters. When purchasing any PFD, a note of caution: Some inexpensive though approved PFDs become waterlogged with repeated use and aren't strong enough to stay in place in rough water, according to the Burrells.

Drownings, outside of those related to hypothermia occur most often when a kayaker is trapped in her boat underwater, or a swimmer gets sucked underwater in a hole or other hydraulic. Rafters can be held underwater if a raft flips on top of them or if they get tangled in lines or struck on the head by a heavy frame or other equipment. When a raft flips, sometimes the force of the collision collapses the deck onto the kayaker's legs, or the feet become jammed under the foot braces. Strong foam pillars (ethafoam or minicell) should be installed in every kayak to help prevent this. However, if they're not installed solidly and braced to stay in place, they can slip, which causes more harm than good.[4]

Immersion hypothermia means the lowering of the body's internal temperature below about 95 degrees Fahrenheit as a result of the cold water. The signs and symptoms are the same as for nonimmersion hypothermia (see chapter 9), but the rapidity of symptom development and its rate of progression toward death is much greater because of the high thermal conductivity of water. Water removes heat from the body much faster than air does. Capsizing a boat or otherwise falling unexpectedly into even moderately cold wilderness lakes or streams is much more serious than many people realize. Many fatal accidents involve recreational boaters who, through decreased sensibilities and reaction time from indulgence in alcohol, don't realize the dangers of immersion until it's too late. The body's internal temperature can drop remarkably fast in cold water. Studies done of people immersed in cold water show that a naked person of average body build will be helpless from cold after twenty minutes in 41-degree water and will die in fifteen minutes in 32-degree water. Deaths in arctic waters have occurred in just a few minutes.

Since hypothermic death is probably most often caused by the heart fibrillating (a rapid series of heart contractions) and then stopping, activities that promote irritability of the heart tissue should be stringently avoided if possible. A prime example of this is movement (active *or* passive) of a hypothermic victim's arms or legs following immersion. If a person is allowed to get up and walk immediately or flail her arms and legs wildly, or if she is jostled while being carried away from the shore, extremely cold blood from these extremities, along with toxic metabolic waste products, will rush toward the heart and induce fibrillation. This is undoubtedly what happened to a group of capsized Norwegian fisherman, who were found alive and who climbed a rope ladder up to the rescue boat. Almost all of them died minutes later on deck.

Even on a warm day, when the surface of the water is warm, the wind can churn cold water up from lower depths in the lake and increase the risk of hypothermia. "We pulled some boaters out of Shoshone Lake in Wyoming in August. They'd only been in twenty minutes and were helpless," says Ernie Naftzger, a canoeist with fourteen years experience. Besides the problems caused by rapidly decreasing body temperature, the functioning of muscles becomes impaired in cold water, making self-rescue difficult, if not impossible. These are reasons why boating is best done with more than one craft to a party, and why it's usually best to stay close to shore.

Should you ever be immersed in cold water, don't take your clothes off thinking they will impede your ability to swim or float, except perhaps shoes or boots. Thick clothing markedly increases the amount of time low temperatures can be tolerated. Even wet layers of clothing help trap warm air next to the body.[5] Don't flail about unnecessarily in cold water in an attempt to keep warm; this only aggravates heat loss, especially in water below about 55 degrees. Studies conducted by the Natick Environmental Research Laboratory have shown that you can slow the loss of body heat in cold water by placing your hands under your armpits and crossing your legs at the knees.

A boater can also get hypothermic in the course of the day after repeated dunkings or during continual rainfall. She may feel like she has reheated after vigorous paddling, but the body may become steadily colder. She may feel nothing wrong because impaired judgment is one of the first signs of hypothermia. Comrades should pay close attention to any group member who seems to become careless about keeping herself warm.

Kayakers should wear a wetsuit if water temperatues are below 50 degrees. If you are a small, slender person or otherwise chill easily, always wear a wetsuit when kayaking. The American Canoe Association urges canoeists to (1) wear a wetsuit when the air and water temperatures add up to less than 100 degrees, (2) always wear a PFD to help retain warmth, and (3) know water-safety and rescue techniques.

Boaters, and indeed all wilderness users, should take at least the basic Red Cross first-aid course and have a thorough knowledge of mouth-to-mouth resuscitation and treatment of hypothermia. CPR (cardiopulmonary resuscitation) is good training for boaters. The procedure, including closed-heart massage, is exactly the same used to save a drowning victim. One important caution, however: Be *sure*, before starting closed-heart massage, that there is no detectable pulse or heartbeat; otherwise an irritable but intact heart can be thrown into fibrillation. A hypothermic's heart may beat exceedingly slowly yet still be adequate in relation to her simultaneously lowered metabolic activity— the "icebox effect". As the body warms, the heart rate will increase.

Kayakers should wear helmets. When you're upside down under-water, you're still moving downstream and can run into rocks. The number of scratches and dents on used helmets attests to the frequency of "kissing a rock." Lightweight racing helmets don't offer enough protection. The ideal helmets are like those used from climbing and bicycling: They have slots designed to let the water drain out, and they don't cover the ears. The helmet should fit well and have a sturdy chin strap and a resilient lining.

Minor Injuries

A boater's hands are akin to a hiker's feet. They continually absorb the small, repeated stresses of rubbing against a hard surface. Just as a hiker would be stupid to go without shoes, so a boater without gloves is asking for trouble. Gloves help prevent blisters. At the first sign of a hot spot, cover the area with cloth medical tape to prevent blisters from forming. It is agony to be forced to continue to paddle when your palms are worn bloody because you overlooked preventive measures. (For the treatment of blisters, see chapter 2.)

Testing the water in a C1. This woman is wearing an ideal helmet for paddling in a C1 or kayak. Photograph courtesy of Nancy Jane Reid.

Contaminated water, bugs, insects, lacerations and bruises are all problems for paddlers. Information about these is given in chapter 2. Many rivers, such as the Middle Fork of the Salmon in Idaho, are so heavily used that boaters are required to carry out their excrement. But because of regulations like these, says Verne Huser, a well-known commercial outfitter and conservationist, some rivers are actually cleaner now than they were ten years ago.

Although heat exhaustion is not one of the first things to come to mind as a hazard of boating, it can occur if you are unwary. Melinda Bowler, an experienced outdoorswoman and nurse, says she once had this problem during a float trip when she didn't drink enough liquids. The prevention, symptoms, and treatment are given in chapter 9.

Sunburning while on the water can be serious because of the reflected radiation. Burns can be greater on areas like the lips, nostrils, nose, and chin. In addition to multiple applications of sunscreen with PABA (para-amino-benzoic acid), use zinc oxide or Glacier Cream to protect the nose and lips. The treatment of sunburn is given in chapter 2.

Snakebites

Rivers are as popular with snakes as they are with people. Snakes are often found sunning themselves on rocks not far from a water source. When traveling in snake country, keep alert for them on the ground, and use a hiking stick in heavy vegetation to warn them of your progress. Always step on top of a log or rock that you cannot see over. (This is a good rule in bear country too.) When climbing, reconnoiter handholds with a stick to avoid surprising a snake lolling there. Always check out a cave before entering. Wear protective boots and clothing. High-topped boots are the best choice.

Death and serious injury from poisonous snakes are rare in the United States, occurring only 2 percent more often than death from bee stings. Young children, the elderly, and those in poor physical condition are the most susceptible. There are only four types of poisonous snakes in the United States: the rattlesnake, water moccasin (cottonmouth), copperhead, and coral snake. The first three have the triangular head, slit pupils, heavy bodies, obvious fangs, and pits between their eyes characteristic of poison snakes (pit vipers). The coral snake is the anomaly, with a slender body and head, round eyes, small fangs, and no pits. It can be distinguished from similar, harmless species by its *yellow* bands in addition to the red and possibly black bands on its body.

The rattlesnake's habitat ranges from the East to the West, but it is most common in arid and semiarid regions. The copperhead is found in swampy, wooded, and rocky areas of the central and eastern United States. The coral snake inhabits the southeastern states primarily; one rare species lives in Arizona. The water moccasin lives in the marshy lowlands in the Southeast.

Patricia Caulfield, a prominent free lance nature photographer, was in an airboat in the Everglades one night. She and a friend had gone out to photograph catching frogs and ran out of gas. The friend waded out for help. The mosquitoes were so bad that as Patricia lay down to sleep, she tied a bandanna around her face. "In a few minutes I heard a strange slither and then a plop in the boat. I had heard stories about water moccasins coming into airboats because they could sense the frogs," she said in an interview with *Backpacker* magazine a few years ago. She was galvanized into action but couldn't get the bandanna off. She couldn't see, but she still managed to get atop the airboat seat, which was about six feet above the hull. She finally got the bandanna off and inspected the bottom of the boat carefully from her perch with a flashlight. Seeing no snakes, she decided that one of the frogs in the bag had jumped. She didn't fall asleep again after that.

Snakes do not strike without provocation. In spite of its poison, a snake should not be killed unless there is no alternative. If you encounter a snake, as with any wild creature, move away from it slowly. Sudden moves are threatening. Be aware that they can be encountered in the water and that they swim well.

The treatment of snakebite is somewhat controversial. On the one hand is the do-nothing approach, in which the injured area is treated with an icepack or immersed in cold water and kept below the heart to slow the spread of the poison. On the other hand is the traditional method of cutting shallow ⅛- to ¼-inch incisions just through the skin over the puncture to draw out the poison by bleeding and suction. The limb should be kept below the heart in this case too. Great care should be taken so that you don't sever tendons, nerves, and blood vessels. This is an especially delicate procedure if the bite is on the hand or foot. Don't try this method unless the person is obviously sick or has been bitten by several snakes or by a large one. You will have to use you own judgement, as is so often the case. Is the injury bad enough to justify the hazards of the treatment? If you think it does, be sure to clean the injured area and use a clean instrument to make the incision. Unless you have sores in your mouth, sucking the venom out of the wound won't hurt you. A restrictive band can be placed above the swollen area to slow the spread of the poison through the subcutaneous tissue. At no time should the band restrict blood flow. Be sure that you can feel the pulse on the far side of the band.

Stress/Overload Injuries

Paddlers get muscle strains probably because of a combination of staying in the same position for a long time, lack of stretching and flexing, the unaccustomed force of the water, and getting cold. About the only form of tendinitis that occurs with any frequency among boaters is in the wrist. Repeated flexing of the wrist extensors when paddling can produce a tendinitis similar to that found in weight lifters who do too many curls.[6]

The prevention of lower-back/stress injuries is discussed in chapter 2. Those that result from trauma such as wrenching and twisting are likely to occur if you don't lift objects correctly. Women are probably more vulnerable because of their smaller size and relative lack of strength. A female "river rat" no doubt wants to be dealt with as an equal, and to do this she will carry her own weight in the literal sense. Although the intention is good, make sure that you're up to it first (remember weight training?) and lift things correctly! Lifting is the most frequent cause of traumatic lower-back injury. Add a twisting motion, say hoisting a dutch oven or food box into a raft, and you have the perfect setup for wrenching your back.

The best single activity to strengthen all the back muscles is swimming. Even if you have been inactive all year, start swimming at least a month before you go paddling. This becomes even more important as you get older because the incidence of lower-back injuries increases with age. Exercises that specifically strengthen the abdominal muscles are important too.

If you do wrench your lower back, be honest with yourself. Are you middle-aged and/or out of shape? If so, you may have hurt a disc. Disc injuries result from the gradual weakening of the ligaments that hold the disc in place. This then causes protrusion of the disc, which is made of cartilage, into the spinal canal. The trauma is only the final insult.[7] The symptoms are a pain that starts in the lower back and radiates to one side through the buttock and down the back of the leg, not in the front or along the inner thigh. Once you have hurt a disc, the problem is more likely to occur in the future. This is why it's so important to keep in shape.

If you strain your back, sleeping on the ground or other firm surface helps relieve pain. Since it's difficult to determine if you have hurt a disc, small muscle, or ligament, the best treatment is one that will do no additional damage. This consists of rest (with hips and knees flexed while awake), a painkiller such as aspirin or Motrin, and an application of cold, such as a plastic bag full of snow. Sunbathing on a warm rock or lying on a campfire-warmed rock may provide additional relief after the first twenty-four to thirty-six hours, especially if a muscle has gone into spasm following the injury.

Long trips in a fixed seated or kneeling position can lead to lower-back pain as a result of fatigued muscles and stretched ligaments. Stretching before, during, and after boating can help a great deal. Be sure to schedule enough rest days (preferably every third day) and rest stops to avoid fatigue and resulting injuries. Muscle cramps can be caused by several things, including electrolyte imbalance, muscle-sugar depletion, and lack of strength in the antagonistic muscles (see chapter 9).

"Housemaid's" knee (or how about houseboy's knee?), is a swelling in the front of the kneecap caused by trauma or stress, such as paddling in a kneeling position. While it looks awful, it's usually not disabling. Knee pads are the best prevention, both those in your boat and extras bought in the drugstore. For mild to moderate swelling, apply a cold pack and wrap the knee with an elastic bandage, and take aspirin or Motrin. If the pain is severe and disabling, the kneecap may be fractured, but this is rare. If you are not able to walk and suspect this, the leg should be splinted behind the knee by a physician.

Boater's elbow occurs when repeated stress is put on the extensor tendon in the elbow during movements in which the hand is bent back at the wrist. As much as the cause of boater's elbow and its dry-land equivalent, tennis elbow, have been studied, the basic prevention remains the same—strengthening the muscles in the forearm. The treatment is cold packs and aspirin or Motrin. Severe, chronic pain requires a doctor's attention. Even so, it may be something you will have to live with. The best remedy is prevention.

The potential for shoulder dislocation is greater in women because of greater flexibility and the related lack of strength. As noted in chapter 10, women are more vulnerable to these kinds of injuries during pregnancy. Once you dislocate a shoulder, it is much more likely to happen again. "The potential stress on a kayaker's shoulder is so great that anyone who has a history of recurrent shoulder dislocations should check with a doctor before taking up the sport," writes Lito Tejada-Flores in *Wildwater*.

Strength training is so important in kayaking that one might seriously question the wisdom of running wild water without first being able to do pullups and pushups. Another means of prevention, as

Tejada-Flores points out, is to not needlessly exaggerate the arm position in the bow draw stroke and to keep your elbows tucked in toward your body. "Cocking your upper arm back over your head every time you come into an eddy won't really improve your technique, and it's a bad habit to get into because in rough water—watch out!" he writes.

Reducing or relocating a dislocated shoulder is advisable only if you are days away from medical help. Even then you must be sure of yourself, and the victim must be willing. It must be done as soon as possible or at least within twenty minutes. The longer you wait, the more severe the muscle spasms, and the harder it will be to put the shoulder back in its socket. Reduction is easier if the injury has occurred before and in persons with less muscle mass. One of the safest and simplest ways to do it is to place the victim on her stomach on an elevated platform, such as an overturned kayak. There should be enough room to allow the arm to dangle free. If not, bend the arm and rig up a neck sling. On the side of the dislocation, elevate the chest slightly with a jacket or towel. The next step is to apply traction. This can be done by hanging a ten-pound weight from a sling around the elbow or by steadily pulling down on the arm. It may take some time—from as little as ten minutes to up to two hours. If it doesn't work within two hours, give up and immobilize the arm in a sling. The traction applied should be even and steady. Don't try to jerk the shoulder into place. If you succeed in reducing the dislocation, make sure that the arm remains immobile until medical attention becomes available.

The procedure must have the victim's full cooperation. If possible, try to document the presence of wrist pulses and of good sensation (especially on the upper, outer part of the arm) before and after you attempt reduction. This information will help a doctor treat the condition later. If a dislocated shoulder is already producing a cold, blue, pulseless hand, at least an attempt to reduce it should be made in hopes of relieving the impeded circulation. The victim should relax as much as possible. If she is unable or unwilling to cooperate and circulation does not appear to be cut off, don't try this procedure. You could damage the nerves or muscles, especially if an associated fracture is present, which it is in about 10 percent of dislocations.

Equipment

Boating can be an expensive way to get in touch with nature. For this reason, it's a good idea to acquire some proficiency before forming a permanent relationship with a boat. The following list of essential, basic boating equipment is in the medium-price range, and most of it can be purchased used. Prices are manufacturer's list as of 1982.

Canoeing		*Kayaking*		*Rafting*	
Canoe	$600	Carrier	$30	Frame	$300
(750 lbs.; carry-capacity		Flotation bags	30	Life jacket	50
Weight 67 lbs.)		Helmet	35	Oars (pair)	130
Carrier	50	Kayak	500	Paddle	15
Life vest	40	Life vest	40	Patching kit	20
Paddle	45	Paddle	75	Pump	50
		Spray skirt	38	Raft (four-person,	1,300
		Wetsuit	60	commercial grade)	

Specialized whitewater gear bags aren't absolutely necessary at first, since you can use heavy-duty plastic trash bags. But they are a good investment in the long run because they won't come open when you dump, and they have carrying straps that can be used to tie the bags to the boat, which makes portaging easier. A set of four bags from Seda Products (Box 997 Chula Vista, California 92012) costs about $107.

One of the advantages of either a canoe or raft over a kayak is that you can carry more gear. Kayakers often run rivers with a support raft because of this; a loaded kayak is unwieldy. You *can* carry all the stuff you need to be self-contained, but it must be crammed into the spaces in front of the foot pegs and behind the cockpit. You have to take out your normal flotation bags and deck brace and insert storage/flotation/bags. These cost $40. If you are a photographer, an absolute necessity is an Army ammo box. Once a camera has fallen into the water, so it's said, about the only reason to pick it up is to throw it farther. Ammo boxes, available from an Army/Navy surplus store, cost between $5 and $10.

There are some interesting alternatives to canoes, kayaks, and rafts. A Klepper foldboat is a kayak with a collapsible wooden frame. It is not a good boat for anything harder than Class III rapids, but it holds much more than any fiberglass kayak, so it is good for expeditions. Kleppers cost about $1,000.

A hybrid between rafts and canoes is an inflatable canoe, which costs about $400. It can carry up to 750 pounds, according to the manufacturer (most likely an overestimate), which is about the same as the claimed carrying capacity of the average fiberglass canoe. Because of their air compartments, they ride higher on the waves and are often called "rubber duckies." Weighing about 36 pounds, half that of a canoe of similar carrying capacity, they're certainly easier to portage.

But they are sluggish on flat water and don't cut cleanly through the water, as does a boat with a keel and hard hull. However, it takes less skill to maneuver them in whitewater. The manufacturer of one model, the Sea Eagle 340, recommends it for long trips in wilderness areas.

A decked inflatable kayak is fairly rare and doesn't seem to have much merit. They cost as much as a fiberglass kayak and are just as likely to tip, but they're not as maneuverable.

A Sportyak looks a bit like a baby's bathtub. Like the inflatable canoe, it's homely alongside the sleek kayak. Often used in tandem with rafts to give the rafters a chance at a more thrilling ride, it is rowed like a raft and is unsinkable and hard to tip over. Made of tough, rigid plastic, it costs about $200 and can be outfitted with a waterproof baggage compartment and spray shields.

Dories are generally used as commercial craft for rapids milder than Class IV. They look something like a large rowboat and are powered by oars. More manueverable than rafts, they can be used in heavy whitewater if loads are kept light. Decks can be added for whitewater camping trips. Because they ride high on the water and are whipped around easily by the wind and have a flat bottom with no keel, dories are not good lake boats. "It's easier to stay dry in them. In a raft you're almost bound to get wet. They're Cadillacs for people who fish. You can take them out on a river in the winter, stay dry, stay warm, and put a hibachi on the floor and cook steaks. Their main drawback is that you need a trailer to haul them," says George Wentzel, a fly-fishing authority who owns a dory. Dories cost about $1,100.

Becoming Proficient

Naturally, how fast you become a good boater depends on how often you get in the water. But other important factors are your physical strength and stamina, desire, natural ability, the skill and patience of your teachers, and sometimes necessity. Two of the women who went on the Hanbury-Thelon expedition had no experience, but within two weeks they became competent paddlers. They *had* to.

The most important general rule is to match your skill level with the water you intend to paddle. People doing their first boating trip are not unlike the skier who on her first time out takes the double chairlift to the top of the mountain, not knowing enough to be aware of the difficulties and dangers.

An international scale of river difficulty, formulated by the American Whitewater Affiliation, is accepted in North America and Europe and is based on a six-point rating system.[8]

Class I	Moving water with a few riffles and small waves. Few or no obstructions.
Class II	Easy rapids with waves up to three feet and wide, clear channels that are obvious without scouting. Some maneuvering is required.
Class III	Rapids with high, irregular waves often capable of swamping an open canoe. Narrow passages that often require complex maneuvering. May require scouting from shore.
Class IV	Long, difficult rapids with constricted passages that often require precise maneuvering in turbulent waters. Scouting from shore is often necessary, and conditions make rescue difficult. Generally not possible for open canoes. Boaters in covered canoes and kayaks should be able to Eskimo roll.
Class V	Extremely difficult, long, and violent rapids with highly congested routes that nearly always must be scouted from shore. Rescue conditions are difficult, and there is significant hazard to life in event of a mishap. Ability to Eskimo roll is essential for kayaks and canoes.
Class VI	Difficulties of Class V to the extreme of navigability. Nearly impossible and very dangerous. For teams of experts only, after close study and with all precautions taken.

Beginning paddlers should start on Class I rapids and work slowly up to Class II and III. Most boaters run Class IV or lower. Take it slowly. Your experience, commitment, and gear should be commensurate with the water.

Most guidebooks will give a rating of the water. However, the difficulty will change drastically according to water level. Generally, the faster and higher the river is running, the more dangerous it is. A river that is Class III in July might be Class V at flood. Important indicators are cubic feet per second (cfs), which is the volume of water moving past a stationary point, the drop of the river, how many narrows there are, and how many sidestreams or rivers feed into it. Wherever a sidestream flows in, there will be rapids formed by the rocks carried into the river. The Colorado River in the Grand Canyon, which is one of the biggest, most difficult rivers to run, drops at an average rate of eight feet per mile, but in volumes of 6,000 to 20,000 cfs.[9] The Chattooga River in Georgia and South Carolina is an exciting whitewater river. Its hardest sections drop at an average rate of forty-four feet per mile, but they usually run at only 200 to 1,200 cfs. This river is extremely narrow in places, which, in addition to its drop, makes it exciting and sometimes dangerous in spite of a relatively low volume.

In addition to guidebooks, most public land agencies, such as the U.S. Forest Service, state and national parks, and Parks Canada, keep track of cfs and should be able to tell you how runable a river will be on a given date. Of course if it rains torrentially, the water will be bigger and contain more debris. A wet season can cause land formations to slump into the river, which can put trees and other obstacles in your path and make the going much more dangerous. Some stretches of river are obstructed by dams. When the water is released, it will be much higher. Look to the dam agency (Army Corps of Engineers, U.S. Bureau of Reclamation) for this information. Topographic maps made by the U.S. Geological Survey may be your only and best source of information for rivers and lakes. The U.S. Coast Guard has aerial photos of navigable water that show river and lake features well. Some central sources of maps are: U.S. Geological Survey, National Cartographic Information Center, Reston, Virginia 22092; Map Source Directory 1982, Map Librarian, York University Library, 4700 Keele Street, Downsview, Ontario, Canada M36–2R2; William Nealy's Maps, Nantahala Outdoor Center, Star Route, Box 68, Bryson City, North Carolina 28713; and Les Jones, Scroll Maps, Star Route, Box 13, Heber City, Utah 84032.

Canoeing

Although this is highly individual, an estimate of getting the basics down for paddling proficiency on lakes or rivers in a canoe is four seasons. "I've canoed for fourteen years and there are times I still

Rafting on the middle fork of the Salmon River, Idaho. Photograph courtesy of Nancy Jane Reid.

don't feel proficient," says Ernie Naftzger. "It's a question of being able to do it well versus just doing it." Schools are the best way to go, but the quality of instruction varies drastically. You're on your own with this one, except to take the usual precautions you would in assessing the purchase of any service—references, certification, safety record, philosophy, and so forth. (For a listing of whitewater schools, send a stamped, self-addressed envelope with your request to *Canoe* magazine, Highland Mill, Camden, Maine 04843.)

Commercial canoe outfitters usually have to teach skills. It's hard to get all the canoes down the river unless the customers help. Allagash Canoe Trips has this to say in its brochure:

> You will receive excellent instruction for the most efficient handling of your craft in all water conditions, the importance of proper loading and unloading, and careful beaching. We can teach you how to pole a canoe in intricate stretches where water is too low to shoot cleanly under blade. And you will learn to read the water, a must for the successful challenge of whitewater. We believe that learning all aspects of properly handling a canoe will make you a superior canoeist.

Allagash has also offered women's canoe trips. If you organize your own group, almost any outfitter will run a custom-made trip for you.

There is a strong history of women canoeists promulgated through such organizations as the Girl Scouts and the YWCA. Not only will a girl learn how to canoe, but she will have female role models. Trish Berglund, a physician's assistant, learned her canoe skills through a YWCA camp. The fact that she learned from women affected the way she perceives them: "I figure they should be able to do anything they want to. My experiences in the outdoors have been really important to me. They've helped me form a baseline of personal strength. Doing things like primitive camping in teepees, lean-tos, and shaliens, and canoeing for five days down the Mississippi, allowed me to acquire personal strength."

Trish taught her husband and brother to canoe during a major excursion. She had a lot invested in the trip emotionally. It was to be a seven-day trip with sixty miles on the water and a thousand miles round trip to the put-in point on the Hudson Bay in Canada. They would then paddle south down to Lake Superior and catch a train back to their vehicle.

> I *did* deal with the men differently than I would with women. For example, on one trip with four women, I was the tacit group leader. There were two novices, and the one experienced woman was very supportive of me.

The group followed my pattern and we were structured. With my husband and his brother, I kept trying to be subtle. Consequently I became the cook and dishwasher. After three days of this I just delegated the responsibilities. Although they did accept my authority and developed a fair amount of respect for my skills, such as starting a fire with wet wood, I did have to be more tactful.

Many men, unconsciously or otherwise, may assume that they should be the leader even if their skills are no better than the woman's. After all, the outdoors has traditionally been the male's province. If you learn to paddle a canoe with a male partner, make sure you get equal time in the stern of the boat. Traditionally, the better canoeist takes the stern position. But the stern person can see everything the bow person is doing, and it's easy and tempting to blame the bow person for mistakes. Of course the bow person cannot see what the stern person is doing, so she or he doesn't know who may be at fault if you spill.

Clubs are an excellent way to acquire skills if you don't want to go to the expense of hiring an outfitter or school. But make sure that the group expectations are the same as your own, or that outing partners are willing to teach you and help you through hard spots. To find out if there is a canoe club in your area, contact the American Canoe Association, Box 248, Lorton, Virginia 22079; or The Canadian Canoe Association, 333 River Road Ottawa, Ontario K1L–8B9.

Kayaking

It takes about two seasons to learn the basic kayaking moves and be able to do them in a river as opposed to a swimming pool or flat water. "There are only three basic paddle strokes in kayaking; thus it is easier to learn than canoeing," wrote Walt Blackadar, a leader in big water kayaking until his death while kayaking in 1978.[10] While there are more canoe strokes to learn—and things become even more complicated with a partner—kayaking is certainly harder than the average canoe trip on flat water. Kayaks are less stable in the water than a lake canoe, and they are harder to control. Walt was probably referring to the whitewater C1.

On one of his early trips down the Middle Fork of the Salmon River in Idaho, Walt took his two kayaks and another person along. This person was an expert swimmer, not an expert kayaker. The Middle Fork is an extremely wild river to begin with, yet they planned to run it at flood. For flotation in his own boat, Walt had a beach ball in one end and a waterskier's belt in the other. The other boat had two inner-tubes for flotation. In the first major rapid the two dumped. Wearing only skimpy ten-pound buoyancy jackets, they almost lost their lives, alternating between drowning, hypothermia, and getting smashed between rocks and boats.

Although they finally managed to get out, the friend almost drowned, primarily because of his inadequate life jacket. Walt lost one of his boats but he learned a great deal. "We were too confident, and relied on our swimming ability. We should have worn wetsuits, as well as good, big life jackets. Of course, our boats should have had full flotation, and we should have known what we were doing before we tackled the Salmon at flood.[11]"

After this trip, Walt enlisted the aid of experts. Thereafter he felt strongly that kayaking should be learned from expert kayakers. But sometimes this isn't possible. Kayaking is still in its infancy as a popular sport, and there aren't that many schools. As of this writing there is no formal certification of kayaking instructors, so you may *have* to learn from books. But most experts agree that you should learn the Eskimo roll in a pool or flat water before venturing onto a river. "Get a good instructor who knows how to roll. I studied movies and still shots of all positions of the roll, and read everything written on the subject, but until I had a teacher standing in the water and helping me, I was lost," Walt said.[12]

The American Canoe Association does issue certificates for canoeists, but according to Fletcher Anderson, a board member of the National Organization for River Sports, the certification standards are so vague and elementary that they would surely leave seasoned whitewater instructors shaking their heads. He is also suspicious that those promoting this among kayakers only want to get the U.S. Forest Service, The Bureau of Land Management, and other agencies that control access to rivers to recognize their certification program, thereby controlling kayaking instruction and driving their competitors out of business. He thinks a more noble pursuit is putting a dam out of business, since these are the principal destroyers of whitewater.[13]

Many professional outfitters give instruction. Contact the Eastern Professional River Outfitters, Box 69, Ohiopyle, Pennsylvania 15470; or the Western River Guides Association, 994 Denver Street, Salt Lake City, Utah 84111. For a list of whitewater clubs contact the American Whitewater Affilation, Box 1261, Jefferson City, Missouri 65102; or the Canadian Whitewater Affiliation, 436 Sitison, Burlington, Ontario L7R–2N9. If you want to help protect wild rivers, contact the American

Rivers Conservation Council, 323 Pennsylvania Avenue SE, Washington, D.C. 20003.

Rafting

In the West, where rafts are popular on big rivers, by far the greatest number of people go with commerical outfitters. Good rafts are expensive (the cheap ones fall apart fast).

If you are interested in acquiring skills from a commercial rafting outfitter, look for the small operator who stresses customer participation. Also look for those that employ women as guides and boat operators, for this will indicate how you yourself will fare.Outfitter/ schools are more common in the East, but one Western company that emphasizes skills is Mariah Wilderness Expeditions (3304 Geary Blvd. Suite 272, San Francisco, 94118). Mariah offers a series of trips entitled "Women on the River." It has a three-day women's whitewater raft clinic ($175) and a seven-day women's mountain/river leadership training course ($385). A company in the East with a similar approach is Nantahala Outdoor Center (Star Route, Box 68, Bryson City, North Carolina 28713).

The nature of many eastern rivers makes it more difficult to take huge oar- or motor-powered rafts down the river. Customers must take paddle in hand and learn. This certainly makes it harder on the outfitter in many ways, but the customer gets a more worthwhile experience. Your trip will be less fun if you're packed with thirty other people on a floating cattlecar.

Commercial outfitters have procured the lion's share of permits on the country's most popular rivers. River-access rights are bestowed by the agency that manages the land. Once issued, they are considered property and are held for life. Like liquor licenses, the number issued is limited, and they can be bought and sold. Some commercial outfitters perform a valid public service and get people on the rivers who otherwise wouldn't have a chance. But in the Grand Canyon, for example, 441 private parties applied for permits in 1979 and 394 were turned down. Private parties may have a seven-year wait to run the Grand Canyon of the Colorado, says Ron Watters in *The White-Water River Book*.

It would perhaps be easier to see it from the outfitter's point of view if in question was the family operation. But an ominous trend is developing in the Grand Canyon, and it is a harbinger of whitewater rafting throughout the United States. As of June 1982, a large corporation has moved to buy up four Grand Canyon river companies and their valuable river-access permits for about $6 million. Prices like this make it impossible for the small operator to get into business, and they are tempting for even the most dedicated outfitter to sell out. The approach of the large operators is resort-oriented and not at all dedicated to preserving the integrity of the river.

The fitness benefits of boating can be high if you do it often and if you stay in shape. Paddling and rowing can be aerobic, but more likely the greatest aerobic benefits will come from your training. The payoff factor to muscle strength will be immediate and obvious. You will get stronger, and you will look it. The psychological benefits in boating are great as well. And there's a good chance that you will become addicted. It's exquisite fun if the weather is good. But it can also be miserable when the rain hammers down on you day after day.

Boating is not the hard work of backpacking, climbing, or cross-country skiing because the water does much of it for you. But it combines the best of both worlds—land and water. Once camped, you can hike, follow trails, fish in side streams, or land lunkers in the river or lake. If motorboats, trail bikes, and so forth are allowed in the area, forget the fishing unless the water is stocked. You can swim if the water isn't too cold, make a sauna from a plastic tarp, with water poured over heated rocks, or lie on the beach, nature's firm, pliable mattress. And you will become more in tune with wildlife.

The moon peeping around the bend in the canyon inspires poetry. Imagine, like Trish Berglund, being on a moonlit lake one summer's eve with a sweetheart, the canoe gliding gently through the inky water. Or imagine floating down the river at dawn. Someone takes out a flute and begins to play. The notes trill over the water. The sky colors gently with the rising sun. Harmony.

Chapter 5

Nordic Skiing and Ski Mountaineering

The differences between Nordic and alpine skiing are several. Alpine skiing is usually done at ski resorts by riding up on a lift and skiing down a developed run. As such, it has less merit for overall physical fitness, especially for ecological fitness. Alpine skis are fat, and the bindings fix the heel of the boot to the ski. In Nordic skiing the skis are skinnier, and the binding attaches only the boot toe, and not the heel, to the ski. It includes touring on a groomed track, back-country touring, and sometimes ski mountaineering and a specialized form of Nordic ski jumping.

In between Nordic and alpine skiing is a whole cross-breeding of equipment, techniques, and access that can get confusing. Ski mountaineering usually means that the skier uses Nordic or alpine equipment and techniques and gets into and up the mountains under her own power. Sometimes a skier will use Nordic equipment on a groomed downhill/alpine run. This is called cross-country-downhill. Using either type of equipment or technique, those who go up the mountain by the lift, then ski down the ungroomed side of the mountain are sometimes called "backcountry skiers." Probably the best definition of all those who fall in between strict alpine and Nordic is "unconventional skiers," a term coined by Paul Ramer, a designer and manufacturer of back-country ski equipment.

Nordic skiing is new enough in this country that there is no set way to do it. There's a slow grace to the basic Nordic downhill Tele-mark turn, which is much like ballet. This turn is most easily performed in powder, which is not abundant on packed alpine slopes. The search for powder is what has led many alpine skiers to the other side of the mountain and to their conversion to Nordic skiing. Powder is to skiing as trout are to fishing; you don't find either at developed sites unless they're artificial.

Adventure: Ski-Racing the Alps

One early skier, Christine L. Reid, of Brookline, Massachusetts, experienced what she terms "a tantalizing taste" of ski mountaineering when she participated in an international roped ski race in the spring of 1933. Christine was a filmmaker and photographer who made training films about skiing. She wrote of her adventures in such publications as *The Canadian Alpine Journal* and the Appalachian Mountain Club's journal *Appalachia*. Excerpts from her article in the June 1934 issue of *Appalachia* are reprinted here by permission of the Appalachian Mountain Club.

The starting line for the race was to be at the Theodule Cabane, situated on the crest of the Theodule Pass, on the border between Switzerland and Italy. Christine was invited by the president of the Swiss Zermatt Ski Club to enter with him as an unofficial duo. She was the only woman of 110 Italian, Austrian, German, French, and Swiss competitors, plus assorted race officials, press correspondents, and an Italian alpine regiment that was to monitor the course. The race covered approximately ten miles. Skiers on each team were required to be roped together, the usual precaution taken on glaciers. If you fall into a crevasse, the fall will be arrested and you can be rescued via the rope.

Christine and her partner took the Gornergrat Railway partway to the race site. On the train they watched with anxiety "huge black and sulphurous-looking clouds steal up behind the Matterhorn, which stood, a massive pyramid of black, alone and majestic against the sky." After getting off the train, they hurriedly donned their skis. They still had to switchback up and over the steep, glazed snow slopes to the upper plateau of the Theodule Pass, then up to the Theodule Ridge, where the mountaineering hut was perched.

The hut was a mere dot on the distant horizon. Facing the rapidly approaching storm, and step-turning our skis with difficulty against its increasingly powerful wind, we had pushed laboriously upward, to gain the high plateau. There we seemed to be in an immense and awe-inspiring vacuum; for across that still white stretch of snow no creature stirred except ourselves, and the soft, sibilant whisper of our skis was the only sound to break the silence.

Then suddenly the storm broke loose in fury! The sky, black overhead like an inverted cauldron, became a seething mass of conflicting forces. Buffeted to and fro by the wind, we climbed the ridge, and reaching the door of the hut skied straight in and slammed it to behind us. Kind and helpful hands relieved us of our skis, and here, in the tiny ill-lighted hall of refuge, we found ourselves surrounded by an immense group of interested and excited skiers.

Before the storm passed, they spent a day in the overcrowded hut. "That evening it was not without quite a few quivers of nervous anticipation that I beheld, hung in a clear blue heaven over the dark silhouette of the Matterhorn, a tiny lemon-peel shaving of a moon that promised a perfect day for the morrow."

Already inspected for the required rucksack, ice-axe and at least one pair of crampons, together with a compass and a first-aid kit, the teams, all roped in squadron-formation, were standing quietly in front of the hut. Before them stretches a smooth and tantalizing track that shusses alluringly down the ridge and disappears with abruptness over the brink to the Theodule Pass—to reappear beyond, a sunlit thread of gold and silver trailing away to the horizon.

As the last slow moments slip by toward the zero hour the first team steps boldly up to the starting line. . . . With muscles taut they stand ready, poised for flight—till suddenly, the flag drops. . . they are off, whoooosh. . . . and out of sight. Fast on their track, down into the gulf of the Theodule, drops squadron after squadron, at three-minute intervals. . . .

At last I stand upon the starting line, clutching my ski poles with frenzied determination and wishing myself anywhere else but here. But the seemingly endless moments of agonizing suspense terminate, and with the drop of the flag and an encouraging flip of the rope from behind, I am off, schussing down into the white blankness.

Throughout the race Christine led on the downhills and her partner led on the upslopes. Following behind his broad back, she kicked her toes up the slope and reveled in the peace of the sunshine and stillness.

There, just beyond us, lies the glistening traverse leading upward to the Breithorn plateau. Our first lung-test, it looks inviting at the moment.

Christine Reid following cog railway tracks to the Gornergrat on a skiing instruction film assignment, about 1933. Photograph courtesy of Ruth P. Chase.

Later, scruff-scruffing along upgrade on my sealskins, I began to wonder if it was so alluring! . . .

Veering now in a southeasterly direction we cut across the wide plateau into Italy, where with skis unmuzzled by sealskins we could taste at last the joys of the downward slope. At least, so I expected; but I had forgotten *that rope*—knotted about my waist and leading back behind me into Bernard's well-held coil. In spite of our efforts to keep it clear, at each moment of ill-conceived concentration, as I tried to turn my skis in graceful arcs, the rope would come squirming surreptitiously up behind me and, like a boa constrictor that engulfs its prey, loop itself about my ski tips, poles, and ankles. Gathering momentum from my half-completed turn, hard down over it I would ride, to become lassoed by its snarls and jerked at last to a sickening stop! . . .

Continuing on down in this (for me) ignominious fashion, we passed between two yellow flags that guided us to safety across a snowbridge spanning a deep and ugly crevasse. Up the slope we herringboned, then crossed through the Verra Pass along a precipitously sloping traverse, over snow unpleasantly frozen to a rock-like consistency. There before us was the great white face of Castor, sneeringly cold. Upon its glistening snow and ice, sticking like flies to a wall, moved tiny specks of squadrons slowly climbing their way upward to the summit ridge; while at the base were others, putting on their crampons in preparation for the ascent. . . .

Panting and pushing, gasping and gripping, we climbed for a seeming eternity upon that great white face. A bit aghast at the immense quantity of space spread out there below me, at the inadequacy of mere hobnails in place of crampons on that icy surface, [Christine had no crampons for the 3,000-foot ascent], and at the increasingly awkward weight of my ski load, I gingerly teetered my way back and forth across the slope as best I could.

Just as they reached the top of the rim and the reward of the glorious panorama of the Italian Alps, a thick fog crept up behind them and blotted it all from view. Worse, they had to make the descent in the fog.

Now we plunged over the rim of the plateau of our last leg to the finish line. Sliding precipitately down the steep slope through that confusing blackness of fog, we were glad to be without skis, for our pace was alarming enough as it was. Down we went to the smoother, undulating surface of the Felik Glacier stretched below. Here we could put on skis; and groping our way from flag to flag in the fog, we at last saw the square gray silhouette of the Sella Cabane rise before us out of the fog. We knew our long race was over. With weary eyes and trembling knees I came to a stop before the hut and glanced at my badly befogged wristwatch. The hands pointed almost on the second to twelve noon—that made, for our total elapsed time, five hours and seven minutes. How silly it sounded, in comparison with the two- to three-minute time-scores of our races back home!

Ski mountaineering is certainly one of the more dangerous and difficult ways to get acquainted with the outdoors. It is the most radical of several options and one that not many women have chosen—or many men for that matter. As a writer for *Cross Country* ski magazine said about winter camping, "a lot of people talk about it, but not many actually do it." While high-risk sports are not necessarily advocated, neither should they be overlooked. It's gratifying to see a woman's name occasionally listed among the male celebrities—such as Jan Reynolds, who holds the women's world altitude skiing record by having skied Mt. Muztagata (24,750 feet) in western China in July 1980 with Ned Gillette and Galen Rowell as partners.

On the other end of the spectrum from ski mountaineering is skiing in a groomed track. This is often what people mean when they speak of cross-country skiing, although this and the term *Nordic* are often used interchangeably. The popularity of cross-country skiing has boomed in recent years. Many attribute this trend to alienation from the cost, crowds, and commercialization of alpine skiing. Another interesting possibility is that skiing itself has calmed down with the aging of the baby boom population. "The baby boom that produced all the hotdog skiers looking for the hardest runs has grown up. The sport has become less macho."[1] Some alpine ski resorts are reported to be modifying their runs to accommodate more beginning and intermediate skiers.

The injury rate among Nordic skiers is much less than among alpine skiers. This is probably true even if you add ski mountaineering. Nordic skiing would almost have to be safer because in order to come down the mountain, you first must get up it under your own power. If you're not in good condition, you probably won't get high enough or far enough to harm yourself or anyone else.

From Novice to Instructor: A Personal Account

Says Kellie Erwin Rhoades, a Colorado Outward Bound instructor who recently organized a course for women in Nordic skiing: "I downhill skied as a child and teenager. But I got bored with it. I wanted to get into the backcountry. When I was a college student I couldn't afford the lift tickets anyway. Maybe if I'd known about skins and Ramer bindings I would have taken up ski mountaineering." She did her first Nordic ski trip when she was in high school. She skied in with several guys who were nationally ranked alpine skiers. "We didn't know anything about avalanches," she shudders. "When we crossed an obvious avalanche slope, at least we had the sense to cross it one at a time. But we didn't have any avalanche rescue equipment. We wouldn't have known what to do if there had been an avalanche."

They didn't start to ski until about 4 P.M. for a ten-mile trip to a mountain cabin. "We'd hiked there before in the summer and figured it wouldn't be that hard on skis. We were wrong." About three-quarters of the way in, Kellie's legs cramped up from ankle to crotch from the unaccustomed stress. One of her companion's feet became frostbitten. They considered turning back, but fortunately didn't: They would have been stuck in the freezing dark without adequate equipment or knowledge. Luckily, when they got to the cabin, two men had arrived before them and dug it out. "We were lucky they had, otherwise we probably would haven gotten hypothermic." They rubbed their companion's feet with snow, then stuck them right next to the fire—both ways to damage frostbitten flesh further. Rubbing the flesh with snow only makes it colder and harms tissue. A foot stuck right next to the fire can be burned without the victim even feeling it.

The snow was too deep to bring in a snowmobile to evacuate the victim, which would have been the best option, so he had to ski out on his own. In this case, it would have been best not to thaw the feet. But they didn't know this. The men who had dug out the cabin came back to find them there. They showed them how to treat frostbite correctly had an evacuation been possible—warm rapidly without endangering the flesh with a burn, like testing the temperature of a baby's bottle. Once thawed, the man's feet swelled so large that he couldn't get his boots on. One of the men wore a size larger and traded his with the victim. Another loaned him a ski tip. It would have been hard to ski out with a tip missing. Although the frostbite damage was not permanent, the victim had to stay in bed for two weeks while his feet healed. "Although it wasn't a good trip because we did so many dumb things, I sure learned a lot," she says.

Kellie eventually set up a course for women because she felt that many women are intimidated by the male predominance. "I worked for the Idaho State University Outdoor Program when I was a student," she says, "and not many women participated in the programs. They'd see a bunch of strong men and think, 'Oh, I'm not capable.' I wanted to do something to bring them in."

In the summer of 1978 Kellie was hired as an instructor for Colorado Outward Bound, a network of schools for backcountry adventure training. It can be as demanding or more so on the instructor as it is on the student. "Once I finished that summer, I knew I was competent and that I could lead. I gained a lot of confidence. Enough to try to get a winter program going for women." With the encouragement of her academic adviser in her major, parks and recreation management, she approached the Outdoor Program director. "I convinced him that it wasn't just a bunch of macho women who wanted to get together to show up men," she says. He agreed to it.

In the winter of 1979 the Outdoor Program sponsored the All Women's Winter Wilderness Workshop in Stanley Basin, in the heart of the Sawtooth National Recreation Area. Kellie posted a trip sheet in the Outdoor Program office. The twelve women who signed up were of greatly differing abilities. "This didn't seem to matter much," says Kellie.

They skied in one mile and once there set up tents and tried building igloos and snow caves. The snow wasn't deep, so they weren't very successful at digging snow caves. The igloo didn't fare too well either. "I wasn't watching. When I did notice what they were doing, they'd built the walls of the igloo straight up and down. The walls have to slant in as you add each block in order to meet in the middle to form the roof. So they had walls and no roof." They also studied avalanche conditions, Pieps (electronic beepers) and how to use them, and map and compass reading. In all, the demands were great enough for the women to learn, but not so much that any real danger was involved.

Kellie held a more ambitious workshop in the winter of 1980. It was done in the Big Hole Mountains, a relatively unknown range in eastern Idaho. The ski in was five miles, and they had to climb a 1,000-foot ridge. They then dropped down into a basin. Instead of tents, snowcaves, and igloos, they used yurts as shelters. Yurts are used by nomads in Mongolia in much the same way that Native Americans used teepees. The yurts were rented from a professional outfitter who had set them up in the Big Holes for the winter.

Kellie distinguishes between teaching and outfitting, in which the guide does most of the work and the customers aren't necessarily expected to learn anything. "There are certain things I consider essential, such as knowing avalanche conditions and Pieps," she says. "But for other things I just ask them what they want to do and we do it."

The third year the outing was offered, so many women signed up that some had to be turned away. "I wanted to keep it to twelve people. There was another woman along who helped guide and teach. We felt that the ratio of novices to experienced women should be low." The workshops are three days long. The first day they ski in, the second

Yurt shelter in the Big Hole Mountains, Idaho. Photograph courtesy of Kellie Erwin Rhoads.

day they explore and learn specific skills, and the third day they ski back out.

Kellie's style of wilderness skills teaching is certainly different than the "scare them into proficiency" method. For the same reason, skiing courses taught by women for women, such as Elissa Slanger's alpine course (see *Ski Woman's Way*), are meeting with similar success. As retired Congresswoman Shirley Chisholm said in her campaign slogan when she sought the Democratic bid for President in 1972, "Someday power will be compassionate."

Training and Preparation

Nordic skiing is about 90 percent aerobic and as such is felt to be the best activity for developing the cardiovascular system. Naturally, this means that it takes a lot of lung and heart power to be good at it. The highest maximal oxygen uptakes on record are those of top cross-country skiers. For women, the highest value is 77 ml·kg·min (77 milliliters of oxygen used per kilogram of body weight per minute). For men the highest is 94·kg·min.[2]

The reason that the $\dot{V}O_2$ max of cross-country skiers is so high is that virtually every major muscle group is used, and in turn every muscle sucks in the oxygen to power itself metabolically. A good cross-country skier bounds along at a pace faster than you can run. The 1976 women's Olympic Nordic ski record for five kilometers is 15:48:69. This averages about two minutes per mile.

Canoeing, backpacking, and bicycling are all good for skiing. Training that best mimics the activity itself produces the most obvious results. Nevertheless, some kind of aerobic training is important if you want to Nordic ski and it becomes essential if you want to backcountry ski or ski mountaineer.

Bicycling is good training for Nordic skiing, and vice versa, because it develops the important quadriceps muscles that power your Nordic stride. Running is good because it does so much for the lungs and heart. Kellie frequently skis with Janene Willer, the bicyclist. Kellie runs to keep in shape. ''I'd say we were about equal. I probably have the edge in lung power, but Janene's thighs are stronger than mine.''

In the best of all possible worlds, you would jog on the trails you cross-country ski. In other worlds, like this one, more likely you jog on a track or road. Although you might feel silly, you can help your skiing even more if you stride along carrying your ski poles as you would in skiing. If you hike, ski poles work well. One woman always carries them when she backpacks; it helps her balance and stride. Although she is in her fifties, she finds that younger hikers are hard pressed to stay on her trail.

If you do jog or hike on a road, one way to increase the specificity of training is to do about one-third uphill, one third level, and one-third downhill. Of course, be sensible. If your knees can't take the downhill, don't do it. You can get a similar training effect with less trauma to the knees and other joints by doing intervals. Another common means of specialized Nordic training is to walk or run stadium stairs. One author even suggests walking them backwards.[3] If you intend to carry a heavy pack when skiing, then also wear a pack while jogging. If you're accustomed to day ski touring, try some of these short trips while wearing a heavy pack before you have to carry it far into the wilderness.

Ski striding and bounding is a specific training method in which you run or jog uphill using long strides. This imitates the movement pattern of cross-country skiing uphill. The difference between ski striding and ski bounding is the difference between walking and running. In the first, you walk up the hill in long strides. In the second, you run up the hill in long strides. This is done in intervals. If you race or ski in areas with many small hills, you may want to do intervals that

Skiing with a full pack requires some getting used to, but it has obvious rewards, such as this winter scene. Photograph courtesy of Kellie Erwin Rhoads.

develop the aerobic system. The way you do intervals depends on your own motivation and the area where you ski. If you know that the chances of doing both distance and intervals is small, do the distance. It's more important to have the basic aerobic stamina.

Rollerskiing is the best training of all. These are skis on wheels, and the poles have a special tip built for the road instead of snow. The U.S. Nordic Ski team rollerskis and runs for training. A pair, including bindings and poles, cost about $200. They can be purchased from Reliable Racing Supply (624 Glen Street, Glens Falls, New York 12801).

Rollerskiing has been found to be as much or more aerobically demanding than running.[4] Most cross-country ski moves can be duplicated on rollerskis, but they are most useful for double-poling and diagonal striding. They should be used with poles that, like those used on the snow, are tall enough to reach to just under your armpit. One serious drawback of rollerskis is their cost. They are also potentially dangerous and should be used only on level road. They have no brakes, and because your toes are clamped into them, it's not easy to dismount. You can't just jump off them like you would a skateboard if you're about to careen into a tree.

A Nordic training device for indoors is the NordicTrack, which is like a treadmill for skiers. It is available from PSI (124 Columbia Court, Chaska, Minnesota 55318) and costs about $500.

Strength training is of particular importance to Nordic skiers. About one-quarter of your propulsion comes from your upper body. As is true of most wilderness sports, women who are disproportionately weak above the waist will have difficulties. The Exer-Genie, available from Reliable Racing Supply for about $40, develops the arms and shoulder muscles used in Nordic skiing. Its tension setting makes it superior to less expensive models. You can get a similar training effect by attaching bicycle innertubes to a clothesline pole, or a fence at about chest height and pulling on them past your hips, as if poling forward on skis. Better yet are the weight-pulley machines in gyms and health clubs. One such machine, the Marcy, accommodates a number of exercises that are good for skiers.

Weight training for skiers should emphasize both all-around strength and that directed to develop muscles and protect you from injury. The body areas that require special attention, both because of the frequency with which they are used and the prevalence of injuries, are the knees, lower back and antagonistic abdominal muscles, the ankles, shoulders, triceps, and hips. That doesn't leave much out!

The following exercises are designed to work the body in the required way. The numbers beside each exercise correspond to the numbered muscle groups. To add or substitute exercises, refer to the weight-training chart in chapter 1. Instructions for calf and toe raises are given in chapter 2.

1. Hips, lower back, buttocks (two exercises)
2. Chest, upper arms (two exercises)
3. Thighs, hamstrings (two exercises)
4. Calves, shins, ankles (two exercises)
5. Shoulders, triceps (two exercises)
6. Abdomen (two exercises)
7. Biceps (two exercises)
8. Forearms, wrists (one exercise)

Free Weights	*Universal or Nautilus*	*No Weights*
Bench fly (2,5,7)	Bench fly (2,5,7)	Abdominal curl (6)
Calf raise (4)	Bent-leg sit-up (1,6)	Bent-leg sit-up (1,6)
Clean and press (1,2,3,4,5,6,7,8)	Bicep curl (7)	Calf raise (3,4)
	Hip and back machine or hyperextension (1)	Dip (2,5,7)
Quarter squat (1,3,4,6)	Leg curl (1,3,4)	Pullups (2,5,7,8)
Toe raise (4)	Leg extension (1,3,4)	Quarter deep-knee bend (1,3,4)
Upright rowing (2,5,7)	Tricep extension or tricep press (5)	
	Roman chair (1,6)	

If you're able to get out frequently during the ski season, most of your muscular workout will come from skiing itself. In this case, you need only weight-train once or twice a week. Otherwise, you should weight-train three times a week.

Warm-Ups and Warm-Downs

Since you start at the bottom and ski uphill on many Nordic ski routes, this can be your warm-up if you start slowly. Pacing is important. Almost every Nordic skier has memories of when she didn't pace herself and became exhausted early in the day, or overestimated how far she could go before sunset. Keep your pace just as you would when jogging or swimming in order to avoid the dangers that come with being overly fatigued. A gentle warm-up is part of the pacing.

Limbering up the body by stretching before skiing is an important habit. Regardless of your aerobic and weight training, you will use muscles and joints at uncustomary angles. The stretches recommended for skiers are the butterfly, hyperextension, lunge, pulldown behind neck, and toe touch. These should also be done during rest stops, or after you're finished for the day.

Injuries and Ailments

As with all sports injuries, it's better to be prepared than caught short. The good news for skiing is that Nordic ski injuries are by and large uncommon, except in the higher-risk sport of ski mountaineering. Records of the U.S. Nordic team show injuries to be extremely rare. In contrast, 79 percent of the female and 88 percent of the male world-class alpine ski racers had at least one serious injury during their careers.[5]

Cold Injuries

In a study done by the National Ski Patrol, about 20 percent of Nordic ski injuries were related to cold, hypothermia, or frostbite.[6] But many cases of frostbite and hypothermia are not reported. Cold injuries are probably the single most common problem among cross-country skiers. Because Nordic skiing is so strenuous, you can sweat a great deal regardless of subzero temperatures. Once your clothing, including your boots and socks, becomes wet from perspiration, the heat loss is much greater.

Frostbite can result from generalized heat loss because the body shunts the blood from the extremities to keep the essential core warm. It's especially insidious in the feet because they don't register cold in most people as quickly as do other parts of the body. The signs, treatment and prevention of frostbite are discussed in chapter 9.

For long tours, including one-day adventures, you need to prepare well for the cold. Skin-tight racing uniforms and other touring garments are not appropriate for extended touring or ski mountaineering. They aren't warm enough and don't protect the skin adequately from cold and wind chill. Superficial cold injury from such tight garments can occur in the breasts in women and the penis in men. Light touring boots and gloves also won't keep you warm.

Starting with the feet and going from the outside layer in, gaiters are your first layer. These keep the snow and wet out of your boots. Overbooties, both commercial ones and simple heavy old socks, can be worn over your boots and are a tried and proved method of keeping your feet warm. Next come the boots. Heavier boots are recommended for the backcountry. Double boots, such as Kastinger Hi-Tour, are warmer still and obviate the need for overbooties. Be sure to take ample pairs of socks and change them when they get wet. Finally, felt pads placed inside the boot form a further barrier against cold.

Taking care of your hands is simpler. Wear good, warm mittens or gloves under long, bulky nylon mitten shells if it is cold and wet.

Take extra pairs of mittens or gloves because if you fall (and you will), your mittens will get wet. If your hands get cold, or show signs of frostbite, warm them under your armpits. If your feet get cold, first make sure that your boots aren't laced too tightly. This can constrict blood to the feet. Cold bare feet can be warmed against the chest of a cooperative friend. If you must, stop and build a fire to get warm. Although damage from frostbite is not always permanent, it can be.

For more information about hypothermia, see chapter 9. Skiers should be particularly aware of hypothermia.

Altitude Sickness

Altitude sickness is discussed in chapter 9. Ski mountaineers should be thoroughly acquainted with its signs and prevention. Day skiers and those who go to high altitudes quickly should also educate themselves about altitude sickness.

Snow Blindness

If anyone should protect herself from snow blindness, it is a skier. The prevention is so simple that most people are ashamed when they get it. Get in the habit of wearing sunglasses. The best are goggles or mountaineering glasses that absorb 90 percent of the reflective radiation. An antifogging agent can be applied. Plastic lenses are less likely to fog and harder to break. Like your skin your eyes can become sunburned, and you may not be aware of it until several hours after exposure. You can get sunburned even on cloudy days. If you break your glasses, substitute a bandanna or cut small slits in a piece of cardboard.

It takes a full twenty-four hours for the cells of the eyes to heal. They should be patched to prevent further irritation and exposure to light and to ease the pain. A cold compress also helps relieve pain, as well as a prescription aspirin-codeine combination or Motrin. Do not use a local eye anesthetic such as pontacaine or tetracaine. These will relieve the pain but can delay healing, and they may result in infection and loss of vision.

Sore Throats

Chronic sore throats are not uncommon when breathing dry, cold air. Take along plenty of throat lozenges. Piro Kramer, expedition doctor for the U.S. Women's Annapurna expedition in 1978, notes that while all members of the expedition were given a generous supply of lozenges, there still weren't enough. *Medicine for Mountaineering* recommends hard candy as being just as effective, less expensive, nutritious, and better than the constant use of an anesthetic or antibiotic, which may be contained in lozenges. A bandanna worn over the mouth or a balaclava pulled up over the mouth can help prevent a sore throat, as can keeping your neck and chin protected. You can also inhale the vapors of steam by water heated on your stove. Cover your head with a towel to trap the steam.

Cuts and Lacerations

Cuts and lacerations, although not especially common, are possible from ski poles and skis with metal edges, especially if you sharpen them. Your first-aid kit should be adequately equipped to treat them.

Traumatic Injuries

Traumatic injuries, as opposed to stress injuries, are more common to Nordic skiers. Yet, the rate of injuries among Nordic skiers is low, estimated at about .5 per 1,000 skier days, which is about half the rate of those among alpine skiers.[7] However, the data for cross-country skiing accidents are almost impossible to gather because so much is done in unsupervised areas.

Among the more common injuries requiring a doctor's attention are "skier's thumb" and shoulder and knee injuries. Since they occur most often when you fall going downhill, you should learn how to fall safely. But preferably you should stop yourself without falling. It is significant that most of the injuries reported in one study were among beginning and intermediate skiers. Presumably these were the skiers who fell most often. Another study showed that most accidents result from exhaustion, poor conditioning, and poor technique.

Your natural reflex to sit down when falling is a good one, and women with their greater fat placement in the derriere and hips are well protected. Skiers who are lower to the ground, through a combination of the skier's crouch and their own height, put less strain on the knees and ankles and don't have as far to fall. Naturally, you don't want to make this your major stopping technique, especially if you ski in groomed tracks. There's no ignominy in dragging your poles as a brake either. Just be sure not to get them tangled in brush. There's also the bush-to-bush method of grabbing friendly bushes when you want to stop. Try not to fall forward, since this endangers the spinal cord, chest, and head.

Although the injury rate among Nordic skiers is relatively low, significant joint injuries do occur. These are related to speed and falls and to the fact that Nordic ski bindings do not release—unless your boots are simply torn out of the three-pin bindings, which happens frequently. Some of the newer racing bindings don't release at all and therefore are more dangerous.

The flexibility of the Nordic boot and three-pin binding system is partially responsible for the lower injury rate among Nordic versus alpine skiers, although the nature of the skiing has a lot to do with it too. Dr. Edward Hixson, coordinator of the medical supervisory team of the U.S. Nordic ski team, has a personal prejudice against devices that fix the heel to cross-country skis. He feels they are not necessary with a good cross-country technique, and they may increase the injury rate to that similar to alpine skiing.[8]

Some alpine skis made specifically for ski mountaineering are sometimes referred to as alpine touring skis. One feature may be a hole in the tip for tying the skis together to made a sled. They are often fitted with bindings that allow up-and-down heel movement for uphill terrain and then clamp down for use on downhill terrain. Because these bindings then hold both the toe and heel in position and are used with a stiff-soled boot, they may cause more injuries than cross-country bindings and flexible-soled boots, as Hixson points out. Of course these bindings give a great deal more control for downhill skiing and to some may justify the greater possibility of injury.

There are conflicting data as to whether injuries occur more frequently to the upper or lower body. It appears that women are more likely to injure their knees when skiing, perhaps because of the way they fall. With a lower center of gravity, they may be more likely to fall on their backsides or sideways, thereby twisting the knee. This doesn't mean that you should fall forward to avoid hurting your knees. It means to develop the strength and flexibility through training and to know how to fall correctly. Women do not have a higher upper-body injury rate than men. It's possible that men with a higher center of gravity may tend to fall forward, thereby sustaining more injuries in the shoulder area.

Possibly the most common Nordic skiing injury is a "skier's thumb." In the Nordic grip the thumb is held between the pole and the strap. In a fall, the thumb may be pulled out of place, which can tear the ligament. Swelling and tenderness on the inner side of the thumb can indicate a severe injury, particularly if you can't pinch or resist pressure. Ice packs and elevation help, but get medical attention if pain and weakness in the thumb persist. Sometimes a plaster cast is needed even if the X-rays appear to be normal. This injury sometimes requires surgery. If not treated properly, it can lead to a permanently weakened thumb.

Ankle sprains occur occasionally in Nordic skiers because the low, flexible boots allow greater twisting during a fall. The toe is held in place by the bindings, and the ski acts as a lever against the ankle. If you have a moderately sprained ankle, you should be able to move your foot up and down with little pain. Tenderness and bruising should be only in the area right in front of the ankle bone. Treatment consists of icing the ankle to relieve pain and swelling, taping to add stability, and a few days of rest. You should be able to walk without great pain. Barring reinjury, which occurs often because the ankle is weak while healing, you should completely recover in at least three weeks.

You may have a severe sprain if swelling, bruising, and possibly pain on both sides of the ankle are present. Not being able to walk or move your foot up and down indicates a severe sprain and possibly a fracture. First-aid for a severe sprain is ice, splinting, and elevation of the ankle. Weight should not be put on the injured ankle. Treatment should definitely be sought, since a permanently weak ankle can result. Any deformity, numbness, severe pain, or poor circulation indicates serious damage and help should be sought immediately.

Skier's fracture, or that resulting from trauma to the shinbone, occurs in cross-country skiing as it once did in alpine skiing before the advent of high, rigid alpine boots. Although there may be no deformity, the bone may still be broken. You may still be able to walk, although there will be pain in that part of the leg. The treatment is ice packs and a few days of rest. Persistent pain after a few days means you should see a physician and that the fracture may require a cast. These injuries appear to be less likely with pin bindings and more likely with cable bindings.

Occasionally you can injure your tailbone if you take a hard fall, and often there's not a great deal a doctor can do. Applying ice periodically for several days should relieve the pain. Once most of the pain is gone, apply heat. It's also advisable to sit on a pillow.

No one predominant upper-body injury has been identified among cross-country skiers. Fractures, dislocations, and damage to the ligaments can occur throughout the shoulder region and neck. The frightening thing about upper-body injuries is the possible involvement of the neck and spinal cord. Anyone whose neck appears to be injured and has pain, numbness, tingling, or a burning sensation in the arms or legs should be moved only by a doctor, trained paramedic, or ski patrol. This basic precaution is taught in every first-aid course for good reason: You can permanently and seriously hurt the person by inept handling. Treat the victim for shock and hypothermia, and get immediate help.

Injuries to the shoulder, such as dislocations and separations, should be treated by applying ice and immobilizing the arm in a sling until a medical evaluation can be made. Broken arms can be splinted and put in a sling. You can hurt your collarbone (clavicle) if you fall hard sideways on your shoulder. This can be very painful because the shock travels through the collarbone to the breastbone. If there is no major swelling in the collarbone area, and if there is no depression indicating an inward dislocation (which is unusual) and both ends of the bone seem okay, simply apply ice to relieve pain. This injury usually doesn't require medical attention unless there is deformity or obvious swelling. A collarbone dislocated inward into the chest is an emergency.

Usually injuries along the clavicle itself, rather than on either end, are fractures. These are common among children. Usually there is swelling, tenderness, and some bruising. These should be iced. The injured person will feel better if she holds her shoulders back. A figure-eight sling can be put on over the clothing to hold the shoulders in this position. It is done by looping cloth or an Ace bandage under the arms and around the back.

Trauma to the Knees

The most common injury among female Nordic skiers is to the ligaments of the knee. These are usually minor sprains. Strength training (especially of the quadriceps) is very important to protect the knee from sprains and strains. Once the knee is weakened, the possibility of hurting it again is greater. There is evidence that an injured joint may be more likely to develop osteoarthritis.

Among alpine skiers, there are strong indications that injury rates are decreasing, perhaps partially because of improvements in the binding system. The state of the art in alpine boot and binding systems is much more advanced than it is in Nordic boots and bindings. Even so, alpine skiers and Nordic skiers who use the clamp bindings can manage to override the built-in safety of their equipment by setting the bindings too tight. Among injured alpine skiers in one large study, some had bindings so badly adjusted that they wouldn't release at all during tests performed by engineers. These excessively high settings were more abundant among those injured than in the control group.

Knees are a problem for all athletes. Women more often tend to be knock-kneed, while men more often tend to be bow-legged. Those who are knock-kneed have problems with a steady eroding of the underside of the kneecap (chondromalacia) and dislocation of the kneecap. It makes sense not only to strength-train to help hold the kneecap in place, but to tape, brace, and pad the knee as needed to protect it from injury.

As noted by the researchers studying downhill ski injuries, lighter, smaller persons and those with little experience tend to sustain more injuries. A woman's lighter bones and more delicate ligaments (both may result from inactivity) might contribute to the greater possibility of knee injuries. It is speculated that possibly 50 percent of all knee injuries could be prevented by proper strength training and conditioning. Strength training won't help prevent all injuries, but it makes sense that the stronger the leg muscles, the less severe an injury will be. Strong thigh and calf muscles are the first line of defense against knee injury. And over a six-month period, most women will see a strength increase of 50 to 100 percent with weight-training exercises.

Knee injuries occur 80 percent more frequently on the weaker side of the body, so devote special attention to strengthening your weaker leg. Exercises such as the leg extension should be done one leg at a time to ensure equal development of both legs. If one leg is shorter than the other, about 90 percent of the time the injury will occur to this leg. (To determine if one leg is shorter, see chapter 2.) If you are able to hyperextend your knee, you should give special attention to strengthening the hamstrings. Remember that about 75 percent of all types of sports injuries take place during the first two weeks of the season. Be sure to be in shape before you start.

If you do injure your knee, wrap it and apply ice. You may need to take the weight off of it too. Consult an orthopedic specialist about the prescribed therapy and rehabilitation.

Overload/Stress Injuries

Stress injuries are not that frequent among cross-country skiers. The snow is softer, and the smooth glide causes little of the stress that you get from pounding over a pavement or rocky trail. However, several overuse problems can develop if you Nordic ski a lot. Lower-back pain is not uncommon. With most lower-back problems, weak abdominal muscles result in an imbalance, which can cause pain. Some of the causes of chronic lower-back pain are given in chapter 2. The prevention is the standard stretching and strength training before and during the ski season. Relief of lower-back pain comes from ice and rest.

A less frequent chronic problem is tendinitis of the triceps because of the action of the arms in poling. The triceps, located on the backside of the arm are the antagonistic muscles to the biceps. Tendinitis develops from too little strength and flexibility and too much use. It may not show up at the beginning of the ski season because the tendon will heal itself of minor tears. However, as the scar tissue accumulates, *it* can tear very easily. When the scar tissue tears, *it* is what hurts.

The treatment for all tendinitis is RICE: rest, ice, compression, and elevation. After you rest for several days you can continue with the sport if the pain is not severe and if you take some precautions. Before skiing, warm your whole body, and especially do stretching exercises for the affected area. Do them fully and slowly. Try to make the area as loose and flexible as you can. Stretch as far as possible, but not so far that you risk further injury. Once you have stretched, warm up further by skiing slowly and getting the body primed for more strenuous work later. Once you quit for the day or take a long break, apply ice or snow to the area as soon as possible. This can be done as necessary three or four times a day. In time the problem usually goes away. You don't need to see a doctor unless the pain gets worse instead of better. Approach the ski season gradually and don't undertake excessive amounts of exercise.

Bunions

Besides a propensity for frostbite, skier's feet can be vulnerable to several other problems. Most of them have to do with the misalignment or mistreatment of the big toe.

A tendency for bunions is inherited and occurs when the bone that connects the big toe to the foot protrudes too much from the side. Bunions themselves are an accumulation of tough connective tissue that eventually calcifies. They may never bother you until you put too much pressure on this part of the foot, either through tight shoes, overweight, or overuse. If you're a runner, you have probably already discovered this problem. When skiing, the constant flexing of the foot right at this joint can cause bunion problems. What to do? Make sure that none of your shoes, including ski boots, are too tight. You can make a bunion "bagel" from a piece of foam rubber with a hole cut out to accommodate the bunion. Or have a bunion pad made by a podiatrist. You can also try an arch support, which makes the arch take more weight, thereby relieving the burden on the ball of the foot.

Skiers can also get what is appropriately named "skier's toe," which comes from the constant flexing of the big-toe joint. It can result in arthritis. Your big toe will hurt and feel rigid. When you move it up and down, it may feel gritty because of calcium deposits in the joint. A solution given by Dr. Murray Weisenfeld, a podiatrist and author of *The Runner's Repair Manual,* is to have a shoemaker put a strip of hard rubber on the outside of your ski boot right across the widest part of the boot. The strip should be just behind the ball of the foot. It should be about ⅛" thick and about 1½" wide and tapered a bit on the edges under the foot so that it won't be lumpy. This will take some of the pressure off the ball of the foot and the big toe.

Avalanches: An Ever Present Danger

Avalanches are to backcountry skiers what getting trapped in a hydraulic is to boaters: The possibility is always there. It's alarming how few cross-country ski books even mention this killer. In the western United States most backcountry users are at least aware of them, since thousands thunder their way down steep slopes every year. Avalanches also occur in the eastern mountains, and the skier who ventures past the beaten track is foolish—no, stupid—not to become knowledgeable about them.

If you ski mountainous country, pay attention here. These paragraphs are adapted from *Hiking the Backcountry: A Do-It-Yourself Guide for the Adventurous Woman,* written by the author and Ann Puddicombe.

> Avalanches are a year-round peril, although they are most dangerous in winter and spring. . . . A complex phenomenon, not completely understood even by experts, they are impossible to predict accurately. The loose snow variety starts at a small point and rapidly increases in size and quantity as it moves downhill in a formless mass.
>
> Most accidents are caused by slab avalanches, which occur when unstable snow breaks away at a well-defined fracture line. Most victims trigger the slides themselves. Their weight on the snow slab breaks the fragile threads that hold it to the slope. Loud shouts, thumps, and noises can also trigger a slide. . . . On a slope with less than thirty degrees' inclination, the chances of an avalanche are not great. Slopes between thirty and sixty degrees are the most likely to avalanche. On those steeper than sixty degrees, the snow tends to sluff off as it falls. Trees, rocks, or heavy brush may anchor the snow and dissipate the onslaught, although avalanches (especially the loose-snow kind) *do* occur in heavy timber and like terrain. Six inches or more of new snow, or layers of old snow subjected to melting—particularly in large, exposed, open areas—are very

dangerous. Convex slopes are more dangerous than concave ones. During midwinter, north-facing slopes pose the greatest threat of sliding, while south-facing slopes become hazardous in the spring and on sunny days, when melting makes the snowpack unstable. Although slopes that protect you from the wind are more pleasant, they are more likely to slide, since snow accumulates there in greater depth and is less compact than that on the windward side.

Avoid avalanche chutes (steep passages where large masses of snow slide down the mountain) and cornices (piled snow that hangs over the edge of a ridge or cliff). The safest routes are ridges away from cornices and slightly to the windward side. If you cannot travel the ridge, the next safest route is in the valley, far from the bottom of the slope. . . . The best times to cross are in early morning or late evening, when the sun is not beaming and cooler temperatures help seal the ice crystals.

If you are alone, it's best not to cross an avalanche slope. The more people in a group, the more there are to dig out a victim—assuming there is only one victim. Everyone should be equipped with avalanche rescue equipment such as Pieps or Skadis electronic beepers, which cost $30 to $50. You need more than one beeper to transmit and receive. The transmission will make the person buried in an avalanche (or the body) easier to locate. Everyone in the party should have a good, strong metal shovel. Ski poles that screw together can be used as probes. One company that makes these poles is Life-Link (Box 2913, Jackson, Wyoming 83001). If you don't have beepers, the alternative is a red avalanche cord (50 to 100 feet), which should be tied to your waist and lined out as you cross the slope. If an avalanche hits, the cord should float to the surface and be visible to observers, but this has never been proven to occur in actual practice.

One person should cross at a time and be closely watched. Sometimes a skier can outrun an avalanche by seeking the relative safety of a clump of trees, rock outcropping, or ridge.[9] Plan your escape route when crossing an avalanche slope. The more you can help yourself, the greater your chances of survival. Before crossing, secure all clothing. The beeper should be hung around your neck and stuffed securely inside your shirt. Remove ski-pole and ski straps and unbuckle your backpack belt so that you can get rid of them should you get caught.

If caught, try to ski to the side of the avalanche where the momentum is usually less. The usual advice is to try to swim to the surface of the snow while the avalanche is still moving. However, a friend who was caught in a slab avalanche while helicopter skiing says that it happened so fast he hardly had time to react. "One minute I was standing in one place. The next I was standing somewhere else," he says. If you are buried, try to form a large air pocket with your hands before the snow slows and sets. Slab avalanches particularly tend to set like cement, and you won't be able to dig this crucial air space once the snow has set.

An avalanche can hit like a semitruck, and victims often die from the impact. Only a few actually suffocate. The chances of surviving suffocation are 50 percent for the first thirty minutes. But you're more likely to live if rescued within ten to fifteen minutes. If you are buried, don't struggle or try to scream. This will only use up oxygen and stimulate heat production. The heat from your breath and face will eventually form an ice mask that may cut off your air supply. This is *very* important: If the snow has not set, try to get your hand above the surface. This will make you infinitely easier to find.

Search for avalanche victims along the fall line. If you find a ski pole or other personal article, often the person will be just uphill. Other places to look are along boulders and trees and other areas where a snow eddy is likely to form.

Discovering the victim won't do much good though if, for example, she's not breathing and you don't know how to resuscitate her. She may also have suffered spinal-cord or head injury, as well as internal injuries. She should not be moved if these are suspected, except by trained medical personnel. Before you try to resuscitate the victim, check for chest injuries and block them to prevent air from escaping the lungs.

This book can only make you aware of the dangers and precautions. More thorough knowledge is a responsibility that goes with the territory. Among the best books is *The Avalanche Handbook* by Ronald Perla and M. Martenelli, Jr. The American Alpine Institute (Box 308, Wilson, Wyoming 83014) gives courses on avalanches and should be able to give you sources in your area.

Equipment

Part of the original appeal of Nordic skiing was the relatively low cost of equipment, clothing, and access when compared to the hotdog glamour of alpine skiing. Here was a means of getting away from the peacock narcissism of the resort to a more personal, reflective realm. And those who loved the adventure and adrenalin of alpine skiing could do that too, sans crowds, commercial exploitation of the mountains, and all the other nonsense that has little to do with skiing but a lot to do with enriching some promoter. Like other forms of wilderness recreation, Nordic skiing is reserved for those who are willing or able to put the effort into getting there under their own power or risking the dangers of the ungroomed slopes: a form of elitism, no doubt, but a more egalitarian one because commitment cannot be inherited.

Nordic skiing is still less expensive and less environmentally destructive than alpine skiing. But curiously, maybe inevitably, as it becomes more popular, specialized, and technologically sophisticated, the two may converge—a sort of dialectical materialism of the mountain. "The two have met in the middle and created something new," says Kate Delate, owner of a backcountry equipment store in Pocatello, Idaho.

The following categories of ski equipment give some idea of the basic approaches and cost of skiing. The cost of alpine equipment is given for comparison. The prices are manufacturer's list as of 1982, and items are in the medium-price range. Naturally, used and sale items can mean a considerable savings. It is also easy to rent ski equipment, so you can forego the cost of buying your own until you know how well you like the sport.

Nordic Racing		General Touring	
Bindings	$25	Bindings	$1
Boots	90	Boots	35
Fannypack	14	Daypack	18
Poles	40	Gaiters	15
Skis	140	Poles	8
		Skis	80

Backcountry/Mountaineering		Alpine	
Beeper	$50	Bindings	$130
Bindings (clamp)	150	Boots	200
Bindings (cable)	55	Poles	35
Boots	160	Skis	250
Gaiters	25		
Poles	20		
Rucksack	130		
Skins	20		
Skis	170		

In general, racing and touring equipment are designed for a groomed track. Skis are lighter and skinnier than backcountry and mountaineering skis. A touring binding usually consists of a toe device that secures by three pins to three corresponding holes in the toe of the boot. Heavier three-pin bindings are now being made for backcountry use. Cable bindings can be affixed to any boot, including hiking boots, and are popular for this reason. The clamp-down release bindings are a little harder to find. The Tyrolia HC is available from EMS (Vose Farm Road, Peterborough, New Hampshire 03458). The pioneer Ramer binding is available from Alpine Research Inc. (765 Indian Peak Road, Golden, Colorado 80401). Skins can also be purchased from Ramer or from Ski Treads (Box 1127, Hamilton, Montana 59840). An intermediate between skins and no skins is the Hill-Climber, a steel-reinforced plastic fin that you install on the ski. When going uphill, the fin digs into the snow; when going downhill, you lock it back into place on top of the ski. It costs $15 and is available from Empire Auto, Ski Products Division (29165 Calahan, Roseville, Michigan 48066).

Most Nordic ski boots are designed for men. Alpinia (Box 23, Hanover, New Hampshire 03755) makes the women's PANA 50/12 all-around touring boot. An important asset is a special flex zone, which, according to the manufacturer, assures ample toe room even when flexed. This should be of interest if you have bunions or skier's toe. Some backcountry/mountaineering boots, such as Kastinger Hi-Tours, incorporate an inner and outer boot. The soft, flexible inner boot molds well to the foot and compensates for the fact that it is not made on a woman's boot last. These and similar boots make an incredible difference in warmth and in ease of skiing and acquiring proficiency because they stabilize your weight over the ski.

Becoming Proficient

The pleasures of Nordic skiing can be immediate—in fact, the first time you put on your skis. You will probably enjoy your first outing more if you start on level or gentle ground, such as a park or golf course. The motion is simple enough, putting one sliding foot in front of the other, then double-poling down the grades. This doesn't take proficiency; rather, it's just a matter of getting acquainted with what it feels like to be on skis. It soon becomes boring, however, as the woods and their snow-dripped shapes beckon.

It takes about four years to become reasonably proficient at Nordic skiing if you are average, says Kellie. This means you're not a natural, but also not a klutz. It also means that you aren't already an alpine skier. If you're good at alpine, you can become proficient at Nordic skiing in one or two seasons. All this assumes that you make about fifteen trips a season. Interestingly, it takes about the same time to start from scratch to become a competent mid-level alpine skier. "It took me years to learn how to alpine ski," relates one woman. "But that's because I skied once a year. Finally I took a season off, bought a pass, and that's when I learned how to ski."

   In Nordic skiing you can get around without any formal training. You can even winter camp and ski the backcountry and mountains. Keep your skins on your skis and walk down the steep parts, then ski down the areas you're prepared for mentally, emotionally, and physically. Many basic Nordic ski moves, such as the diagonal stride and double-poling, can be learned from a book. But this isn't to imply that you can forego learning good technique, and for this you need a qualified instructor. Also before you tackle steep mountains and ungroomed slopes, for your own protection and enjoyment, formal instruction is recommended. After your first Nordic season, you will probably want an instructor anyway. You'll need one to learn the Telemark turn. If you want to learn the alpine techniques, such as the parallel and stem-christy turns, you will need additional instruction. (An aside about "instruction": Ask at your local ski shop.)
   One woman tells of skiing with a close male friend. He criticized her form. It seemed awkward to him because she leaned forward farther than he. Of course she did—her center of gravity is in a different place! Naturally he didn't know that and neither did she, so she spent a lot of time trying to remedy it.
   To become really proficient, well, that's a never-ending quest. Even the best continue to refine their techniques. Lito Tejada-Flores, author of *Backcountry Skiing,* who has taught skiing for more than fifteen years, says his own backcountry skiing has become more efficient, more sophisticated, more carefree. "There's no inherent virtue in a certain ski, a certain binding, a certain turn. . . . Both equipment and technique [are a]. . . means to an end—that old white magic." Which leads us to ski mountaineering and backcountry skiing. Since these often combine the skills of both sports, it would seem reasonable that, with simple arithmetic, it would take eight years to become competent. This is probably true if you start at the absolute beginning with no skills whatsoever. But obviously not so if you're already good at either Nordic or alpine.
   Obviously there are sure hazards involved in going about anything cold. "I've seen alpine skiers who've made dangerous mistakes when trying to ski the backcountry," says a woman who has meshed alpine with ski mountaineering. "One time my husband and I kicked steps in the snow up to a ridge in the Tetons. The formation is called Twin Slides because of its two adjacent avalanche chutes. These alpine skiers followed right up over the stairs we'd made, then proceeded to ski right down the avalanche chute!"
   Ski mountaineering and winter camping are still very much a male domain. Although many men would like to share it, there's still some

resistance on the "hard-core" expedition stuff, which requires a level of expertise and depth that most women don't have yet. Even the "hot" female skiers still meet some resistance.

"Men don't think about it, but they do trips together all the time," says Kellie. "It's just an unspoken assumption. With women, because it's unusual, you have to state specifically that it's an all-women's trip. Desperately needed are more women in the key decision-making ranks. Kellie wants to be an examiner for the Nordic Division of the Intermountain Ski Instructor's Association. If the timing is right, she will be the first. But being first is less important than getting women on these licensing boards. Elissa Slanger, an alpine ski instructor, was the first female examiner in the equivalent, alpine certification program. She felt her presence was important because the men on occasion unknowingly would not take female applicants seriously. And until more women find key positions in ski clubs themselves, there simply won't be enough coverage, role models, and encouragement to give other women the confidence and impetus to try.

Nordic skiing is the queen of aerobic exercise. If you have the opportunity to do it consistently, there is absolutely nothing better for your cardiovascular system. Can beginning and intermediate Nordic skiers get the same kind of workout and its attendant benefits? The answer is a definite yes.[10] There's a cornucopia of muscular benefits too—the shoulders, biceps, triceps, chest, quads, calves, and buttocks. This is what you get from just skiing. If you weight-train for it too, the benefits are lavish indeed.

Another important benefit of Nordic skiing is that it isn't hard on the joints, tendons, and ligaments. And it's a good exercise for those with arthritis because there are few stress/overuse injuries associated with it. The overuse injuries that accompany the summer road training of the U.S. Nordic team disappear once they get on the snow. The body-fat content of women on the U.S. Nordic team also speaks well of Nordic skiing's benefits. Their's was only 16 percent—5 percent less than their alpine counterparts and about 10 percent less than most women in their twenties. Nordic skiing is an excellent way to lose both excess fat and weight. It burns about 800 calories per hour, and much of this is painless because it goes toward keeping the body warm.

Nordic skiing can be as easy or difficult as you wish. You choose the terrain. Because the country is wide open, there's no baby hill on which beginners are sectioned off like so many guppies. Because so many adults have just discovered its pleasures, a novice won't feel intimidated; it doesn't require the same skill level to keep on your feet initially as alpine does. You can spend more time in a vertical position, and it won't be so obvious that you're a beginner.

Like the mastery of any sport, Nordic skiing can build confidence. This applies equally to physical mastery of our bodies and to the willingness to do things on our own, lead, take reasonable risks to accomplish a goal, and shape the society in which we live.

Kellie sums it up well: "Some male students will try to test me, my knowledge, my courage. If it gets too bad, I'll confront them. They have to learn to trust me. Usually I'm not authoritarian except if it's a peak climb—a life-and-death situation. Since I'm the one who's set the fixed lines on an ascent, they've got to entrust their lives to me. Some students aren't used to women taking that much responsibility or having that kind of ultimate control."

This mastery of self through competence, independence, insight, and responsibility is not something that comes with one trip, one season, or even one lifetime. It's a constant process, and it's wrought with emotional avalanches, personal risks, and the ambiguity of dubious trail markers. But the moments of clarity, accomplishment, and pure joy transcend the difficulties. Such is the backcountry.

Chapter 6

Physiology: The Strength of Women

She is hardly a hothouse flower, but a rancher who has bucked hay, broken horses, and hunted deer with the new moon of October. She runs three to five miles at a stretch three times a week, and in good weather she bicycles the twenty-mile roundtrip from the family ranch into the city, where she is studying for her bachelor's degree in business.

But during her first backpacking trip, she loaded close to fifty pounds on her lean 110-pound frame. She recollects how through sheer willpower she managed to stay with her husband on the four-mile-long heavily wooded path with the 1,000-foot elevation gain. She was dumbfounded by the weight of the pack, but she felt that she could take backpacking with the same resolve that she trained horses for show. Her husband speculated that she should be able to carry the equivalent of one-half her body weight. But here she was five pounds under the guessed load limit, and she could hardly move. She kept on her feet primarily by balance, teetering forward, then backward, under the weight. If she began to lose her balance, she would grab a tree to push herself back up. But then they came to a clearing, where there was nothing to brace against. She fell, and pinned under the weight of the pack, couldn't get back up. She felt like a turtle on its back.

While there's something to be admired in this illustration of true grit, there's nothing particularly pleasing about being overpowered by a lump of dead weight. This woman knows now that most men would be hard pressed to carry a proportionate burden. A rule of thumb is that the average woman can expect to pack about one-fourth her body weight. As she gains muscle, aerobic strength, and experience, she can expect to increase this to the male standard of one-third.

Of course some women defy gravity and statistics, like Deanne Shulman, a 130-pound wilderness firefighter who can carry the emergency-required 110 pounds of gear under the duress of a forest fire. But Shulman devoted intensive strength training and several years of her life to become in 1981 the first female smokejumper in the United States. So long as she is equal to the rigors of the job, she will reap the high pay, satisfaction, respect, camaraderie, and danger that come with parachuting out of a helicopter onto the lip of a burning forest.

The seemingly obsessive interest of increasing numbers of women in their physical abilities and their concurrent eagerness for adventure is not a fad. The implications regarding the women's movement are obvious. But an underlying factor that encompasses everyone is the insistent evidence that the Machine Age and its dependence upon fossil fuels are over. Many have come to the conclusion that we not only need to learn to walk again, but that we will and should do for ourselves what cheap energy sources, including human labor, used to do for us.

As women continue to become more active, they will not be without disappointments, setbacks, injuries, and even death as the boundaries of achievement and self-reliance are pushed outward. But the beauty in the midst of change and all the hoopla about what women can, can't, should, and shouldn't do is that at least now we have the option and motivation to try.

An astonishing amount of research has been done on women's physical capabilities in the last five years or so. The harvest is enormous, confusing, fascinating, and intricate. Many of the implications are uncertain or unknown. Conflicting information abounds, since the topic is addressed in everything from traditional magazines for homemakers, to the fleshy women's fitness slicks, to the most erudite, stuffy, and conservative medical journals.

Some women who have done the most to advance the research about and opportunities for women in outdoor adventures and physical fitness are the most reluctant to discuss their findings on a comparative basis to men. This is for fear that some of the results will be used to

Climbing has been almost exclusively a male domain, and only recently have significant numbers of women taken the lead in such demanding efforts as bouldering. Photograph courtesy of Sue Giller.

deny opportunities to women. But none of the research seems to prove a gender difference great enough to keep women or men out of any outdoor adventures. However, it is useful to know the differences and what to expect because the majority of women take their outings with male partners. What it really comes to is framing the question in the classic doughnut or hole analogy. Do we take inspiration from the ever swifter, stronger, more disciplined female world-class athletes and adventurers and the more common examples of small and great courages among our friends and peers, or do we become frustrated by the narrowing gap between these women and their male counterparts?

Size, Shape, and Body Type

The elusive "average" woman and man in the United States were pinned down in 1974 by two physiology experts who gave the couple an identity. These researchers compiled the statistics from detailed measurements of thousands of women and men. The resulting "reference" woman and man are shown here.

The reference woman is four inches shorter and twenty-nine pounds lighter than the reference man. Her shorter height alone means less total muscle mass because of volume. The four-inch difference means that the taller person will be able to lift a 1.06-times greater weight. The ability to exert force, for example on a stationary bicycle, will be 1.12 times greater.[1] This advantage will come into play in such activities as hitting a ball, rowing or paddling, or in contact sports such as wrestling, karate, and football. Greater height is also an obvious advantage in high jumping and other tasks that require reach. Men also have longer arms in relation to the trunk of their bodies, which amplifies their reaching ability. On the other hand, smaller dimensions are an advantage when lifting one's own weight and in accelerating the body. A shorter person also has a lower center of gravity, which helps in maintaining balance. Size is not a factor in running speed.

Women have narrower shoulders and less chest girth than men. This partially explains why they have less upper-body strength. Women also have a wider pelvis, longer bodies in relation to their arms and legs, and greater fat placement in the hips and thighs. A man has greater fat placement in the abdominal and upper regions of the body. This, combined with his greater musculature and size in the upper body, places his center of gravity even with his diaphragm. A woman's center will usually be in the hips. Her lower center of gravity makes her more stable and will help in sports such as gymnastics and skiing. However,

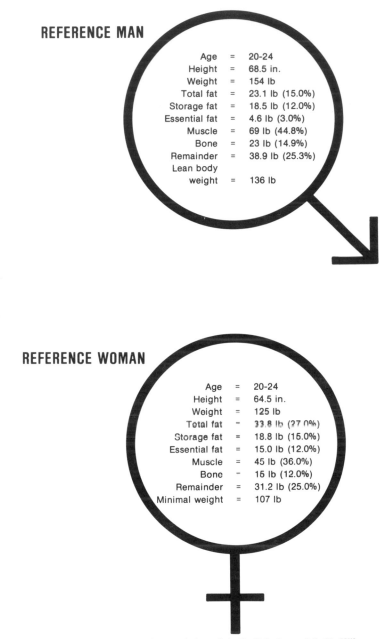

REFERENCE MAN

Age	=	20-24
Height	=	68.5 in.
Weight	=	154 lb
Total fat	=	23.1 lb (15.0%)
Storage fat	=	18.5 lb (12.0%)
Essential fat	=	4.6 lb (3.0%)
Muscle	=	69 lb (44.8%)
Bone	=	23 lb (14.9%)
Remainder	=	38.9 lb (25.3%)
Lean body weight	=	136 lb

REFERENCE WOMAN

Age	=	20-24
Height	=	64.5 in.
Weight	=	125 lb
Total fat	=	33.8 lb (27.0%)
Storage fat	=	18.8 lb (15.0%)
Essential fat	=	15.0 lb (12.0%)
Muscle	=	45 lb (36.0%)
Bone	=	15 lb (12.0%)
Remainder	=	31.2 lb (25.0%)
Minimal weight	=	107 lb

Reference Man and Woman. With permission of A. R. Behnke and J. H. Wilmore, *Evaluation and Regulation of Body Build and Composition* (Englewood Cliffs, N.J.: Prentice-Hall, 1974). Drawing adapted by Janis Rockwell.

this lower center will make her more inert and less agile in turning, results that one author says will surely decrease speed.[2]

There are different body types among women themselves of course, but the division of people into tall and thin (ectomorph), short and fat (endomorph), and in between (mesomorph) is almost useless, since most of us are mesomorphs. Many consider this concept obsolete. Shortness doesn't have much to do with fatness, and those who are tall aren't necessarily thin.

Athletes tend to cluster in various sports according to body type, but the variety is much more complex than an Abbott and Costello stereotype. You probably won't be a top competitor in an activity for which you are not built. Heredity is a factor in the amount of body fat you are likely to possess, but so is lifestyle. Women who are old enough now to have been in school when this method of body typing was popular may well have been told that they were not suited for athletics because they were endomorphs or borderline. Since compared to men most women are endomorphs, the old method of body typing seems suspicious.

Fat and Muscle

Perhaps the most significant compositional difference between women and men is a woman's greater percentage of body fat. As shown by the reference woman, this is 27 percent of total body weight versus a man's 15 percent.

The amount of fat a person carries is important because it is non-working tissue. It is the muscles that provide mechanical movement and supply all the metabolic (heat) energy. Fat decreases performance in prolonged, weight-bearing exercise, which includes practically all the activities that an outdoorswoman would be likely to engage in. The only exception is aquatic sports, where body fat provides insulation against cold and facilitates floating.

In one study women and men were measured for differences in body-fat percentages, cardiorespiratory capacity, and two other factors to determine why the women ran slower. Trained runners were used for this test. Fat explained 74 percent of the difference, and cardio-respiratory capacity explained 20 percent.[3]

It is not known definitely how much a woman's extra body fat is the result of biology rather than upbringing. This test was significant because it matched women and men of similar fitness levels. In the past researchers have often measured sedentary women against active men, and of course the disparities were great. Since the emphasis on strength and fitness in women in our culture is so recent, there is not the long-range evidence available to make sound conclusions about how much body fat is and isn't good for women.

Victor L. Katch, professor of physical education at the University of Michigan, has done research about breast size and how it contributes to body fatness. "Breast weight accounted for 3.5 percent of the total weight of body fat, and at most, twelve percent of the estimated quantities of sex-specific fat," he and coresearchers noted.[4]

Some health professionals believe that 25 percent body-fat content in women is fine, and that getting below 12 or 13 percent can be undesirable. It is important to make the distinction between subcutaneous (beneath-the-skin) fat and essential fat, that stored in the organs, bones, and central nervous system. The reference woman has 12 percent "essential" fat, while the reference man has only 3 percent. The implication is that women somehow *require* more fat. We do not know why this would be. Some feel that the woman who reduces below the 12 percent level will harm her health. This would seem to be a likely prospect if the woman has low fat content yet also has little muscle and is simply underweight, underfed, and physically weak. However, physiologists point out that the 12 percent figure is only an estimate based on theory rather than on actual data.[5]

Perhaps a good indicator of an optimum that could be expected in the general population is shown by women cadets in the military academies and others who were tested for the design of a training program for the first women admitted to West Point in 1975. In the West Point test, sixty high school girls underwent a training program. Before training they averaged 24.5-percent body-fat content. With training they were able to reduce this to 19 percent. Among the cadets, the women seldom dropped below 12 percent.[6]

So it seems that among the general female population, excluding natural athletes, a woman who has between 12 and 19 percent body fat is doing well, unless she is simply wasting away under a diet regime with no exercise. A lifetime body-fat content of 20 percent in women is considered very good.

Muscle is more dense than fat, it weighs more by volume. This means that an active person may weigh more than someone who is sedentary, although both may have the same measurements. On the average, women have 50 percent of the muscle mass of men. When figures are adjusted for size, the difference decreases to 80 percent.

In a 1980 study of the U.S. Ski Team, among alpine and cross-country skiers, the women averaged 33 percent less of the strength of men in the quadriceps (front thighs). When strength was measured relative to weight, the difference narrowed to 18 percent.

The amount of muscle you have in relation to your size is usually more important than absolute muscle power in outdoor activities. Success in most activities requires only that you be able to move your own body. When an outside force is added, such as the moving water in kayaking or rafting, the greater muscle mass is an undeniable advantage.

In an interesting twist to compensate for the differences in upbringing, a recent study compared untrained men with women basketball and volleyball players. Here the absolute strength of women in their lower bodies was 71 percent of the men's. But in the upper body it dropped to 55 percent of absolute strength and 56 percent of relative strength.[7]

The difference in upper-body structure probably has something to do with men's greater relative strength. There is also some evidence that the genes located on the X (female) chromosome may inhibit the development of large muscles.[8] Further, the increase in a male's upper-body strength begins to show up at puberty and is believed to be the result of male hormones. But many people are coming to believe that a great deal of this disparity is cultural, not biological.

According to the late Dr. John L. Marshall, a renowned sports doctor who coauthored a book about fitness for women, the President's Council on Physical Fitness concluded that the quality of muscle (the ability to contract and exert force) is similar in women and men, and that the strength differences are related to muscle use in daily life. Marshall and numerous others conclude that the lack of emphasis for strength and sports for teenage girls and women explains most of the differences in upper-body strength.

It has been fairly well publicized that women will not develop the same degree of muscle enlargement as men no matter how much they train. This is the result of fewer male sex hormones in the female. Dr. Jack Wilmore, former president of the American College of Sports Medicine, says that women can increase strength by 50 to 75 percent without increasing bulk. But as women who have weight-trained know, there may be some increase in muscle size and certainly an increase in muscle definition. The muscles that were formerly hidden beneath the layer of body fat will be more obvious.

A new subject of debate is whether or not female upper-body muscle is attractive. In women's body-building competitions, the criteria by which women are judged is creating controversy. Should the traditional disparity between upper- and lower-body development in women be continued, or should symmetrical strength and muscle definition be expected? This is an important distinction for outdoorswomen, since a weak upper body will limit many outdoors activities. Being strong is not just a question of utility, but one of health and beauty. Shoulder dislocations, tennis elbow, widow's hump, sagging breasts, flabby underarms (bat wings), and forms of arthritis that are age-related are aggravated by a lack of exercise.

A male's greater muscle mass is not always an advantage. Studies show that high-strength men are not able to sustain a muscle contraction for as long as men with lower strength. The reason may be that lower muscle endurance is the result of the increase in muscle size brought on by heavy anaerobic strength training, such as power lifting. As the muscle increases in size, there is not a corresponding increase of capillaries to feed oxygen-bearing blood to the muscle. There is also evidence of a significant decrease in mitochondrial volume density with this kind of extreme muscle enlargement. The mitochondria are the oxygen converters within the muscle cells. Since the muscle needs oxygen for exercise of more than a minute and a half, the oxygen-starved cells will not hold up as long.

Women don't reach the same degree of muscle enlargement as men, and one study showed that no difference exists in the endurance times of high- and low-strength women.[9] So a woman should be able to increase strength without decreasing muscle endurance. She also won't need to worry about the massive growth of muscle tissue, which may decrease a man's flexibility.

Women are generally more flexible than men, in part because of their lesser degree of muscle enlargement. Women are also generally more loose jointed. Greater flexibility is a boon in activities such as gymnastics and climbing, but it is not without its hazards. A woman's loose joints may be the result of weak ligaments and tendons because of a lack of strength. Loose joints make her more susceptible to dislocations, especially in the knees and shoulders. If the loose joints are accompanied by a lack of strength, the odds for injury are even greater. Exercise, especially during youth, makes the ligaments and tendons stronger. Exercise also strengthens the muscles. Overall, exercise reduces the chance of injury.

In a comparison of injuries among high-school girls and boys in the United States, the girls had a significantly greater number of knee and ankle injuries. The researchers cited joint laxity, more stress on the knee because of a wider pelvis, slighter bone structure, and less muscle mass as predisposing factors.[10] Since teenage girls are generally less active than teenage boys, lack of exercise also increases their chances of injury.

Body strength, a much overlooked essential for all women, is especially important to the outdoors woman who takes on the challenges of the untamed and natural world, be it a wild river, a granite face, a wind-chopped lake, or a mountain pass.

The Cardiovascular System

Of course the story doesn't stop there. It comes full-circle to the cardiovascular system. Muscle is just so much dead weight without substantial amounts of oxygen to power through the easiest to the most difficult task. The cardiovascular system consists of the heart, lungs, arteries, veins, and capillaries. Cardiovascular fitness refers to how well each unit operates and how well they interact in performing their primary function, which is to get oxygen and nutrients to the muscles and to remove waste products.

Your heart rate, blood pressure, vital capacity, stroke volume, and so forth each tell you something about your level of fitness. Physiologists refer to the overall ability of the body to use oxygen as maximal oxygen uptake. It is also variously termed maximum oxygen consumption, maximum aerobic power, or simply $\dot{V}O_2$ max, which means the maximum volume of oxygen consumed per minute per kilogram of body weight.

When $\dot{V}O_2$ max is measured without taking body weight into consideration, women do not compare favorably with men. This is simply because they're smaller on the average. Using this method of determining $\dot{V}O_2$ max, women have ranged from a low of 59 percent $\dot{V}O_2$ max of that in men to 78 percent in a compilation of thirteen studies done over a twenty-six-year period.[11] But of greater interest is the $\dot{V}O_2$ max in relation to body size. This tells the most about a woman's ability to power her own body effectively over long periods.

When the women in the compilation study were compared on this basis, they did much better. $\dot{V}O_2$ max was measured by milliliters of oxygen consumed per minute per kilogram of body weight. Here the women on the lower end of the scale still did much better, with 65 percent of the men's $\dot{V}O_2$ max, and those women near the top had 87 percent of the male $\dot{V}O_2$ max. The two groups in this study were American high-school athletes and Swedish physical education students and teachers. For more information about $\dot{V}O_2$ max and how to measure your own, see chapter 7.

A final method of measuring $\dot{V}O_2$ max is to assume that persons measured had *no* body fat. Naturally this gives women another boost, and among Norwegian Nordic skiers in the same study the $\dot{V}O_2$ max

Cross-country skiing in the Big Hole Mountains in Idaho. Photograph courtesy of Kellie Erwin Rhoads.

according to "lean body weight" was 82 percent of that of the men. A more dramatic increase appeared among the worst-case females in the compilation study. Here the percentage was boosted from 66 to 85 percent when the women's fat was discounted. The lean-body-weight figures are of marginal value for our purposes because body fat is stubbornly present whether or not you compensate for it in your calculations. The overfat person will have to work harder and will tire sooner than leaner companions. These figures underline the dramatic effect that fat wreaks upon work capacity.

A woman's heart-stroke volume is proportionate to her body size, so it does not help to account for her still relatively lower $\dot{V}O_2$ max. During exercise a smaller person's heart may beat more rapidly to compensate for the lower stroke volume. Although stroke volume is relative to size, a woman's vital capacity is about 10 percent lower than in men of the same age and size. Vital capacity is the maximum amount of air that can be expelled from the lungs following maximum intake.

$\dot{V}O_2$ max is dependent upon vital capacity. The highest vital capacity recorded is nine liters for a Danish rower, according to Doctors Per-Olof Astrand and Kaare Rodahl, Scandinavian physiologists. The average values are four to five liters in young men and three to four liters in young women. It is not unusual for a tall person to have a vital capacity of between six to seven liters, they note. The $\dot{V}O_2$ max potential increases slightly more than proportionately with an increase in vital capacity.

By looking at the effect of fat and vital capacity upon $\dot{V}O_2$ max in women, we can almost solve the puzzle as to why it is lower for women even when size is taken into account. The final missing piece turns out to be the ability of the blood to carry oxygen, and possibly the ability of the muscle cells to use the oxygen once it is delivered.

The red blood cells carry the molecule hemoglobin. Hemoglobin, composed of iron and protein, in turn carries the oxygen. The greater the amount of hemoglobin per unit of blood, the more oxygen that can get to the muscle. In women the average hemoglobin concentration is between 12 and 25 percent less than in men. It is still an open question as to whether or not the muscle cells in women and men differ in their ability to use the oxygen once it gets to them.

The good news in all this minutiae is that work capacity ($\dot{V}O_2$ max) can be improved with training, especially if the training begins in the teens. For example, training during adolesence can eventually increase a person's optimum vital capacity. After age thirty, optimum vital capacity usually decreases. While the highest $\dot{V}O_2$ max is usually reached at age eighteen, if training continues or studiously begins, it can be maintained at this level or even increased for approximately another ten-year period.

Among healthy sedentary people, $\dot{V}O_2$ max can be increased by 10 to 20 percent. If you are an athlete or are very active, it will be harder to increase the $\dot{V}O_2$ max because you have already been operating at or close to your peak. This is where you will hit the hereditary wall, and it's one reason why not everyone can be a marathon winner. In a backhanded way the average woman has this advantage over a man when she embarks on a training program. Her improvement will be more dramatic, since she probably has farther to go before she reaches her optimum. If you are in your thirties and start a program, chances are good that you can become stronger than you recall ever having been in your life. A man, however, will probably notice a decline in strength at this age.

All the things that contribute to $\dot{V}O_2$ max—stroke volume, the efficiency of the lungs, the amount of capillaries, the concentration of hemoglobin per unit of blood, higher lean to fat ratio—can be increased with training. For example, largely because of stroke volume, endurance athletes may have a $\dot{V}O_2$ max that is twice that of the average person.

Age

$\dot{V}O_2$ max is approximately 10 to 20 percent less in eleven- and twelve-year-olds than it is in young adults. In children muscle strength increases with age because of an increase in size. The development of the central nervous system also contributes to strength increases by about 5 to 10 percent per year. About one-third of the increase in height occurs between the ages of six and twenty, but four-fifths of the development of strength takes place at this time.[12]

Young children sustain fewer and less damaging injuries in sports partly because they have less muscle mass and because their bones haven't become rigid (ossified). Before puberty there are no major differences between girls and boys in size, strength, endurance, or $\dot{V}O_2$ max. So there is no reason to separate girls and boys at this age in either contact or noncontact sports.

Because girls mature earlier, between the ages of ten and fourteen, they are in many cases larger and stronger than boys and can surpass them in performance. One writer comments that when the law started to force equal access for girls in sports, many Little League coaches had to reassure their boys that one day they would grow to be as good as the girls on the team.[13]. However, boys become significantly stronger than girls after the onset of puberty. They develop larger muscles, greater cardiovascular and muscle endurance, and generally become taller and outweigh the girls. They also become better at gross motor skills, so they outperform the girls in almost all contests. This is also the time when the gender differences in percent of body fat and hemoglobin concentration develop and widen.

The male sex hormone androgen is responsible for the increase in growth in both sexes. In girls it is thought that the adolescent rise in the female hormone estrogen causes the bones to mature and prevents further growth. Male hormones are also responsible for the increase in muscle size and strength. However, it is thought that the female sex hormones inhibit the growth of large muscles and cause the greater fat deposits and lower hemoglobin concentration.

Although men usually have a greater degree of muscle enlargement than women, this doesn't mean that mere size is an advantage. Muscle strength is not necessarily related to muscle size. Women can become exceptionally strong without developing large muscles. In addition, despite biological differences, evidence shows that cultural expectations have a profound influence on the greater physical weakness of females. Given sex roles that traditionally have expected girls to be less competent in order to be attractive, it is no wonder if girls fall behind. Fortunately all this seems to be changing. But the influence in the past has been so pervasive that many records of top performance among women are being substantially increased every year. While records are still being set by men as training becomes more specific and sophisticated, the increases are not proportionately as great as those among women.

The loss of estrogen during menopause, which takes place between the ages of forty-five and fifty, may precipitate bone thinning (osteoporosis) and increase the possibility of fractures. However, regular exercise and calcium supplements may reduce the degree of bone thinning. On a sad note, some hip fractures in elderly women may occur when the fragile bones give way under the increasing burden of fat associated with aging. A lifetime of exercise is one defense against this.

The indomitable Margaret Mead often characterized the increase of energy and feeling of well-being experienced by some middle-aged women as "postmenopausal zest." The zest could be the result of the ending of the mild anemia that often occurs with the loss of blood during menstruation and the ceasing of the mood swings, which may accompany monthly hormonal changes. Postmenopausal women have been reported to have 20 percent less grip strength but 18 percent more grip endurance than premenopausal women, and 23 percent more grip endurance than men. The researchers thought that this must obviously be the result of menopause itself, but more likely it is the result of aging.[14]

Among both women and men, there is evidence that as the body ages the composition of the muscle fiber changes so that there are more endurance fibers and less of those responsible for strength. This would account for the decrease in strength and the increase in endurance experienced with age in both sexes.

Muscle strength declines gradually. The strength of a sixty-five-year-old will be about 75 percent of what she had when she was twenty. But the proportionate differences of strength between women and men increase with age. In one study women slid from 80 percent at age thirty to 50 percent at age sixty of the muscle strength of men of the same age.[15] Since the women studied were either homemakers or held office jobs and the men were factory workers, this is a good illustration of the principal of "use it or lose it." Undoubtedly, the women lost such massive amounts of strength by simple failure to use their muscles.

When it comes to VO_2 max, both women and men at age sixty-five have about 70 percent of that of a twenty-five-year-old. But the average man at sixty-five will have the same VO_2 max as the average twenty-five-year-old woman.

Other physical changes that come with age are an increase in body weight and fat, decreased stroke volume and heart rate, and a decline in fine motor coordination and flexibility. In both sexes the body metabolism slows with age. This means that the body needs fewer calories to sustain itself while at rest. Older persons need about 100 fewer calories per day for each decade after age thirty.

Although aging is inevitable, it can be slowed with exercise. Two female swimmers, both in their seventies, who averaged about one-half mile of swimming a day five times a week, had only 24 percent body fat. The average sedentary woman of seventy has 44.6 percent body fat.[16] Female distance runners with an average age of forty-four who train between thirty-six and sixty-six miles per week showed only 18.3 percent body fat as compared to the average of 34 percent of a sedentary woman of that age.

Aging does not prevent acquiring strength. When fifty-nine-year-old women underwent a fitness program the gains they made were proportionately similar to those made by twenty-year-olds.[17] There is also some evidence that habitual training helps retain protein (muscle) and thus delays strength losses during aging.

If the male of the species has the advantages of strength, the female definitely outclasses him in the arena of survival. She is a heavyweight genetically, hormonally, and immunologically. Although more males are conceived (about 140 for every 100 females), only 106 of these survive to birth. In the first months after birth, the death rate among boys is 15 per 1,000 but for girls it is 11 per 1,000. Of the 190 birth defects recorded, more than 71 percent occur primarily in males and 25 percent in females. This is believed to be a result of the configuration of the male and female chromosomes.

Females are more resistant to certain bacterial infections. Estrogen appears to enhance the female immune system. It also acts as the protective mechanism against coronary artery disease (CAD). In men the male hormone testosterone is thought to increase the risk of CAD. The effect of the male hormones is illustrated by a study that showed that castrated men live longer, the more so the earlier the age of castration.[18]

In a recent issue of *Science Digest*, writer Paula Dranov notes that the dire predictions that changing sex roles would result in increased female vulnerability to heart disease and other life-threatening ailments simply aren't coming true. She says that a recent woman's health survey showed that women in the work force are healthier than those whose contributions don't show up in the gross national product. She concludes that the most pressing question seems not be whether new women's roles will erode their health advantages, but if these female survival secrets can be tapped to prolong the lives of men.[19] It would be equally compelling to see if the male physical strength secrets couldn't be tapped to enhance the quality of life for women.

Whether you choose to call the traditional role of woman a pedestal or a prison, a privilege or a privation, her exemption from physical labor and sports activities has also exempted her from many of life's greatest rewards and pleasures. The canyons and summits, and the wind- and water-born fulfillment of mind and spirit lie open to her as never before.

Chapter 7

Fitness: Tests and Incentives

Why does strenuous exercise kill the appetite? Why can you hike for several hours and feel no pain yet sprint up a talus slope or stumble downhill over an eroded trail and be reminded of the effort by the fatigue and aches that set in a few hours later? How can you prevent or minimize these occupational setbacks? Why do some apparently healthy people fatigue more easily than others? Why is the water tank a better measure of fitness than a tape measure or bathroom scales? Why do smoking and air pollution decrease your immediate energy capacity? Are you expecting too much or too little of yourself? And how do you determine your present level of fitness?

Many outdoorswomen have large libraries that contain the where-fores, wherewithals, and whatsoevers about physical fitness. And the more you know, the harder it becomes to tell yourself that these questions make little difference. In fact, the more you know about health and fitness, the more motivation you will have to become healthier and stronger.

Energy

The human body produces energy in the muscle cells through three systems: one operates with oxygen (aerobic) and two operate without oxygen (anaerobic). The action of the two anaerobic systems is symbiotic.

The anaerobic systems produce short-term energy. The explosive power that a ski racer uses at the starting gate is an example of the energy produced by the ATP-PC (adenosine triphosphate-phosphocreatine) system, the first anaerobic system. The small stores of this muscular dynamite are exhausted within fifteen to ninety seconds.

The second anaerobic system supplies energy for ninety seconds to three minutes. This is done by the cellular breakdown of sugar without the aid of oxygen. But much of the muscle sugar is wasted. The byproduct of this incomplete use of sugar is lactic acid, and this system is referred to as the lactic-acid system.

The body's use of the three energy systems is like a pyramid. At the top is the ATP-PC system. In the middle is the lactic-acid system, and at the base is the aerobic system, which replenishes the stores of the lactic-acid system and supplies the majority of the body's energy.

The aerobic and anaerobic systems are different enough that training for only anaerobic power will do little to enhance the aerobic system. Someone who rock climbs, which is generally an anaerobic exercise, won't at the same time help her cross-country skiing performance. Cross-country skiing, in contrast, closely parallels marathon running as one of the most highly aerobic exercises.

The anaerobic systems are more dependent upon the aerobic system, which explains why a rock climber would benefit more from cross-country skiing than the skier would from rock climbing. If the climber wishes to recoup her anaerobic power between spurts of energy, she will be better able to do so by having developed her aerobic power. However, because aerobic endeavors always require starts and stops and short bursts of muscle power, aerobic training alone is generally not adequate for outdoor activities.

$\dot{V}O_2$ max is the measurement of the aerobic system. Few of us have any way of knowing what percent of $\dot{V}O_2$ max we're using at any given time. However, you can get a rough idea by calculating it according to heart rate. To estimate your maximal heart rate, subtract your age from 220.

Maximal Heart Rate (percent of)	$\dot{V}O_2$ max (percent of)
50	28
55	35
60	42
65	49
70	56
75	63

80	70
85	77
90	83
100	100

The aerobic system is the most efficient of the three energy systems at using available fuel. Through a chemical process, blood sugar (glucose) is converted to glycogen in the muscle cell. The energy output of glycogen by the aerobic process is 13 times greater than it is by the anaerobic process.[1] Without oxygen, only 3.5 percent of the calories available in the glucose are converted to energy.[2]

The more and the faster oxygen outside the body gets to the muscle cells, the better your performance will be and the less you will tire. For every five calories of energy expended, the body uses about one liter of oxygen. To supply this much oxygen and to replenish the muscle sugar stores during intense exercise, the body must divert much of the blood supply line to the working muscle. At maximal exercise this requires 85 percent of the total blood supply (cardiac output). During rest it is only 15 percent. This is one reason why intense exercise reduces appetite. The blood circulating to the stomach is diverted to the working muscle. Herein lies the truth of the old adage of not to eat heavily less than two hours prior to strenuous exercise.

The aerobic system is also more efficient because it does not create the waste product lactic acid. As lactic acid builds up in the blood and muscle, it produces fatigue. If you are hiking uphill, for example, and cannot supply enough oxygen to the muscle to get to the top of the switchbacks, your anaerobic system will pull you up the final few feet. The more often this occurs throughout the course of the day, the greater the buildup of lactic acid and the greater the fatigue.

Lactic acid does not cause the actual ache in the muscle as many mistakenly believe. The soreness is thought to be caused by minute tears in the muscle fiber. It does play a complementary role, however. The more tired the muscle, the less efficient it is and the greater the likelihood of injuries, from soreness to sprains. While the role of lactic acid in muscle injury may seem academic, in practice it isn't. If you are simply tired, light exercise will help disperse the lactic acid and aid recovery. If the muscle is actually damaged to some extent, rest is in order.

The point at which the body cannot supply enough oxygen to power the muscles, referred to as the "anaerobic threshold," is an important measure of physical fitness. The body begins to use the anaerobic system to make up for the energy that the overtaxed aerobic system is unable to supply. Those who have not done any endurance training are likely to reach their anaerobic threshold at about 75 percent of their maximal heart rate, or 63 percent of $\dot{V}O_2$ max. This is about the level of heart rate suggested for aerobic training. Those who do aerobic endurance training can push this threshold up as far as 87 percent of maximal heart rate, or 80 percent of $\dot{V}O_2$ max.

This is of particular value to women, since many of the factors that contribute to high $\dot{V}O_2$ max are determined by gender and size. However, the ability to use $\dot{V}O_2$ max without lactic-acid accumulation is the result of training. You may never be able to get up a hill as fast as a male partner, but you may be able to go farther without tiring, provided you go at your own pace. Some studies show that the anaerobic threshold in trained women and men is either independent of gender or occurs at a higher percentage of $\dot{V}O_2$ max in women than it does in men.[3] This appears to be the only basis to the widespread belief that women have more endurance capacity than men.

Air Pollution and Energy Production

Tobacco smoke and other air pollutants decrease the amount of oxygen that gets to the working muscle. They irritate the mucous membranes of the airways, leading to increased airway resistance. At rest this probably won't be noticed, but as greater demands are placed on the respiratory system, it will be. The chronic smoker tends to show a decrease in lung function, although in younger people this may have little effect upon physical performance.

Carbon monoxide is contained in both tobacco smoke and the exhaust fumes of vehicles. Hemoglobin has a 200 to 300 times greater affinity for carbon monoxide than it does for oxygen. When you inhale carbon monoxide, whether or not by choice, the blood will carry this, rather than oxygen, to the muscle cells. Even small amounts may noticeably reduce your oxygen-carrying capacity.

Ozone, a common air pollutant, can cut down cardiovascular performance by as much as 10 percent with as little as .5 parts per million. In cities such as Los Angeles and Tokyo it is not uncommon for ozone levels to reach concentrations of 2.5 parts per million.

Some of the ill effects of smoking can be reduced by abstaining forty-five minutes to twenty-four hours prior to exercise. Forty-five minutes allows the blood to clear itself of some of the carbon monoxide. It takes approximately twenty-four hours to clear the blood completely of the extra pollutant. If you live in an area of substantial air pollution, you may notice an increase in energy once you get away from the smog. Smoking elevates the heart rate by as much as ten to twenty beats per minute. More crucial, it elevates blood presure, which puts more stress on the heart and vascular system. Perhaps the principal way in which women are voluntarily destroying their greater survival capacity is through this habit.

Cigarette smoking may be one of the single best indicators of whether or not you will get coronary artery disease. The probability of CAD in smokers is almost twice as great as in nonsmokers. The increase in the death rate from CAD in women in the United States closely parallels their increased consumption of cigarettes. In *The Whole Heart Book*, James J. Nora states that "smoking is not only a major contributing factor in cardiovascular disease, but is the most striking, preventable, environmental hazard causing death and disability in America."[4]

Most top athletes do not smoke. Among those who do, studies show that most take part in sports that do not require great endurance and aerobic capacity. If trends continue, and as those who participate in such anaerobic sports as ski jumping and rock climbing recognize the value of aerobic training, there will likely be a decrease in smoking in these quarters too.

If you do smoke, it would be to your benefit in outdoor endeavors to leave your cigarettes at home. This would also be a good time to quit. A break in routine, such as weekends and vacations, has been found by some to be the easiest time to quit. Of course other health hazards are associated with smoking and air pollution, among them cancer, emphysema, asthma, black and brown lung disease, and lead poisoning. Ridding your environment of tobacco smoke is one way to safeguard yourself. But this solution is inadequate without enforced clean air regulations and occupational protections from other hazardous airborne substances.

Fitness Testing

Fitness testing and prescription have become extremely sophisticated in recent years with the wedding of great public interest and space-age technology. It has given rise to the interrelated fields of sports medicine and preventive medicine. The standard height and weight charts of a decade ago have in many cases been replaced with analyses of body density, blood chemistry, muscular strength, muscle fiber typing, and aerobic capacity.

Sports and preventive medicine professionals include cardiologists, exercise physiologists, gerontologists, internists, nutritionists, orthopedic surgeons, podiatrists, and a number of other health professionals. Many hospitals, clinics, universities, and fitness centers have programs available to the public that are designed to foster fitness and prevent disease. The cost can range from a $10 course on high blood pressure at the YMCA to a $400 to $1,000 comprehensive analysis consisting of a medical profile, nutritional analysis, CAD risk factor, cardiovascular evaluation, body composition analysis, musculoskeletal evaluation, flexibility test, blood chemistry test, and exercise prescription. This is available at clinics for athletic training and rehabilitation.

Unless a doctor or other health professional specializes in sports or preventive medicine, you often can't obtain sufficient information to determine your present level of fitness or to construct a training regime. That is not necessarily a criticism, since such diagnosis requires specialized equipment and knowledge. A program that uses the services of several types of health professionals is more likely to be able to give you a comprehensive analysis. If one is not available or the cost is prohibitive, you can piece together the information by coupling certain tests with an overall knowledge of what to look for.

$\dot{V}O_2$ max Tests

The measure of $\dot{V}O_2$ max must be done by a professional. It is usually performed on an ergometer (stationary bicycle), uphill treadmill, or by means of the bench-step test.

To be measured accurately, $\dot{V}O_2$ max must be analyzed by sophisticated lab equipment that determines the amount and content of the gases you exhale as well as the amount of oxygen you take in. For women it is important to include body weight in the $\dot{V}O_2$ max calculation. Women fare much better when the equation is measured by consumption of milliliters of oxygen per kilogram per minute as opposed to consumption of liters of oxygen per minute only.

You can get a rough estimate of your own $\dot{V}O_2$ max by taking the following test. Designed by James R. White, exercise physiologist, Department of Physical Education, University of California, San Diego, it is part of a larger cardiac risk analysis.

FITNESS LEVEL ($\dot{V}O_2$ max)

Most people would like to know how physically fit they usually are. Fitness can be measured on a treadmill while breathing into a gas analyzing machine. A less expensive method is the check-off fitness rating. To use the check-off method circle the number in each of the four categories that most accurately describes your present exercise practices. The tables are designed so that the sum of the four numbers is an excellent estimate of your $\dot{V}O_2$ max.

FITNESS LEVEL ($\dot{V}O_2$ max)—*continued*

	Points:	
Your present age:	MEN	WOMEN
15–25	10	10
26–35	9	9
36–40	8	8
41–45	7	7
46–50	6	6
51–55	5	5
56–60	4	4
61–65	3	3
66–70	2	2
71+	1	1
How often do you exercise?		
6–7 days per week	18	16
4–5 days per week	16	14
2–3 days per week	12	10
1 day per week	9	7
2–3 days per month	7	6
Infrequently or almost never	4	3

	Points	
The duration of your exercise sessions is:	MEN	WOMEN
60 or more min.	20	16
50 min.	18	15
40 min.	16	14
30 min.	14	12
20 min.	12	10
10 min.	10	8
Less than 10 min.	8	7
The intensity or vigor of a typical exercise session is best described as:		
Sustained forceful breathing (160 heart rate, distance training)	20	17
Sustained vigorous breathing (150 heart rate, running at 7:30 mile pace, jumping vigorously)	17	14
Sustained brisk breathing (140 heart rate, running at 8–8:30 mile pace, jumping vigorously)	13	10
Intermittent forceful breathing (racquetball, squash, basketball, singles tennis)	11	10
Sustained comfortable breathing (130 heart rate—jogging, bicycling, swimming, jumping for joy)	11	10
Intermittent vigorous breathing (volleyball, softball, etc.)	10	8
Sustained light breathing (walking, hiking, jumping lightly)	8	6

Occasional very light exercise (golf, doubles tennis, gardening, etc.)	4	3
No exercise	2	2

ENTER YOUR SCORES HERE

Age	_____
Frequency	_____
Duration	_____
Intensity	_____
Total	_____ mlO$_2$/kg/min

This represents your estimated fitness level. If you are curious, see how you rank with other people your age and sex from the following chart.

EXERCISE LEVEL	AGE	FITNESS mlO$_2$/kg/min Men	Women
World Class	18–28	78–94	71–73 +
Very Highly Trained	18–28	65–77	58–66
Highly Trained	18–25	62	53
	26–35	60	51
	36–55	58	49
High Fitness Category	56–69	52	44
	70–79 +	42	36
Moderately Trained	18–25	50	43
	26–35	45	37
	36–55	40	34
Average Fitness Category	56–69	35	31
	70–79 +	30	29
Untrained	18–25	42	37
	26–35	35	32
	36–55	30	28
Low Fitness Category	56–69	25	24
	70–79 +	20	19

Source. *Jump for Joy*, Goldfield Books (1301 Goldfield, San Diego, California 92110).

Getting a lab analysis of $\dot{V}O_2$ max is of course preferable to a rough estimate, but it is more expensive. $\dot{V}O_2$ max is genetically endowed and can be improved with training by 10 to 20 percent. Where you stand as to $\dot{V}O_2$ max will tell you a great deal about your natural abilities.

To test your $\dot{V}O_2$ max, try the exercise called the twelve-minute run. The distance you can run during twelve minutes is a good measure of your overall cardiovascular fitness. Unless you are in good physical condition to begin with, do not attempt to run the whole twelve minutes. If you have to, slow to a walk until you regain your breath. This test is measured in miles.

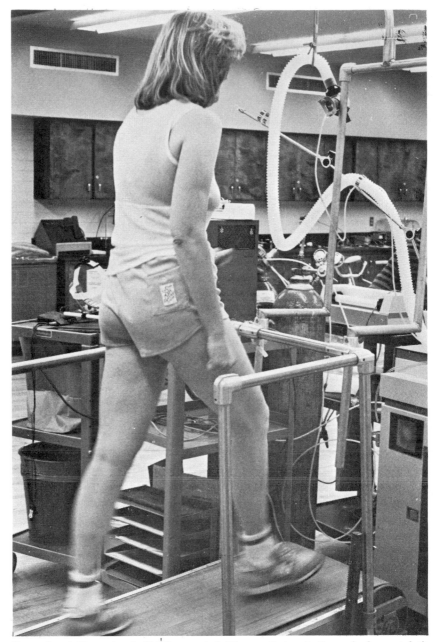

The author taking a treadmill $\dot{V}O_2$ max test. The mouthpiece to the expired gas analysis equipment will be inserted a few minutes prior to exhaustion. Test courtesy of Lanny Nalder, Ph.D., Utah State University. Photograph courtesy of Ralph B. Maughan, Ph.D.

Age	Under 24	25–34	35–44	45–54	55–64	65–74
Excellent	1.65	1.59	1.48	1.36	1.25	1.13
Good	1.5	1.45	1.34	1.24	1.13	1.03
Fair	1.25	1.2	1.1	1	.9	.8

Heart Rate Recovery

The speed with which your heart returns to its resting pulse after a bout of strenuous exercise is a good measure of your stamina and heart efficiency.

An approximation of the original Harvard Step Test is to run in place for three minutes. Lift your knees as high as possible to imitate the amount of work it would actually take to step up and down from a platform as is done in the Harvard test. When you stop running, immediately take your pulse for ten seconds and multiply by six to compute your pulse rate per minute at the same rate at which it was beating while you performed the test. You then take your pulse at one, then two, minutes after recovery.

To find your heart rate recovery, use the following formula:

$$\frac{\text{peak pulse minus one-minute recovery pulse}}{\text{peak pulse minus resting pulse}} = \text{percent of recovery}$$

Use the same formula to find your two-minute recovery rate, but substitute the two-minute recovery pulse in the equation. This is how you stand:

	One-minute Recovery Pulse	Two-minute Recovery Pulse
Good	above 75 percent	above 90 percent
Average	55–75 percent	70–90 percent
Poor	below 55 percent	below 70 percent

Because you are measuring your own peak heart rate against your resting and recovery heart rate and not that of someone older or younger than you, this test does not need to be weighted for age. Unlike VO_2 max, you can do a great deal to improve your recovery heart rate, and one of the best ways is by exercising.

Blood Pressure

Blood pressure measurement consists of the systolic and diastolic readings. Systolic pressure is generated by the contraction of the left ventricle of the heart. At rest, the highest normal pressure generated by this contraction is about 120 mmHg (millimeters of mercury) on the column of the blood-pressure gauge (sphygmomanometer). During the relaxation phase of the heart cycle the blood-pressure gauge measures the diastolic pressure. This reading is usually 70 to 80 mmHg.

Most physicians agree that a systolic/diastolic reading of greater than 140/90 over several serial determinations suggests a risk of cardiovascular disease. Some data place the beginning risk as low as 120/80. It is an unsettled controversy if the systolic or the diastolic reading is more or equally important as an indicator of risk factor. Both systolic and diastolic blood pressure can be reduced significantly with a regular program of endurance exercise. In one study, middle-aged men with readings of 139/78 at rest reduced this to 133/73 after four to six weeks of training.[5]

Static exercise, such as lifting heavy weights, causes a large and rapid rise in blood pressure. This strain can be harmful to those who have cardiovascular disease, chest pain, and high blood pressure. Seek your physician's approval before undertaking a weight-training program if you have such problems.

Flexibility

Flexibility varies with each joint, but the flexibility of your trunk appears to be a fairly good indicator of general flexibility. If you can touch your palms to the floor while standing with your legs together, knees locked, your flexibility is good. If you can touch the floor with the tips of your fingers only, your flexibility is average. Your flexibility is fair if you can touch the top of your toes or instep. If you cannot get past your ankles, your flexibility is poor. When taking this test, do *not* bounce. Do the test slowly to avoid overstressing the back. Try this test after you have warmed up with a slow trunk rotation and with alternate toe touches, in which your feet are placed about even with your shoulders.

Flexibility is of importance in the prevention of injury in sports. Many trainers, coaches, and sports medicine physicians feel that serious, concentrated, stretching before and after activity could prevent the majority of sports-related injuries. Another important factor contributing to injury, especially in women, is muscle weakness, which causes imbalances of and stress upon other muscles as well as decreasing the protection afforded by the muscles to the joints.

Lower back pain is often related to poor flexibility of the hips and back, poor elasticity of the hamstring muscles, and weak abdominal muscles. It is possible to be strong and have plenty of endurance capacity yet be inflexible. An exercise program of sit-ups to strengthen the abdominal muscles and stretching to become flexible is in order if you don't pass this test. Almost one-third of adults in the United States suffer from backache. In an estimated 85 percent of the cases, the cause is simple muscle weakness, tension, and inflexibility.

Muscular Strength

One measure of muscular strength consists of five tests: modified pushups, flexed-arm hang, dips, bent-knee sit-ups, and wall sits. These tests will give you a thumbnail portrait of your muscular strength and indicate where you need to do the most work. By way of caution, these are values for the average woman. The active outdoorswoman eventually will need to score above average, since, for our purposes, the average woman is not fit.

Modified Pushups: The average woman cannot do one unmodified pushup, so modified pushups are used instead. Do these until you are able to do the unmodified version. When doing pushups, be sure not to sag in the middle. The back of your hands should be just under your shoulders when you are in the lowered position.

Age	Under 24	25–34	35–44	45–54	55–64	65–74
Excellent	42+	30+	28+	25+	22+	19+
Good	32	23	21	18	16	14
Fair	22	16	14	13	11	9

Flexed-arm hang: This test requires a chinning bar or equivalent. Use an overhand grip in which the palms face away from the body. Lift yourself so that your chin is above the bar. In this position your hands should be parallel with your ears. Hold this position for as long as you can. This test is measured in seconds.

Age	Under 24	25–34	35–44	45–54	55–64	65–74
Excellent	14+	10+	9+	9+	8+	7+
Good	12	8	7	7	6	6
Fair	8	6	6	5	5	4

Dips: In this measure of upper-body strength, you stand between two parallel bars or other stable surfaces of equal height. Suspend your body weight while keeping your arms straight. Lower yourself by bending your elbows. You should go about one-third of the way down. Do as many as possible.

Age	Under 24	25–34	35–44	45–54	55–64	65–74
Excellent	11+	8+	7+	6+	5+	4+
Good	8	6	5	4–5	4	3
Fair	6	4	3	3	2–3	2

Bent-knee sit-ups: Straight-leg sit-ups are no longer recommended because of possible strain to the lower back. With your knees bent, your feet anchored, and your hands clasped behind your neck, do as many repetitions as possible in one minute.

Age	Under 24	25–34	35–44	45–54	55–64	65–74
Excellent	48+	46+	32+	24+	20+	16+
Good	37	35	26	22	18	14
Fair	30	28	24	20	16	12

Wall sits: This measures the strength of the important quadricep muscles, those that cover the front of your thighs. The quadriceps are your main line of defense against knee injury because they support the knee joint and help hold the kneecaps in place. To take the test, press your upper back against the wall and lower your body to a position as though you were sitting in a straight-back chair. Your hips and knees should be at a ninety-degree angle to each other. Hold this position for as long as possible. This test is measured in seconds.

Age	Under 24	25–34	35–44	45–54	55–64	65–74
Excellent	100+	100+	90+	80+	70+	60+
Good	95	95	85	76	67	57
Fair	90	90	81	72	63	54

The Lean-to-Fat Ratio

Fat, at least how to get rid of it, is a popular subject. One can hardly talk about fitness without addressing fat because it has such a profound impact on the body's ability to function. This is not to say that you cannot be a good skier, mountaineer, or kayaker if you're overfat. But you see few overfat climbers, hikers, bicyclists, and so forth because it's just too much work to be much fun if you must carry the excess fat. Don't let excess fat or self-consciousness stop you of course. Motivation can play an enormous role, and people who are overweight should no more confine themselves to little or no activity than should those over sixty. But at the same time, you will be exceptional if you can keep the same pace as leaner partners.

Average Weights for Women Age 25 and Over
(Between 18 and 25, subtract one pound for each year under 25)

Height (bare feet)	Small Frame (pounds)	Medium Frame (pounds)	Large Frame (pounds)
4'8"	92–98	96–107	104–119
4'9"	94–101	98–110	106–122
4'10"	96–104	101–113	109–125
4'11"	99–107	104–116	112–128
5'0"	102–110	107–119	115–131
5'1"	105–113	110–122	118–134
5'2"	108–116	113–126	121–138
5'3"	111–119	116–130	125–142
5'4"	114–123	120–135	129–146
5'5"	118–127	124–139	133–150
5'6"	122–132	128–143	137–154
5'7"	126–135	132–147	141–158
5'8"	130–140	136–151	145–163
5'9"	134–144	140–155	149–168
5'10"	138–148	144–159	153–173
5'11"	142–152	148–163	157–178
6'0"	144–156	152–167	161–183
6'1"	148–160	156–171	165–188
6'2"	152–164	160–175	169–193

You may have spent the last several years getting your weight down only to discover that the fitness experts have produced a tougher standard. This is the lean-to-fat ratio. No longer is it sufficient to be the right weight for your height. The real litmus test is how much of that is lean (bone and muscle) weight.

The most accurate way to measure the lean-to-fat ratio is by hydrostatic weighing, in which you are immersed in a swimming pool while suspended from a scale. The scale works by the same method as you weigh produce in the supermarket. Your weight is first determined on a standard scale. You are also measured for vital capacity and residual lung volume, the amount of air left in the lungs after you exhale forcefully.

When your weight is taken underwater, the fat does not register on the scale because it floats. What does show on the scale is lean body weight. Residual lung volume is subtracted, and other factors are taken into account, such as the density of the water at specific temperatures. The test should be repeated approximately five times to get an accurate reading. While under water, you mentally count to ten and exhale as much air as possible.

The results may be disappointing and this test might be enough to inspire an increased emphasis on aerobic and muscular strength. If you are overweight in addition to being overfat, you can do a great deal by losing the weight. If you are only five pounds overweight, you are probably at least thirteen pounds overfat. If you are not overweight but just overfat, you must work to exchange fat tissue for muscle.

A new method that is currently being developed for estimating body fat was reported in the August 1982 issue of *The Physician and Sports Medicine*. It uses an X-ray of the upper arm. In preliminary studies, the method appears to be almost as accurate as underwater weighing, and is a much simpler and cheaper test to perform.

Another experimental method of measuring body density is by ultrasound. In this process, sound waves are aimed at the body and a receiver picks up the results. Different materials characteristically alter sound waves. Ultrasound could conceivably give a more accurate assessment of the percentage of muscle versus bone and organs than hydrostatic weighing.

A second method of determining body fat is the skinfold or "pinch" test. This is a fairly involved procedure that uses calipers to measure the skinfold thickness at various sites on the body. Calipers and an

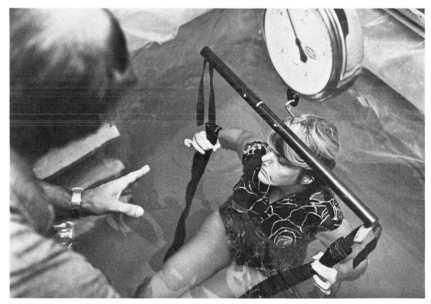

Hydrostatic weighing. Test courtesy of Alex Urfer, Ph.D., Idaho State University. Photograph courtesy of Lloyd Furniss.

instruction manual can be obtained for a small fee from Fat Control, Inc. (Box 10117, Towson, Maryland 21204).

A final method, which is reasonably accurate, consists of taking various body circumference measurements and computing their outcome according to values given in the following charts. The charts and formulas were designed by Frank I. Katch, chairman, Department of Exercise Science, University of Massachusetts. They are adapted here with permission from William D. McArdle, Frank I. Katch, and Victor L. Katch, *Exercise Physiology: Energy, Nutrition, and Human Performance* (1981).

The measurements should be taken at (1) the abdomen, one inch above the belly button; (2) the right upper thigh just below the buttock; (3) the right forearm, maximum circumference with the arm extended in front of the body with the palm up; and (4) the right calf, widest circumference midway between the ankle and the knee.

Formula: Percent fat = Constant A + Constant B − Constant C
              − 19.6 for young women
              − 18.4 for older women

For example, a woman of twenty has an abdominal measurement of 30.7 inches (Constant A), a thigh measurement of 22 inches (Constant B), and a forearm measurement of 9.5 (Constant C). She weighs 125 pounds. Her formula would be:

$$41.11 + 45.77 - 40.95 - 19.6 = 26.33\% \text{ body fat}$$

Suppose this woman has the same measurements but is fifty years old. Instead of the forearm measurement for Constant C, her calf measurement would be used. Suppose her calf measurement is 13.4 inches, which, according to the chart for older women, would give her a Constant C of 19.52. Her formula would be:

$$36.51 + 27.2 - 19.52 - 18.4 = 25.79\% \text{ body fat}$$

If you aren't sure whether to rate yourself "young" or "older," you can use either set of measurements and constants, since the effect upon the calculated percent of body fat should not be great.

If you want to estimate your necessary weight loss given a certain percent of fat desired, use the formula:

Weight of fat = percent fat/100 × body weight
Lean body weight = body weight − body fat weight
$$\text{Desired body weight} = \frac{\text{lean body weight}}{1.00 - \text{percent fat desired}}$$

Suppose our hypothetical woman wanted to reduce her percentage of fat to twenty by losing weight. This is how she would calculate her needed weight loss:

$$\text{Weight of fat} = 26.33/100 = .2633 \times 125 \text{ lbs} = 32.91 \text{ lbs.}$$
$$\text{Lean body weight} = 125 \text{ lbs} - 32.91 \text{ lbs} = 92.09 \text{ lbs.}$$
$$\text{Desirable body weight} = \frac{92.09}{1.00 - .20} = \frac{92.02}{.80} = 115 \text{ lbs.}$$

Before assuming that weight loss is the only way to reduce body fat, remember that it is entirely possible to be the correct weight yet be overfat. In this case it would be better for your outdoor endeavors and your health to build muscle, not to lose weight.

Conversion Constants to Predict Percent Body Fat in Young Women

	Abdomen		*Thigh*		*Forearm*
Inches	*Constant A*	*Inches*	*Constant B*	*Inches*	*Constant C*
20.00	26.74	14.00	29.13	6.00	25.86
20.50	27.41	14.50	30.17	6.50	28.02
21.00	28.07	15.00	31.21	7.00	30.17
21.50	28.74	15.50	32.25	7.50	32.33
22.00	29.41	16.00	33.29	8.00	34.48
22.50	30.08	16.50	34.33	8.50	36.64
23.00	30.75	17.00	35.37	9.00	38.79
23.50	31.42	17.50	36.41	9.50	40.95
24.00	32.08	18.00	37.45	10.00	43.10
24.50	32.75	18.50	38.49	10.50	45.26
25.00	33.42	19.00	39.53	11.00	47.41
25.50	34.09	19.50	40.57	11.50	49.57
26.00	34.76	20.00	41.61	12.00	51.73
26.50	35.43	20.50	42.65	12.50	53.88
27.00	36.10	21.00	43.69	13.00	56.04
27.50	36.76	21.50	44.73	13.50	58.19
28.00	37.43	22.00	45.77	14.00	60.35
28.50	38.10	22.50	46.81	14.50	62.50
29.00	38.77	23.00	47.85	15.00	64.66
29.50	39.44	23.50	48.89	15.50	66.81
30.00	40.11	24.00	49.93	16.00	68.97
30.50	40.77	24.50	50.97	16.50	71.12
31.00	41.44	25.00	52.01	17.00	73.28
31.50	42.11	25.50	53.05	17.50	75.43
32.00	42.78	26.00	54.09	18.00	77.59
32.50	43.45	26.50	55.13	18.50	79.54
33.00	44.12	27.00	56.17	19.00	81.90
33.50	44.78	27.50	57.21	19.50	84.05
34.00	45.45	28.00	58.26	20.00	86.21

Abdomen		Thigh		Forearm	
Inches	Constant A	Inches	Constant B	Inches	Constant C
34.50	46.12	28.50	59.30		
35.00	46.79	29.00	60.34		
35.50	47.46	29.50	61.38		
36.00	48.13	30.00	62.42		
36.50	48.80	30.50	63.46		
37.00	49.46	31.00	64.50		
37.50	50.13	31.50	65.54		
38.00	50.80	32.00	66.58		
38.50	51.47	32.50	67.62		
39.00	52.14	33.00	68.66		
39.50	52.81	33.50	69.70		
40.00	53.47	34.00	70.74		

Conversion Constants to Predict Percent Body Fat in Older Women

Abdomen		Thigh		Calf	
Inches	Constant A	Inches	Constant B	Inches	Constant C
25.00	29.69	14.00	17.31	10.00	14.46
25.50	30.28	14.50	17.93	10.50	15.18
26.00	30.87	15.00	18.55	11.00	15.91
26.50	31.47	15.50	19.17	11.50	16.63
27.00	32.06	16.00	19.78	12.00	17.35
27.50	32.65	16.50	20.40	12.50	18.08
28.00	33.25	17.00	21.02	13.00	18.80
28.50	33.84	17.50	21.64	13.50	19.52
29.00	34.44	18.00	22.26	14.00	20.24
29.50	35.03	18.50	22.87	14.50	20.97
30.00	35.62	19.00	23.49	15.00	21.69
30.50	36.22	19.50	24.11	15.50	22.41
31.00	36.81	20.00	24.73	16.00	23.14
31.50	37.40	20.50	25.35	16.50	23.86
32.00	38.00	21.00	25.97	17.00	24.58
32.50	38.59	21.50	26.58	17.50	25.31
33.00	39.19	22.00	27.20	18.00	26.03
33.50	39.78	22.50	27.82	18.50	26.75
34.00	40.37	23.00	28.44	19.00	27.47
34.50	40.97	23.50	29.06	19.50	28.20
35.00	41.56	24.00	29.68	20.00	28.92
35.50	42.15	24.50	30.29	20.50	29.64
36.00	42.75	25.00	30.91	21.00	30.37
36.50	43.34	25.50	31.53	21.50	31.09
37.00	43.94	26.00	32.15	22.00	31.81
37.50	44.53	26.50	32.77	22.50	32.54
38.00	45.12	27.00	33.38	23.00	33.26
38.50	45.72	27.50	34.00	23.50	33.98
39.00	46.31	28.00	34.62	24.00	34.70

Abdomen		Thigh		Calf	
Inches	*Constant A*	*Inches*	*Constant B*	*Inches*	*Constant C*
39.50	46.90	28.50	35.24	24.50	35.43
40.00	47.50	29.00	35.86	25.00	36.15
40.50	48.09	29.50	36.48		
41.00	48.69	30.00	37.09		
41.50	49.28	30.50	37.71		
42.00	49.87	31.00	38.33		
42.50	50.47	31.50	38.95		
43.00	51.06	32.00	39.57		
43.50	51.65	32.50	40.19		
44.00	52.25	33.00	40.80		
44.50	52.84	33.50	41.42		
45.00	53.44	34.00	42.04		

Benefits of Fitness

Cardiovascular

In a comparison between sedentary and endurance-trained young women, those who had run twenty to thirty miles per week for one year had an average resting heart rate of fifty-one beats per minute. The sedentary women had a resting heart rate of seventy-one beats per minute. In addition, a well-known aerobic training effect, enlargement of the left ventricle of the heart, had occurred in the women who had trained.[6] The enlarged ventricle of the aerobically trained person allows for an increased stroke volume, which gets more blood to the muscle tissue per beat. This person does not have to work as hard to accomplish the same task as the person who is not in condition.

In addition to an enlarged left ventricle and stroke volume, the number of capillaries in the muscle increases with training. In one study this was by 41 percent.[7] Training may also increase the number of intermediate vessels between the capillaries and the arteries. These arterioles are thought to be opened up for use because of the increased blood flow.

The increased number of capillaries helps both in receiving and delivering oxygen. More come in contact with the lungs to take up the oxygen, and more come in contact with the muscle to deliver it. Once the oxygen gets to the muscle, it is taken up by the mitochondria, a sort of microscopic power plant in which the production of aerobic energy takes place. In fit people the mitochondria and related enzymes may double in number and activity. There is some speculation that in women the mitochondria do not increase with training in the same proportion that they do in men. As yet, the evidence is not firm enough to have found many defenders.

Finally, the muscle stores of sugar can as much as double in those who have undergone long-term physical training. Fat (triglyceride) stores in the muscle have been shown to increase by up to 83 percent in the same person.[8] This occurs in both the endurance (slow twitch) and power (fast twitch) muscle fibers and aids both power and endurance performance. The increase of triglyceride stores in the muscle is not the same as an increase in stored body fat. Rather, it is a concentration of body fuels in a more convenient place, the muscle, for conversion to energy.

Longevity

There is no conclusive evidence that exercise actually increases longevity, but there is plenty of evidence to show that it slows the physical decline and many of the disabilities associated with aging. Increased age is usually accompanied by decreased physical activity and increased body fat. The collection of fat deposits makes the person less inclined to physical activity and vice versa. They both conspire to accelerate the aging process. But unlike aging itself, they are a matter of choice for most people.

On the average, $\dot{V}O_2$ max declines with age; by age seventy-five it is about half what it was at age twenty. But when sixty-year-old male endurance athletes were matched with eighteen-to twenty-seven-year-old endurance athletes, their $\dot{V}O_2$ max was only 15 percent smaller. When matched with untrained middle-aged men, their $\dot{V}O_2$ max was 60 percent greater.[9]

Maximum heart rate on the average declines about 8 percent with each decade after adulthood. This would add up to an overall decrease of 32 percent by age sixty. But the endurance athletes had only 14 percent less maximum heart rate than the young athletes. Their body fat was about 10 percent as compared to about 9 percent in the young men and about 20 percent in the middle-aged men, showing that they had experienced little loss of muscle to fat. Finally, the resting heart rate in the sixty-year-olds was fifty-five beats per minute, in the young athletes fifty-nine beats per minute, and in the middle-aged men seventy-three beats per minute. This is not to suggest that everyone can be an endurance athlete. But it does show how much impact a lifetime of exercise has on the rate of bodily decline.

While it is true that you become slower as you grow older, when active sixty-four-year-old women were measured against twenty-year-old women for reaction time, they did quite well. Compared to inactive young women, their reaction time had declined by only 5.5 percent.

The reaction time of inactive sixty-four-year-olds had declined by 14.5 percent.[10] This confirms the studies that show that the more nerve cells used, the less likely they are to deteriorate.

Bone thinning (osteoporosis) is a problem most common in older women, particularly in women who are short to medium in height. It has been found that the bones in tall women are more dense than the bones of their shorter sisters, hence they are not as subject to osteoporosis. Studies done at the University of Wisconsin show that bone loss in aged females may be reversed and maintained at a higher level through physical activity and/or calcium and vitamin D supplements.[11] Studies in animals have shown that exercise prevents the joints from deteriorating. Older persons who exercise have been found to have less arthritic changes in their hips than older sedentary persons.[12]

The role of exercise in reducing the risk of CAD is well known. *The Whole Heart Book* by Dr. James J. Nora well explains risks and remedies. Whether or not regular physical exercise improves job performance has not been proven. But it has been shown that a regular fitness program adhered to for more than a year resulted in a decrease of hospital days and all types of medical claims. In the study, the benefit was seen in everyone in the company not just those in the fitness program. This suggests that the lowered health care costs came from an overall improvement of everyone's habits (power of suggestion?), rather than from partipication in the classes.[13]

It is beyond the scope of this book to outline all the methods of increasing longevity. One book that shows how to compute your chances of reaching old age based on present lifestyle and insurance actuaries is *The Longevity Factor* by Walter McQuade and Ann Aikman (Simon and Schuster, 1979).

Gynecology

Several benefits of exercise relate specifically to women's reproductive organs. One is the relief of premenstrual tension. Water retention is higher just before menstruation because of female hormonal production. Water retention may affect the brain because of increased pressure. It also causes swelling in other body tissues and can lead to discomfort and weight gain. Vigorous exercise causes the sweating away of some of the body's salt and hence some of the retained water. There is also evidence that athletic women have less menstrual pain. Some physicians believe that exercise itself can relieve or prevent cramping. This is advocated both before the onset of pain and during the cramping itself. In addition, women who are in good shape physically tend to have easier and quicker deliveries when they have children.

Even toxic shock syndrome may have something to do with a lack of exercise. Among 80 women so afflicted, it was found that they exercised significantly fewer times per week then did 160 controls matched for age, sex, and neighborhood. Among the many variables measured, two other factors were significant. One was that the onset of toxic shock syndrome was between 6 A.M. and noon, possibly the result of wearing a tampon too long, such as overnight. The other was that the women wore more absorbent tampons. Of the three variables of importance, it seems odd that only the last two were widely reported in the press.

Weight Reduction

Among the direct benefits of exercise to weight reduction is that it drives up the body temperature, and the increased body temperature reduces the appetite. The exercise itself also decreases appetite because the blood is not circulating to the stomach and the hunger mechanism is suppressed. In addition, because of a phenomenon known as dietary-induced thermogenesis, after a meal the metabolism heats up and calories are burned at a greater rate. The higher your aerobic capacity, the more heat you lose after a meal and the longer your metabolic rate remains elevated. This effect is known to last for two and a half hours.[14]

Intelligence

Athletes, especially those in individual sports, tend to be above average in intelligence. Distance runners measured in a Canadian study averaged IQs of 128, three points higher than the average person with a doctorate or medical degree and in the top 4 percent of the national population.[15] Physically fit persons have also been found to be more imaginative. The highly imaginative are often described as "unconventional, absorbed in ideas, enthralled by inner creations," said the researcher. These are all good traits for those who must put up with long, repetitive exercise sessions. Maybe the imagination is developed as a means of entertainment.

Another compelling argument for aerobic fitness is that it may increase both immediate and long-term intelligence. A number of studies have shown significant increases in intelligence that result with aerobic training. For instance, one researcher found that IQ and other measures of mental performance increased significantly among subjects after only ten weeks of walking/jogging. Another found that the IQ scores of mentally retarded boys increased significantly after twenty days of a fitness program.

It seems reasonable that if fitness increases the oxygen supply to the muscles and allows them to work more efficiently, the same would hold true for the brain. Tests have shown that increased fitness is accompanied by increases in fluid intelligence. Fluid intelligence depends upon the neurological functions of the brain. Among average persons, neural signals drop about 2 percent each decade, probably because of lack of oxygen. As we have seen, the average seventy-year-old can take into her lungs only about half as much air as she could at twenty. If you increase the amount of oxygen that you can take in, it follows that more should get to the brain. As might be expected, the most active retirees, according to Mark Crooks, who studied residents of a retirement community, were the sharpest mentally. Of course it's possible that both their greater activity and mental abilities were the result of their being healthy. Forced inactivity because of illness can and often does affect mental abilities. Nevertheless, the "normal" decline in mental ability is due primarily to the decline in physiological ability. This decline, to some extent, can be forestalled or reduced with aerobic exercise.

Even memory, termed "crystallized intelligence" by psychologists, may improve with aerobic exercise. People experimentally deprived of oxygen and those suffering from altitude sickness show many traits of advanced aging, such as impaired vision, hearing, memory, and judgment. On the reverse, senile patients administered pure oxygen became much more alert and scored as much as 25 percent higher on memory tests.

Other studies show immediate benefits to intelligence as well. Aerobic exercise stimulates the mental processes and fends off mental fatigue. One researcher had his subjects solve problems displayed on a screen while they ran on a treadmill. The faster they ran, the faster they solved the problems. Even more unexpected, they did best when running at 97 percent of their maximal heart rates.

This mental stimulation appears to linger once the exercise is finished. Several studies have shown that mental functions increase after mild physical activity. It may therefore be a good idea to jog a couple of miles before taking a test or writing an essay. The mild exercise also increases physical performance such as stamina, speed, and visual acuity. It may also account for a reduced accident rate noticed among Soviet textile workers after they had adopted an exercise program. Although you might feel foolish doing calisthenics trailside, it may increase your safety factor to get your heart rate up and your system flushed with oxygen before climbing a difficult pitch, running a set of big rapids, or crossing a slippery log over a turbulent river.

Sex

The grand finale in the exercise-benefits column is that speculation about increased sexual prowess and drive may have something more to it than wishful thinking. Naturally, as Masters and Johnson noted, the better condition you're in, the better the potential if the desire is there. But what about exercise itself?

It seems that an increased heart rate intensifies sexual attraction or aversion. It does not matter what stimulates the increased heart rate, whether it's rock and roll music, running in place, or listening to comedy. If you find a person attractive to begin with, a heightened heart rate may increase your enthusiasm. If the person is not attractive to you, the quickly beating heart may make him seem less so.[16]

Some studies seem to hold out the possibility that exercise may increase sex drive. Male sex hormones are thought to be responsible for sex drive in both women and men. Anaerobically trained females, such as weight lifters, have registered significantly higher levels of the weak male sex hormone androstenedione.[17] In another study, levels of the stronger testosterone increased significantly in men but not in women immediately after weight lifting. Finally, levels of both hormones tended to be somewhat higher in both sexes after anaerobic and aerobic exercise. But because the effect of blood levels of these hormones upon human behavior has not been clearly established, all this remains conjecture.

Chapter 8

What Is Sensible Nutrition?

The optimal diet is one that promotes the best physical and mental performance, provides the greatest resistance to illness, and does not hasten the aging process. It is agreeable, inexpensive, and easy to prepare. But is it possible? No one diet suits everyone under all conditions. Your genetic makeup, age, gender, food preferences, and the kind of outdoor activities you take part in all affect your nutritional needs. Nutritionists generally agree about the basics of a good diet, but not about the specifics. Many vitamin and mineral requirements and functions remain unknown. However, broad guidelines have been set for most of these nutrients.

Despite this country's wealth, nutritional deficiencies in the American diet remain. Some are the result of poverty, but many are the result of affluence—too many calories, too much sugar, fat, and protein, and too little fiber. While protein is essential to good health, the days of the twelve-ounce T-bone steak are numbered. In addition to the ethical considerations gorging on a product that requires ten calories of energy for every one of food output, as do feedlot beef and distant fishing, is the simple fact that there are better things to do with your money. But it is also true that many claimed health foods are energy-intensive, expensive, or of dubious nutritional value.

Nutritional Basics

Sensible nutrition may sound suspiciously like sensible shoes—unattractive and boring. But it doesn't have to be. It does require some knowledge of the basics of a good diet and how these can be applied by women in various outdoor and training situations. Included here are the methods to determine your nutritional needs. How well you apply them to your own activities, preferences, means, and requirements will determine whether or not your diet is optimal.

The cornerstones of nutrition are the right mix of carbohydrates, fats, and protein, the appropriate number of calories, adequate fluid and fiber intake, and sufficient quantities of minerals and vitamins. To cover these requirements, nutritionists offer a dietary shorthand, which consists of four food groups. It can also be applied to a vegetarian diet.

The four food groups may be too high in calories and may not supply the iron necessary for women of all ages. Depending upon which foods you eat, it may also be too high in fats and too low in certain of the B-complex vitamins. Variety is the margin for error against getting too little or too much of some nutrients. If your diet is repetitive, even if it meets the criteria of the four food groups, it may lack certain nutrients. The main idea behind the four food groups is to provide a guideline to ensure that you get the recommended dietary allowance of nutrients.

Daily Four Food Groups
(Omnivorous or Ovo-lacto Vegetarian)

Servings Recommended
(adult minimum)

I. High-Protein Group
(2 or more servings)
or
1 c. legumes: beans, split peas, lentils, garbanzos.
(2 or more servings)

2–3 ounces of lean cooked meat, poultry, fish, or shellfish; 1–2 eggs; 2–3 oz. cheese, cottage cheese.

4 T. peanut butter; 4 oz. soybean curd (tofu); 1½ T. nuts, oil, or seeds (sunflower).

Protein
Thiamine
Iron
Niacin
Riboflavin
Vitamin E
Phosphorus

II. Milk Group
(Child: 3 servings or more
Teenager: 4 servings or more
Adult: 2 servings or more
Pregnant: 3 servings or more
Lactating: 4 servings or more)

8 oz. whole, skim, buttermilk, or evaporated dry milk, reconstituted; 1 c. yogurt; 1 c. baked custard; 1 c. malted milk; 1 c. soymilk; ½ c. cottage cheese; 1½ oz. cheddar-type cheese; 1 c. ice cream; 1 c. chocolate milk.

Calcium
Protein
Riboflavin
Vitamin D*
Phosphorus

III. Vegetable-Fruit Group
(4 or more servings)
1 c. raw salads
½ c. cooked fruits or vegetables
½ c. juice

1 good or 2 fair sources of vitamin C	Good sources: grapefruit or juice, orange or juice, cantaloupe, strawberries, brussels sprouts, green pepper, sweet red pepper, papaya, mango, guava, and broccoli.
	Fair sources: honeydew melon, lemon, tangerine or juice, watermelon, asparagus, cabbage, cauliflower, collards, garden cress, kale, mustard greens, potatoes and sweet potatoes cooked in jacket, spinach, tomatoes or tomato juice, turnip greens.
1 good source of vitamin A at least every other day	Good sources: dark green and deep yellow sources such as apricots, broccoli, cantaloupe, carrots, chard, cress, collards, kale, pumpkin, spinach, sweet potatoes, winter squash, turnip greens and other dark green leaves.

IV. Bread-Cereal Group (4 or more servings)	Only count if whole-grain or enriched. 1 slice bread; ½–¼ c. cooked cereal; 1 oz. ready-to-eat cereal; 1 roll, biscuit, or muffin; ½–¾ c. cooked macaroni, spaghetti, noodles, or other pasta.	Thiamin Riboflavin Niacin Iron Protein Magnesium Phosphorus

*Vitamin D: Most liquid and dry milk has been fortified with vitamin D. It is also synthesized by the body from sunlight. Strict vegetarians may have trouble getting enough, but not if they are exposed to sunlight.

Adapted from Marie V. Krause and Kathleen L. Mahan, *Food Nutrition and Diet Therapy*, 6th ed. (Philadelphia: W.B. Saunders, 1979), p. 201, and F.J. Stare, P.J. Cifrano, and J.C. Witschi, "What Everyone Should Know," in *The Complete Diet Guide for Runners and Other Athletes*, Hal Higdon, ed. (Mountain View, Calif., World Publications, 1978), pp. 39–40.

An outdoors diet should also be based on the four food groups. You may have to add calories according to your activities, but don't overdo it. During an outdoor leadership school training session, the male leaders assumed that the caloric needs of the women and men students were the same and urged too much food on the women. Likewise, if you're burning 400 to 1,000 calories a day running or swimming while at home, your caloric needs in the wilds might not be that much greater. Getting a *balanced* diet rather than enough calories is a harder task in remote areas, even with freeze-dried foods and other innovations. But high-protein and milk sources should not be that great a problem, since dried milk, peanut butter, cheese, and nuts are relatively easy to pack.

The potential problems arise with the vegetable-fruit group. The woman on an extended trip of one to two months is at risk of becoming deficient in some minerals and vitamins because of the lack of fruits and vegetables. On extended trips, you might want to take a multivitamin, which contains both fat- and water-soluble vitamins and minerals. However, the quantities of minerals and fat-soluble vitamins should not greatly exceed the recommended daily requirement (RDA), since you could get a toxic overdose if you take excessive amounts over an extended period.

The common ailment of trail constipation results in part from a lack of fiber, since fresh fruits and vegetables and whole grains may not be available. Plant fiber is now recognized as an important factor in good nutrition. While an RDA has not been set by the National Academy of Sciences/National Research Council, which sets RDA in the United States, its estimated average intake between .8 to 3.2 grams daily is not enough. It takes about ten grams of fiber to form a bowel movement. This is about the equivalent of four pieces of fresh fruit and a large salad.

To help prevent constipation on the trail, take two tablespoons of bran or a handful of prunes daily. Insufficient fluid intake may be the most important contributor to constipation, so drinking lots of fluids will often solve the problem. Consider a laxative only if you become uncomfortably constipated in spite of preventive measures. Suppositories are preferable because, unlike oral laxatives, they are fast-acting and don't upset the entire digestive tract. However, excessive laxative use can permanently harm the ability of the bowels to function. No laxative should ever be taken if appendicitis is suspected.

Calories

Caloric needs are determined by your body composition, age, gender, activity level, and climate. What is commonly referred to as a calorie is 1,000 calories and is really a kilocalorie (kcalorie). Basal metabolism is the minimum amount of energy the body needs to maintain itself at rest while fasting. It can vary among individuals by 10 to 15 percent depending upon the above factors. Women in general have a 10 to 15 percent lower basal metabolic rate (BMR) than men of the same height and weight. This is probably because they have less proportionate muscle. It requires less energy to maintain fat than muscle. Some of the BMR differences between women and men may be the result of hormones. During menstruation, when the amount of female hormones in the body decreases, BMR increases somewhat.

The BMR is highest during periods of rapid growth, as in early childhood, and to a lesser extent in adolescence. During pregnancy the BMR increases by about 13 percent. Overall, when taking into account the mother's augmented weight, the increase averages about 28 percent.[1] After age thirty, BMR declines about 2 percent each decade. This may occur partly because of less physical activity and the resulting decrease in muscle.

Athletes and others with a high proportion of muscle tend to have at least a 5 percent higher BMR. Exercise itself appears to be the only way around an internal "thermostat," through which the body will conserve energy by decreasing its metabolic rate when food intake is decreased. This has been shown in voluntary and involuntary deprivation and starvation situations. It could easily be the reason why many a baffled and frustrated dieter has found that even with greatly reduced caloric intake, the weight does not come off, or at least not at the rate it should. To repeat, the only way to circumvent this seemingly contrary response of the body to a diet appears to be exercise, where you force your body to increase its caloric expenditure. Exercise also increases the metabolic rate after the exercise itself has stopped. Until you have completely cooled off, you will have an increased BMR. Food itself, for a reason that is not understood, increases the metabolic rate. Carbohydrates and fats increase heat production by about 5 percent of total calories consumed. If you were to eat only protein, the increase might be as great as 30 percent.

Next to BMR, physical activity is the most important factor that determines your caloric needs. A sedentary activity level burns under 150 kcalories per hour. Sedentary activities are those in which you sit most of the time. They burn few kcalories despite the difficulty of the mental task. While the brain needs oxygen, it is not a muscle that increases oxygen uptake with workload. Persons who have sedentary jobs yet exercise frequently should probably classify themselves in the light-activity category.

Light activity (150 to 300 kcalories per hour) encompasses occupations such as food service, hairstyling, domestic work, plumbing, carpentry, and sales. In short, they are occupations in which you stand a great deal of the time. Light recreational activities include golf, bat and ball games, and leisure walking. Moderate activity (300 to 450 kcalories) might include janitorial work, gardening, or working in a laundry. Moderate recreational activities include circuit weight training, fencing, gymnastics, horseback riding, roller skating, tennis, and volleyball. Heavy activity (450 to 900) applies to only a few occupations. These have traditionally been male-only endeavors. They include timber cutting, foundry work, coal mining, and fire fighting. It is estimated that the energy it takes to carry a load up and down stairs is eleven times greater than on level ground. (Backpackers, take note.)

The disparity in the Dietary Allowances of Kcalories and Protein chart between females and males for protein intake is the result of a smaller total base of calories for the females. If a female's body-fat content is close to the male average of 15 percent, she may need to increase calorie and protein intake toward the male standard. The protein allowance is somewhat greater in this chart than in others in order to make up for the approximate 30 percent of protein that is not used efficiently by the body. The minimum recommended in most cases is 9 percent protein intake. Pregnant and lactating women need more proportionately because of the growth of the fetus and milk production. Persons over fifty are thought to need more; although the kcalories needed to maintain body weight tend to decrease with age, protein requirements do not. It is also with age that chronic disease is more likely to take its toll, and protein requirements are higher to aid the healing process.

Dietary Allowances of Kcalories and Protein
(per pound per day, by activity level)

Age	Kcalories			Protein (grams)		
	Light	Moderate	Heavy	Light 9%	Moderate 12%	Training 15%
Females						
11–14	24.7	28	32	.56	.74	.93
15–18	17.6	20	24	.40	.53	.66
19–22	16.4	19	22	.37	.49	.62
23–50	15.6	18	21	.36	.47	.585
51+	14	16	20	—	.42	.525
Pregnant	19	22	25	—	.62/13%	.71
Lactating	20.3	23	26	—	.61	.76

| | Kcalories | | | Protein (grams) | | |
| | | | | Light 9% | Moderate 12% | Training 15% |
Age	Light	Moderate	Heavy			
Males						
11–14	29	32	37	.65	.87	1.09
15–18	22.4	25	28	.50	.67	.84
19–22	20.4	22	26	.46	.61	.765
23–50	17.5	19	23	.40	.52	.66
51+	15.6	18	20	—	.47	.59

Source: Based on data from Joint Food and Agricultural Organization/World Health Organization Ad Hoc Expert Committee, "Energy and Protein Requirements," in *World Health Organization Technical Report,* no. 522 (Geneva, Switzerland, 1973), p. 74; and National Academy of Sciences, *Recommended Daily Dietary Allowances,* 9th ed. (Washington, D.C., 1980), pp. 39–51.

Many activities of the outdoorswoman require a heavy energy expenditure. Some are hard to classify because they depend upon how rugged the terrain or water; the condition of the snow, ice, or rock; how fast your pace and how heavy the load; the efficiency of your equipment; and weather conditions.

The estimates in the Energy Expenditure chart were gathered from a number of sources and are averages only. They will be in error for those whose weight isn't 150 pounds, the average used for most charts. But they do give a good idea of the relative effort of each kind of activity.

Energy Expenditure per Activity

Activity	Kcalories per hour	Activity	Kcalories per hour
Aerobic dancing	280	Running (10 mph)	1,000
Backpacking	450–750	Scuba diving	450
Bat and ball games	250	Skiing, alpine	500
Canoeing (2½ mph)	230	Skiing, cross-country	800
Climbing, ice	900	Snow shoeing	700
Climbing, rock	700	Squash, racquetball, handball	600
Cycling (6 mph)	275	Surfing	600
Cycling (13 mph)	650	Swimming, breaststroke	450
Fencing	300	Swimming, crawl	800
Fly Fishing (in stream)	300	Table, tennis	360
Golf	200–350	Tennis, doubles	350
Horseback riding (trot)	350	Tennis, singles	400
Ice skating (10 mph)	400	Volleyball	350
Jogging (5 mph)	500	Walking (brisk)	300
Judo	650	Water skiing	480
Kayaking	400	Weight training (circuit)	350
Rafting	300	Wind surfing (circuit)	650

The Role of Carbohydrates, Fats, and Protein

Normally the foods we eat provide energy for the next day. We get calories from three of the six nutrients essential to the human body: carbohydrates, fats, and protein. The noncaloric nutrients are water, minerals, and vitamins. The amount of calories in foodstuffs is about four per gram of carbohydrates, nine per gram of fat, and four per gram of protein.

Estimates of how much we need of these respective foodstuffs vary. Most nutritionists, dieticians, and physiologists agree that carbohydrates should comprise between 50 and 60 percent of the diet. Actually, carbohydrates make up only 45 percent of the average diet in the United States. Of this, 54 percent comes from sugar, which amounts to 23 percent of the total caloric intake!

Opinions about optimal fat consumption vary drastically, although most agree that the present 42 percent is far too high. Estimates from those in the health establishment range between 25 and 35 percent. A low of 10 percent is advocated by Nathan Pritikin, founder of the Longevity Research Center, who has treated heart patients with some success. On the other extreme is cardiologist Robert Atkins, whose now discredited high-fat diet eliminated carbohydrates almost entirely.

Estimates of optimal protein intake also vary, but not so conflictingly. They range from 8 to 25 percent. Many of the differences are logical ones based on such factors as childbearing, growth, age, total caloric intake, whether you are attempting to add muscle, and the quality of the protein. The protein in milk, eggs, meat, fish, and poultry is complete. This means that each source supplies all of the eight amino acids not produced by the body. The protein in milk and eggs is used more efficiently than animal protein, so relatively less of it needs to be eaten. Vegetable protein is called incomplete, in that some of the essential amino acids may be lacking or present in smaller amounts than in animal sources. Of vegetable sources of protein, legumes (peas, beans, peanuts, and especially soybeans) are in the same category as meats. One cup of cooked soybeans boasts twenty grams of protein, which is equivalent to one-quarter pound of hamburger or three ounces of cheese, according to *Jane Brody's Nutrition Book* (W.W. Norton, 1981).

Carbohydrates

Carbs have long taken a backseat to protein in the public's estimation of nutritional importance. But they supply most of the body's energy as well as most of the world's food supply. All sugars and starches fall into this category. The principal sources are sugars, syrups, fruits, vegetables, and grains. Carbohydrates are important to the outdoorswoman because they are the body's first choice of fuel for the nervous system and brain. While the rest of the body can be powered on fat or carbohydrates, the nervous system and brain cannot use fat as a fuel. Protein can be recruited from the muscle and organs if no carbohydrate is available, but this takes longer and requires the breaking down of lean body weight. Carbohydrates are the predominant food fuel during short-term, heavy exercise. All three foodstuffs can be used in the aerobic system, but only carbohydrates are used in the anaerobic system.

While fat is the prevailing fuel for low-intensity, long-term efforts, carbohydrates are still important because they supply the majority of energy (60 percent) during the first twenty minutes of submaximal effort. At this point, the fuel balance begins to shift and will reverse by the third hour, when you will be using 70 percent fat and 30 percent carbohydrates.[2]

Another way of looking at it is the lower the oxygen uptake, the more the body is using fat as a fuel source. The harder you work, the more carbohydrates your body uses. The better conditioned you are, the less hard you have to work and the more the body will rely on fats for fuel. If you are not in good condition, you will need to eat and rest more frequently to replace lost carbohydrate stores.

High altitudes and long expeditions present the problem—especially for men, it seems—of marked weight loss for various reasons, including malabsorption, dehydration, and loss of appetite (anorexia). Appetite suppression at altitude is greatest in the first few days and decreases with acclimatization. Carbohydrates appear to be more palatable at higher altitudes than fats or proteins. One vivid experience was related of a meal served by a well-meaning Sherpa shortly after arrival at 16,000 feet in the Himalayas. It consisted of fried eggs, fried cheese, and fried yak meat! This combination, difficult to tolerate at *any* altitude, brought waves of nausea to some, who couldn't bear to eat it, and groans of indigestion to those who did.

A high-fat meal may reduce the oxygen content of the blood, while in short-term experiments, high-carbohydrate diets had the opposite effect.[3] Physician Charles Houston, a well-known mountaineer and researcher of altitude adaptation, says that a carbohydrate-only diet will give you an adaptational advantage at moderate altitudes (14,000 to 17,000 feet) as though you were 2,000 feet lower. Overall, during early exposure at least, a high-carbohydrate diet seems to increase

Transporting just enough food and fuel to get adequate nutrients, whether carbohydrates, fats, or protein, is a major logistical problem on long expeditions. Photograph courtesty of Shari Kearney.

tolerance to altitude, reduce the severity of mountain sickness, and reduce some of the loss of physical performance.

One problem of a high-carbohydrate diet in the mountains is the difficulty of obtaining and transporting enough food to supply caloric needs. Because fat contains the highest amount of calories per gram (nine kcalories) of the three foodstuffs, it may have to supply a larger quantity of calories than is desirable. One potential solution might be a high-carbohydrate intake during the early stages of altitude exposure, with the proportion of fat gradually increased as acclimatization is reached. Another is to eat only carbs on days when you're exercising and fats and protein on rest days, when oxygen metabolism is not so crucial. At the highest altitudes (about 20,000 feet), where acclimation may never adequately occur, at least one famous mountaineer and many wise Sherpas prefer to eat only *tsampa*, roasted barley flour—high carbs, some protein, low fat.

While it might seem logical during low- or mid-altitude excursions to eat a diet high in fat because fat is an "endurance" food, even at low altitudes this will not allow you to function as well as you would if you supply the excess calories you need in the form of carbohydrates. Carbs are important to the recovery process. Without ample supplies, you are setting yourself up for long-term fatigue.

Sugars provide energy but next to nothing nutritionally, so they are referred to as empty calories. But those who use them judiciously in outdoor activities, and not as a substitute for the health-protecting foods, will find them an asset because they do supply quick energy.

Generally, the simpler the chemical structure of a carbohydrate, the quicker it is available for energy. This is the meaning of simple sugars. The most simple of them all is glucose because it and blood sugar are one and the same. Ordinary table sugar is more complex and takes a slight but not appreciably longer time to be converted to energy. But most sugars are the simplest form of carbohydrates and therefore provide energy quickly.

Among the foods themselves, unrefined fruits are high in sugar, grain is high in complex carbohydrates, and vegetables are high in the most complicated carbohydrate of all—fiber. This is all relative of course, since all these foods contain varying amounts of all three kinds of carbohydrates—simple, complex, and very complex.

Most carbohydrates are converted in the body into two fuel forms, glucose and glycogen. Glucose is the basic working form of carbohydrate. Glycogen is the storage form of glucose and the body's preferred source of anaerobic fuel. Some blood glucose is converted into glycogen and stored in the liver and muscle. Normally about 225 grams of glycogen are stored in the muscle, seventy-five to nine grams in the liver, and ten grams of glucose circulates in the blood.

The liver, with its relatively large storehouse of glycogen, can boost low blood-sugar levels when needed. If levels get too high, the liver will take up the excess and store it as glycogen or convert it into fat. While muscle stores of glycogen are higher still, they cannot be used as readily for endurance exercise because they must first be broken down into lactic acid, then carted down to the liver to be changed into glucose.

With long-term training, muscle glycogen stores have been shown to double. Since the emptying of muscle sugar stores occurs in tandem with fatigue and exhaustion, training, which increases these stores, is a boon. However, the use of muscle glycogen of necessity produces lactic-acid waste and fatigue. This can be avoided somewhat, by frequent rest stops to allow the muscles to recover. Small, frequent sugar intake during exercise will also help reduce fatigue by reducing the drain on the muscle glycogen. Of course aerobic training helps because this also reduces the need for muscle glycogen.

Sugars, then, are quick energy boosters if taken in small quantities. Small means about two tablespoons of sugar (102 kcalories) added to one quart of water, one quart of Kool-Aid mixed about one-third strength, or one ounce of hard candy. Larger amounts of sugar will slow the rate that the sugar is taken into the bloodstream. Fat, like nuts in a candy bar, will also slow the digestive rate. The effect is probably not critical except in competitive or dangerous situations. Taking sugar drinks while exercising in heat retards the movement of liquid out of the stomach. This may in effect promote dehydration. On a hot day, drink plain water while exercising, and save the sugar for a rest stop.

In strenuous situations such as snowshoeing, cross-country skiing, backpacking uphill, or mountaineering, in which you operate above 75-percent $\dot{V}O_2$ max, even the liver cannot supply sugar long enough to keep you going for more than about an hour and a half. If you exercise at this rate without replenishing liver and blood sugar, you could get hypoglycemia (dizziness, nausea, confusion, and even partial blackout). This is so even without depleting muscle glycogen stores. Hypoglycemic symptoms involve the central nervous system, which cannot get energy from fat sources. Once you take in about one tablespoon of sugar, symptoms should disappear within about fifteen minutes. Hypoglycemia in this physiological sense means simple loss of fuel. Runners sometimes refer to it as "bonking." It is *not* the unprovable, ephemeral "disease" of recent debate.

Even with mild exercise (30-percent $\dot{V}O_2$ max), the liver glycogen can be depleted in about four hours. But studies have shown that those who were given carbohydrates while working at 60 percent of $\overset{,}{V}O_2$ max—comparable to rowing or paddling in still water, backpacking on a level surface, or hiking rapidly—were able to keep going for six hours, and their blood sugar remained more or less unchanged.[4]

In essence, the body is not like a dry-cell battery that you can stoke up every four hours and hope to operate at your best or even at a safe level during strenuous outdoor activities. It is obvious that the outdoorswoman should eat small snacks at frequent intervals, the more so the heavier her work load. Hypoglycemia is something to consider if you have symptoms resembling mild altitude sickness (headache, dizziness, nausea). If a piece of candy or dried fruit alleviates these symptoms, you have confirmed the diagnosis. Dehydration can cause similar symptoms, which can be almost as quickly relieved by ingesting sufficient fluids.

Because it's hard to cook up a plate of spaghetti while putting a route up a rock face, and because it's difficult to secrete a loaf of French bread in your pocket for easy access while kayaking (although this is a popular custom among French mountaineers), emphasis has been placed on concentrated sugars, the carbohydrates that are easily portable and quickly digested. But this is definitely not to suggest that they are the most important source of carbohydrates.

The carbohydrate content of the various concentrated sweets is: sugars, 99.5 percent; candies, 70–95 percent; honey, 82 percent; jam and jelly, 55–75 percent; and beverages, 10–12 percent. The content of dried fruits is: bananas, 86 percent; raisins, 77 percent; apples, 72 percent; apricots, 67 percent; and prunes, 59 percent. The content of fresh fruits is: pears, 35 percent; bananas, 15 percent; sweet cherries, 17 percent; pineapple, 16 percent; oranges, 12 percent; apples, 13 percent; strawberries, 14 percent; peaches, 10 percent; and grapefruit, 5 percent.

If you don't need easy, fast energy, or if the restraints of gear and the activity don't require concentrated sugars, complex carbohydrates are far better for you. Technically, complex carbohydrates are several sugar molecules that combined to make a larger molecule. Glycogen is one of them.

Complex carbohydrates are found in most abundance in grain. The carbohydrate content of some grain products is: dry cereal, 68–85 percent; flour, 70–80 percent; plain cookies, 77 percent; saltines, 72 percent; bread, 48–52 percent; pasta and rice, 23–30 percent; and cooked cereals, 10–16 percent. The carbohydrate content of certain boiled vegetables is: corn, white and sweet potatoes, lima dried beans, and peas, 15–26 percent. That in uncooked carrots, onions, and tomatoes is 5–7 percent. In leafy vegetables such as lettuce, asparagus, cabbage, greens, and spinach, it is only 3.4 percent because the bulk of these is water.[5] Unrefined and lightly cooked starch sources are also relatively high in varying amounts of vitamins, minerals, and incomplete proteins. Although many products, especially white bread, flour, and cereals, are enriched to replace many nutrients lost in processing, they certainly don't contain dietary fiber.

In addition to their energy supply function, carbohydrates are necessary for fat metabolism and seem to improve the body's use of protein when eaten at the same meal. If not enough carbohydrates are eaten, the body will convert muscle (protein) to glucose to provide energy. This is because the central nervous system cannot use fat as fuel, so a diet low in carbohydrates weakens the body. It illustrates why a complete water fast is not a good idea. Even if you have a bovine look about the hips, if you fast, the body will go after glucose and glycogen stores and the protein. The protein will be taken from muscle in every organ of the body, and this can lead to weakness and possible damage to the organs. Of course the fat stores will be mobilized too, but most of your weight loss will come from water. Water is stored along with muscle glycogen, and when the glycogen is used, the water is freed and you lose weight—along with strength and energy. Fasting also lowers the white blood cell count, thereby weakening the immune system and making you more susceptible to disease. (A complete fast is not to be confused with a liquid fast, such as taking fruit juices, which does not present the same hazards because some nutrients, including sugar, are supplied.)

If you don't feel like climbing a mountain or poling upstream every day of an outing, there is good reason. You're tired. Often the excitement or the necessity of reaching an objective, or peer pressure of not being the first to admit fatigue, will keep you going beyond what your body would do if you gave it a choice. If you are taking part in prolonged, continuous exercise scheduled for longer than several days, carbohydrates are one main line of defense against chronic fatigue. The other is rest.

Each day of continuous, relatively heavy exercise reduces the glycogen stores, and your energy level dips ever downward. Only a small amount of glycogen would be replaced even after five days of rest if you were to eat no carbohydrates. One day of rest or lighter activity plus a high-carbohydrate diet will restore glycogen to about 70 percent of normal. It takes forty-six hours of rest or light activity to restore glycogen completely *if* a high-carbohydrate diet is eaten.

When planning long trips, try to schedule the most difficult passages for every third day. Granted, sometimes this isn't possible, and weather conditions are likely to interfere. But once you have decided how many days a trip *should* take (great expectations), rethink it in terms of adequate days of rest. Intermittent exercise, in which you rest every few minutes to the point that your heart rate returns to normal, does not present the hazards that endurance exercise does. It does not require a higher than normal carbohydrate diet. Complete recovery on either a normal or high-carb diet requires twenty-four hours in these circumstances.[6]

An excessively high carbohydrate diet would not be healthy on a long-term basis. But a 70 percent intake while on a trip should do much to maintain energy and help prevent fatigue. Look objectively at your level of exertion. Are you trundling along at an easy pace, or are you breathing hard? Are you climbing mountains, or are you covering some 500-foot rises in the course of a five-mile trip? If the outing is casual, you don't need to load up on carbohydrates.

High-carbohydrate intake of about 82 percent is of interest to competitive runners, cross-country skiers, and others in endurance events in which winning, for whatever reason, really matters. In the granddaddy experiment that gave seed to carbohydrate loading, it was shown that those whose diets several days prior to exercise were high in carbs could run longer and faster than those on mixed and high-fat diets. The high-fat eaters became exhausted after an hour and a half. The mixed-diet runners were exhausted after two hours. But the high-carb runners lasted for four hours![7]

There is ample evidence that carbohydrate loading works. In its strict form, it involves a depletion phase, in which muscle sugar (glycogen) stores are brought to a low through exhaustive exercise and a diet low in calories and carbohydrates: It also involves a packing phase, in which the glycogen is restored and augmented by a high-calorie, high-carbohydrate diet. This phase forces the muscle to store large amounts of glycogen, which is then available as fuel during the event itself. A complete exercise and food plan appears in *The Complete Diet Guide for Runners and Other Athletes*, edited by Hal Higdon. The drawback of the depletion phase of carbo loading is that it makes you feel tired and ill. It also requires that you closely monitor your diet. The packing phase, however, can be beneficial to the outdoorswoman if three days prior to a demanding endurance activity she increases her carb intake to 78 percent.

Carbohydrate loading in its depletion/packing form is not recommended more often than a few times a year because the long-term effects are not known. It can cause an accumulation of toxic substances in the blood and can lead to kidney damage. This danger can be offset somewhat by drinking at least eight glasses of fluids a day. Older persons and those with kidney and liver diseases should not undergo the depletion phase at all. Those who have a significant risk for CAD should be wary of either phase of carbohydrate loading because it may cause an accumulation of glycogen in the heart muscle, which could lead to cardiac abnormalities. There is also a weight gain, because for every gram of muscle glycogen stored, an average of three grams of water is also stored.

Fats

The emphasis upon carbohydrates shouldn't mislead anyone to believe that fats are not important. Percentage wise, you don't need as much of them as carbohydrates because they are such a potent energy source. Indeed, they are the most concentrated source of energy; one gram supplies nine kcalories, about twice that of carbs and protein. For women, they are the body's largest store of potential energy. As a fuel source in endurance activities, fat in the blood (free fatty acids) supplies 11 percent of the energy; stored fat supplies about 32 percent. Together they provide 43 percent of the energy. During rest, fat furnishes two-thirds of the body's energy.

Like carbohydrates, fats free the protein for its principal job, which is to build and repair body tissue. Since it takes three and a half hours to digest, fat slows the emptying time of the stomach and delays hunger. Fats also act as a carrier for fat-soluble vitamins (A,D,E, and K) and minerals, such as calcium. A diet too low in fat, below 25 to 30 percent, can result in vitamin and mineral deficiencies. A deficiency of certain fatty acids in test animals has been shown to lower energy utilization and lower the skin's resistance to ultraviolet light.

The ability of the body to use fat as a fuel source depends upon your oxygen-carrying capacity. Since training increases aerobic capacity, it also increases your ability to use fat as a fuel source for aerobic exercise. This proves to be an advantage for prolonged work at submax levels because fat stores are so much greater than carbohydrate stores. Because women possess a higher percentage of body fat, some have thought that women might thereby have a relatively greater amount to use as a fuel source. Since the use of fat for fuel decreases reliance on the limited glycogen stores and the fatigue resulting from the lactic-acid system, women would be able to last longer in endurance exercise if this were true. This interesting theory has yet to be tested or proven. While some research shows that women and men use similar amounts of free fatty acids during moderate exercise, it doesn't rule out the possibility that women might be able to continue to exercise longer.[8] The important point here is that the exercise be submaximal. The evidence that women do not reach their anaerobic threshold as quickly as men may suggest that they're using fats as an energy source for a longer period of time.

Another advantage of extra body fat would be on expeditions in which the woman literally carries a larger food supply. Arlene Blum, in her book *Annapurna: A Woman's Place*, commented: "In fact, the higher we climbed, the better we all looked—slim, tanned, and healthy. Many men, in contrast, take on a haggard look after a few weeks at altitude." When the time to choose the summit teams was drawing close, she noted:

> I had assumed all along that by the time we were ready for the summit push, natural selection would make the choice of the summit teams obvious. On many expeditions, after months of hard work at high altitude, some climbers are too tired physically or psychologically to try for the top. But there had been little attrition on this climb. Indeed, most of the members were growing stronger and more determined by the day.
>
> Physiology may have been a factor in this. The average woman's body is 25 percent fat, while an average man's is only 15 percent fat. This extra fat is an energy reserve that can help women to remain strong and healthy under the most severe conditions; it is said to give women a higher tolerance for cold, exposure and starvation.[9]

The proportion of fats and carbohydrates you eat does affect which will be used for energy. Although there is intense interest in carbohydrates because of the performance they deliver, too much of a good thing will force the body to use glucose when it normally would use fats. In one experiment, this shift from fat to carbohydrate took place with ingestion of about three and a half ounces of sugar. This is about the amount of carbohydrate in three doughnuts. So, once again, sugars are desirable for quick energy if taken in small, not large, quantities.

Excess fat of course, both in the diet and stored as tissue, does decrease longevity. A long-term study of women indicated that the greater the amount of fat in the diet at middle age, regardless of whether or not the woman was obese, the shorter the life span.[10] The average adult in the United States gets about 40 percent of her calories from fat and probably 45 percent from carbohydrates. This is 10 to 15 percent too much fat and, correspondingly, too little carbohydrate, according to the American Heart Association. Among the principal fat sources are butter and margarine, 81 percent; lard and vegetable oil, 100 percent; salad dressing, 50 percent; cheddar cheese, 33 percent; egg yolk, 29 percent; nuts, 26 percent; red meat (trimmed), 13 percent; avocados, 13 percent; cream, 12 percent; and whole milk, 3.5 percent.

You can hardly talk about fat and longevity without addressing cholesterol. Cholesterol itself is not a fat, but it is found in combination with animal fats. This has led many researchers to conclude that saturated fats (animal fats) are more unhealthy than vegetable fats. It is now believed that simply decreasing the amount of saturated fat in your diet does not reduce cholesterol levels unless overall fat intake is reduced.

Protein

Protein as a carrier of genetic information is what separates living organisms from rocks, air, and water. Sustaining protein's life-building function are the amino acids, nine of which are considered essential. Food from both plants and animals contains protein, but only animal protein is complete. Thus it helps for most vegetarians to be "ovo/lacto." This means that they include eggs and dairy products in their diet. (Many vegetarians do not eat eggs because they are considered animal in nature.) Without one of these sources of complete protein, it requires a little forethought to combine incomplete vegetable proteins effectively. The basic rules for combining foods are to eat legumes at the same meal as grains; legumes with nuts or seeds; and eggs or dairy products with any vegetable protein. Specific recipes and suggestions can be found in the landmark book by Frances Moore Lappé, *Diet for a Small Planet*.

Protein is essential to human growth. The body's needs are greater when new tissue is being formed. Thus infants, children, teenagers, and pregnant and lactating women need relatively greater amounts.

Heavy endurance exercise may lead to short-term destruction of muscle tissue and lowered hemoglobin levels. Consequently, a person may need slightly more protein than the 9 percent RDA set for most adults. A replacement level of 12 percent seems better. If you are in training and attempting to add muscle, you may want to increase this to 15 percent. Growing youngsters in training may need even greater amounts of protein.

You can calculate your own protein needs based upon caloric intake and training/activity level. One gram of protein yields about four calories of energy. For example, a twenty-three-year-old woman, who weighs 125 pounds and is moderately active will need about 2,250 kcalories. Her protein intake at 9 percent will be about 202 kcalories, which is fifty-one grams of protein. To meet this she might drink a glass of whole milk (9 grams), eat a 3.5-ounce serving of lean meat (31 grams), a 1-ounce serving of cottage cheese (5 grams), and one egg (6 grams). Common foods and their amount of protein are: lean meat, 2.5 ounces, 22 grams; whole milk, 8 ounces, 9 grams; navy beans, ½ cup, 7.5 grams; nonfat dry milk, ¼ cup, 6 grams; small green peas, ½ cup, 4 grams; soybeans, ½ cup, 3 grams; bread, 1 slice, 2 grams[11]; and hulled sunflower seeds, 3.5 ounces, 100 grams.

It is generally agreed that the typical adult intake of protein of 20 percent is too high. The life of amino acids is probably only a few hours, and protein cannot be stored. Therefore, what you eat in excess of what you need is simply stored as fat: This is a waste, since most protein, with the exception of soybeans, is expensive.

Vitamins and Minerals

A thorough explanation of vitamins and minerals would require another two chapters, and the information is available in basic nutritional textbooks. These are suggested as a reference source, since many popular books often advocate massive doses of one or more of these nutrients, which can lead to imbalances and toxicity. Knowledge about vitamins and minerals has advanced rapidly in the last decade. Consequently, any source you use should have been copyrighted or revised within the last few years.

A diet thoughtfully based on the four food groups should supply most if not all of the needed vitamins and minerals. Supplements with high amounts of fat-soluble vitamins (A,D,E, and K) are not recommended because they are stored in the body fat and excess amounts are not excreted. Water-soluble vitamins are excreted if the intake is too high, so they do not present the same potential toxicity problem. But no one knows the ultimate effects—for example, on the kidneys—of ingesting and thus having to excrete megadoses of water-soluble vitamins.

The Recommended Daily Allowance chart shows the RDA of most vitamins and minerals on a per pound basis. The standard RDA assumes that all women weigh 120 pounds, and it usually recommends less for women than the average 154-pound man. But a large woman wouldn't need fewer vitamins than a man of similar weight. This is why the RDA is given on a per pound basis, except for vitamin D.

Recommended Daily Allowance per Pound

Water-Soluble Vitamins

	Vitamin C Ascorbic acid (mg.)	Vitamin B[12] Cyanocobal amine (ug.)	Folacin (ug.)	Vitamin B[3] Niacin (mg.)	Vitamin B[6] Pyridoxide (mg.)	Vitamin B[2] Riboflavin (mg.)	Vitamin B[1] Thiamine (mg.)
Females							
11–14	.5	.03	4	.15	.02	.01	.01
15–18	.5	.025	3.3	.12	.02	.01	.01
19–22	.5	.025	3.3	.12	.02	.01	.01
23–50	.5	.025	3.3	.11	.02	.01	.01
51+	.5	.025	3.3	.11	.02	.01	.01
Pregnant	.67	.03	6.6	.13	.02	.01	.01
Lactating	.83	.03	4.2	.15	.02	.01	.01
Males							
11–14	.50	.03	4	.18	.02	.02	.01
15–18	.41	.02	2.8	.12	.01	.01	.01
19–22	.39	.02	2.6	.12	.01	.01	.01
23–50	.39	.02	2.6	.12	.01	.01	.01
51+	.39	.02	2.6	.10	.01	.01	.01

Fat-Soluble Vitamins

	Vitamin A Retinol (ug./RE)	Vitamin D Calciferol (I.U.)	Vitamin E Tocopherol (mg./TE)
Females			
11–14	8	400	.08
15–18	7	400	.07
19–22	7	300	.07
23–50	7	200	.07
51+	7	200	.07
Pregnant	8	400	.08
Lactating	10	400	.09
Males			
11–14	10	400	.08
15–18	7	400	.07
19–22	6	300	.06
23–50	6	200	.06
51+	6	200	.06

Minerals

	Calcium (mg.)	Phosphorus (mg.)	Iron (mg.)	Iodine (ug.)	Magnesium (mg.)	Zinc (mg.)
Females						
11–14	12	12	.18	1.5	3	.15
15–18	10	10	.15	1.2	2.5	.12
19–22	7	7	.15	1.2	2.5	.12
23–50	7	7	.15	1.2	2.5	.12
51+	7	7	.08	1.2	2.5	.12
Pregnant	10	10	*	1.5	3.7	.16
Lactating	10	10	*	1.7	3.7	.2
Males						
11–14	12	12.4	.18	1.5	3.5	.15
15–18	8	9	.12	1	2.8	.10
19–22	5.2	5.4	.06	1	2.3	.10
23–50	5.2	5.2	.06	1	2.3	.10
50+	5.2	5.2	.06	1	2.3	.10

mg.: milligrams.

ug.: micrograms; ug./RE, retinol equivalents; ug./TE, tocopherol equivalent; I.U.: International Unit.
* 30–60 mg. supplement recommended for pregnant and lactating women until three months after pregnancy.

Source: National Academy of Sciences, *Recommended Daily Dietary Allowances*, 9th ed. (Washington, D.C., 1980), appendix.

Let's take a closer look at those vitamins and minerals that are particularly important to the outdoorswoman.

B-complex Vitamins: These vitamins contribute to energy production. A diet based on the four food groups may be deficient in one or more of these vitamins, which include B^1, B^2, B^3, B^6, and B^{12}. The B vitamins should be taken together because inadequate intake of one may impair the function and uptake of the others. When you take oral contraceptives, your need for the B vitamins and vitamin C increases. Heavy exercise and other stresses increase the need for thiamine (B^1). A deficiency of this vitamin can weaken the heart muscle. Riboflavin (B^2) is essential for growth and is thought to help in the forming of red blood cells and blood sugar. Pyridoxine (B^6) can help overcome premenstrual tension. Elevated levels of estrogen, which occur at this time, indirectly deplete pyridoxine. Cyanocobalamine (B^{12}) is important for treatment and prevention of nutritional anemia. Because it is present only in animal protein, including dairy products, strict vegetarians commonly have low levels of this vitamin.

Vitamin C: Since foods containing vitamin C (ascorbic acid), such as fruits, fruit juice, and raw leafy vegetables, are often hard to pack and preserve for backcountry activities, a supplement is a good idea for extended trips. Vitamin C might well be called the healing vitamin because it promotes the healing of wounds, fractures, and bruises, and it may reduce susceptibility to infections. It is especially recommended for outdoorswomen. By increasing the acidity of the urine, it makes the urine less hospitable to bacteria. The likelihood of urinary tract infections, which are more common in women to begin with, may be greater in the backcountry because of reduced hygiene opportunities. This is especially true if you have sexual intercourse, during which bacteria may be pushed into the urethra. An increased vitamin C intake of 200 mg. to 1 gram per day may also be of value in outdoors endeavors because stress, both physiological and psychological, increases its excretion. But unlike other water-soluble vitamins, ascorbic acid excesses are not entirely excreted and may cause undesirable side effects.

Among the minerals and trace elements for which RDAs have been established, calcium and iron are important because intake of both is frequently low among women. Insufficient amounts contribute to osteoporosis and iron-deficiency anemia, respectively.

Calcium: It is hard to meet the RDA of 800 mg. without milk or milk products. Even a balanced diet from the four food groups supplies only three-quarters of the RDA. An 8-ounce glass of milk or 1 ounce of cheddar cheese supplies about 250 mg. Some situations increase the need for calcium, such as immobilization (being confined to a tent during a prolonged storm); a low-protein, low-fat diet; physical or emotional stress; and strenuous activity. More calcium is also needed by pregnant and lactating women.

Inadequate calcium intake over a period of time may contribute to osteoporosis, a disease more common in women than in men. Researchers have shown that in women between the ages of thirty and seventy, bone mineral decreases by 24 percent, at a rate slightly under 1 percent a year. Significant bone-mineral increases have been obtained when eighty-year-old women were given 750 mg. of calcium and 375 units of vitamin D per day. (Vitamin D is necessary for calcium absorption.) A preliminary recommendation of 1,000 mg. of calcium per day has been made for women above forty to prevent bone thinning and to restore bone tissue that has already been lost.[12]

Iron: Iron deficiency has been cited as the most common of all nutritional deficiency diseases in both undeveloped and developed nations. It is the only dietary supplement recommended for women by the American Dietetic Association. One study by the Department of Health, Education and Welfare showed that 50 percent of all women of childbearing age may be iron-deficient.[13] Dr. Dorothy V. Harris, director of the Center for Women and Sport at Pennsylvania State

University, found that 32 percent of the moderately active women she studied were iron-deficient, while only 8 percent of the sedentary women were. She noted that the whole question of iron deficiency is particularly important to the female athlete, since physical performance depends to a large degree on the ability to take in and use oxygen. Iron deficiency harms oxygen uptake because of decreased red blood cell formation. It has also been shown in one study to lower the anaerobic threshold, thereby increasing fatigue during exhaustive exercise.[14]

Exercise is a known stimulus to blood formation, but women who are not iron-deficient have enough iron stores to accommodate the demand. Why would some women, especially active women, be more prone to iron deficiency? Strenuous exercise and lack of rest periods between strenuous outings may actually destroy red blood cells. Decreased oxygen at altitude puts even more strain on a person's iron stores. One situation or a combination of them certainly can put women into the deficient zone.

Nutritionists note that an otherwise adequate diet supplies only 75 percent of the RDA for iron. Since active outdoorswomen may have even greater needs, it is easy to see why they may become iron-deficient. Harris writes that iron from animal tissue is absorbed by the body better than iron from vegetable sources. "Liver of all kinds is tops on the list; oysters are the next best food. Vegetarians must pay close attention to getting sufficient amounts of iron. Good sources are prunes, dates, kidney beans, and baked beans.[15] But even these may require ingestion of huge amounts to fulfill the iron requirements of an active, menstruating vegetarian female. An illuminating chart in Christine Haycock's *Sportsmedicine for the Athletic Female*, entitled "Selected Sources of Iron," reveals the huge difference between meat and nonmeat sources of iron.

One case in point occurred in one of the members of the 1980 American Women's Expedition to Dhaulagiri I in Nepal. An ovo/lacto vegetarian for ten years, she reported never having experienced the "classic" symptoms of iron deficiency—tiredness, fatigue, and lack of energy. In fact, she had trained vigorously for the expedition and felt quite fit. However, she noticed that she took an inordinately longer time than most of the other women to carry loads from camp to camp on the mountain. It was not until months later, back home, that she discovered she was anemic. In retrospect, she remembered that on most of her excursions into the mountains, on foot or on skis, she had gotten used to lagging behind others, assuming that she was simply the least fit. After a month of iron supplements, she was thrilled to note that she could not only keep up with her peers but even share the leads.

Simply checking your hemoglobin and hematocrit—the ratio of the volume of packed red blood cells to the volume of whole blood—may not reveal anemia. A nonanemic iron deficiency will show normal hemoglobin. Because it can exist without detection in hemoglobin tests, other blood tests—in particular, serum ferritin, serum iron, and/or total iron-binding capacity—may be required. The amount of serum ferritin is highly correlated to the bone marrow storage of iron. A "latent anemia," in which iron stores in the bone marrow are low, likely won't show up until they're called upon, such as during prolonged exercise. Another form of anemia may also occur with endurance training. It is postulated that even though one's blood volume has actually increased, hemoglogin and hematocrit levels drop because the total hemoglobin has not increased proportionately. This is called "pseudoanemia," and it may be an indication to back off somewhat in training or perhaps increase ingestion of iron in hopes of boosting hemoglobin production.[16] Two periodic tests, hemoglobin and serum ferritin, are suggested to keep a line on anemia. Exact amounts of iron supplementation can be determined in consultation with a physician. Different preparations are tolerated better by different individuals. Ferrous gluconate is an especially popular choice. While too much iron can cause constipation, it is easy to tell if your intake is too high when taking iron supplements because it will markedly darken the color of the stool.

Salt: Salt use in the United States and in other countries where foods are manufactured and preserved for mass distribution is too high. The RDA for salt itself has not been set, but the estimated recommendation is between one-half to three grams daily. The average person in the United States ingests between six to eighteen grams daily.

High salt intake contributes to high blood pressure. Since canned foods (especially soup), convenience foods (TV dinners, pot pies), snack and fast foods are the biggest offenders, elimination of these will do much to reduce your salt intake. Many freeze-dried foods are also high in salt. Among the dehydrated noodle and soup combinations in the grocery store, salt is sometimes listed as the second ingredient, and one serving often contains one gram.

Inadequate salt intake is probably not a problem for the outdoorswoman, unless she has deliberately eliminated salt from her diet. In this case it would be wise to increase salt intake in situations (heat, exertion, sweating) in which your salt loss will be high. This means salting foods lightly, not taking salt tablets.

Water

In general, you should drink about one quart of fluid for every 1,000 kcalories of food you eat. This rule applies when you aren't losing great quantities of water by sweating or rapid breathing. A way of measuring your own fluid loss is to weigh yourself before and after a training workout. For every pound of weight lost, you need to replace one pint of water.

In extreme conditions of heavy work in heat, fluid replacement should be about three to five ounces several times an hour. Almost all precautions regarding dehydration are directed to those exercising in heat. However, plenty of water can be lost when you're exercising in cold or average temperatures, as any sweating cross-country skier or high-altitude climber will attest. Sweating is only one avenue of fluid loss; fluids still need to be replaced abundantly. Urinary output increases with exercise, cold, and altitude, and much water is also lost from the lungs, especially during exertion at altitude, which translates into dry air plus faster breathing.

Dried or dehydrated foods, gorp, beef jerky, and other trail items all supply calories without giving the fluid that you would get from a normal diet. We normally get about two quarts of water each day in the foods we eat. Consequently, the more you substitute these dry trail foods for moist foods, the greater your liquid intake should be.

Because the amount of fluid a woman loses during heavy exercise and/or heat has not been determined, an absolute recommendation cannot be made. In men the fluid loss is known to be high, as much as two quarts in a single hour in extreme heat and heavy exercise. To be safe, about one quart of water an hour needs to be replaced in situations of extreme exertion and heat. At moderate exertion in cool or cold conditions, four quarts a day should suffice. At altitude, six to eight quarts a day is normally advised. However, more than one quart of water per hour won't be absorbed by the body, so your fluid intake in camp may need to be high to replace what you lost during the day.

The risk of not drinking enough water to protect yourself from heat exhaustion and dehydration is greater among those who are not accustomed to heat, be it environmental or the heating up of your own body. In general, you need to drink more than you are thirsty for, since thirst is a poor indicator of fluid loss. This is obviously an inconvenience when you must purify your water source, such as melting snow or boiling water. But in some situations it is crucial to protecting your life.

Stimulants

Caffeine has been shown to increase endurance in moderately strenuous exercise. It takes about 330 mg. (the equivalent of about three cups of coffee) taken an hour before exercise for this effect to be noticeable. However, it doesn't work for everyone, most notably those who are already heavy coffee drinkers. Caffeine increases endurance by indirectly causing the release of free fatty acids. This spares muscle-sugar stores and reduces lactic-acid fatigue. In effect, the release of free fatty acids would appear to increase the available energy supply during endurance exercise. Another nice effect noted in one widely quoted experiment is that those who took caffeine did not *feel* like they were working as hard.[17] Another study has shown that caffeine increases both $\dot{V}O_2$ max and maximal heart rate in some persons to a small but significant degree.[18] The use of caffeine by pregnant women is still in question. It has been implicated as causing birth defects and is also a well-known diuretic that can stimulate dehydration if water intake is inadequate.

Amphetamines have no value in increasing endurance, speed, reaction time, and other measures of physical performance. However, they have been shown to increase alertness and to reduce fatigue during mental tasks. Their prescription is discouraged because they are potentially addictive, may suppress the perception and response to pain, heat, and fatigue, and may make a person overestimate her abilities. Like the currently popular over-the-counter diet pills containing phenolpropanolamine, amphetamines increase blood pressure.

Some people have substituted chewing tobacco or snuff for smoking. These habits have had some popularity among outdoors enthusiasts who like nicotine but find the inconvenience and hazards of carrying a lighted coal too great for the field. Smokeless tobacco is undeniably not as bad for your health as smoking. Snuff presents some hazard of lip cancer because it is held in the same place inside the cheek and irritates the mucous membrane. One man, a former smoker, says that every few years he has these cells on his lip surgically removed. He prefers this procedure, which can be done in a doctor's office, to the possibility of emphysema and CAD. Of course, any form of tobacco puts a substantial jolt of nicotine in the system. The amount received from either chewing tobacco or snuff is greater than that gotten from smoking. Nicotine is a stimulant with the side effects, such as elevated heart rate and sleeplessness, associated with other stimulants.

Chapter 9

Small Miracles: Female Adaptation to Environment

Part of the miracle of human physiology is that it's so dynamic. Every cell in every organ is active and constantly changing. Participation in outdoor sports involves immersing this body into the diverse and often stressful environment of "the elements." Somehow it has been written into our biological computers to adapt and survive, and even to perform, in such vastly different environments as heat, cold, and altitude. While the basic mechanisms of adaptation are common to all human beings, some differences between female and male adaptation exist. Because so little has been known about how women actually do adjust, differences in symptoms or behavior were often judged to be weakness.

Of late, much rethinking has been done on the topic of women as competent outdoorspersons. Research and resulting useful information regarding how women adapt has only just begun to emerge. The ultimate purpose of investigating comparative adaptability is not to defend weaknesses or to flaunt the strengths of either sex, but rather to help both men and women understand and enhance their performance.

Adapting to Heat

The average woman is not as heat-tolerant as the average man because she is not as fit as the average man. Heat tolerance is directly related to aerobic capacity, but like aerobic capacity it can be improved with training. Excess body fat is a liability when working in the heat. Fat increases the body's insulation more than muscle does, and it slows the movement of heat away from the core of the body to the skin. Excess fat also increases the work load of the heart, resulting in a double bind when exercising in heat. When fit women are compared with men of similar fitness, the picture changes drastically and suggests that in a number of ways a woman adjusts better to heat.

The most obvious difference between the sexes is that women do not sweat as much as men. Women have a slightly lower skin temperature, which may reduce the need to sweat, and their sweat threshold is generally higher than men's. This means that the internal body temperature must increase more before sweating starts. Because a woman's sweat glands are distributed more evenly, and because she has more of them that are active than a man, on the average the evaporative process is more equal all over the body. In other words, says one researcher, although the male sweats sooner, the female may sweat better.[1]

Although the female sweat rate increases with fitness levels, it does not reach the same rate as that in men. One study showed no difference between male and female sweat rates during exercise in dry heat, while the women had significantly lower rates in humid heat.[2] One mechanism that helps women dissipate body heat with less sweating is that in humid conditions they maintain higher blood volumes than do men. The greater volume aids in the removal of heat from the core of the body to the surface. Although the man continues to sweat in humid heat, he simply loses fluids without the benefit of cooling because the water in the air does not permit the sweat to evaporate.

Fit women experience less water loss than men operating under the same workload. This is a benefit for a woman in situations where potable water is not readily available or when water losses occur for other reasons, such as in heat or at altitude. Another possible way in which women adapt better to heat than men is that our lower basal metabolic rate may reduce the need for evaporative cooling. Finally, women have been found not only to have lower sweat rates, but if fit, lower increases in heart rate when under heat stress.[3]

The sweat rate increases in women as they become more fit, and fitness and acclimation to heat reduce their sweating threshold. These two facts underscore the importance of sweating. A possible explanation—and this is only speculation—is the greater percentage of muscle tissue in men and trained women than in sedentary women. About one-third of the water available to the body for temperature regulation comes from the release of water when muscle stores of glycogen are used. With less muscle and hence less "muscle water" available, women sweat less. But as a woman becomes more fit and the percentage of muscle increases, she may gain this "male" advantage while retaining her own.

The "sweat" question and others about women's adaptations to working in heat have more than just curiosity value for two reasons. First, erroneous biases have been used to exempt women from work and sports in hot environments. Second, the more that is known, the more women can avoid heat exhaustion and heatstroke, "salt" cramps, and fainting. A case in point is that we have no guidelines as to just how much water women should consume while in a hot environment. Plenty is known about the needs of men, but not of women. The most that can be said is that water replacement is extremely important for both sexes. Water loss not only increases fatigue, but it can put you dangerously close to heat exhaustion or heatstroke. And because a woman doesn't sweat as much, it might seem safe to assume that she doesn't need to replace water quite as often as a man in similar circumstances. But how less often or how much less? Listening to your body sounds logical, but thirst is not an adequate indicator of fluid loss, although an increase in thirst does seem to come with experience and heat acclimation.[4]

No doubt spurred by the historic participation of men in competitive sports, military combat, and heavy industry, there are volumes of published research about how much fluid men need for what conditions. For example, during strenuous activity in temperatures of 100 degrees Fahrenheit, a man can lose up to two quarts of water in a single hour. Water replacement for men is about three to five ounces several times an hour when exercising in heat. The best that can be recommended for women at this point is to follow the general guidelines for men. It is far better to err on the side of caution. But keep in mind that an otherwise healthy person cannot consume too *much* water.

Among the less serious, although admittedly frightening effects of too much heat is fainting (heat syncope). It has been thought to be more common in women, although this has not been documented. Fainting occurs when a large proportion of blood is dispersed into the peripheral blood vessels as a result of their dilation from the heat, thereby shunting blood away from the vital organs, including the brain.

Standing for long periods worsens the situation because blood becomes pooled in the legs from gravity. Dehydration, which causes a decrease in total circulating volume, may also be a contributing factor. The result is that not enough oxygen gets to the brain. To treat fainting, move the person to a cooler place, lie her on her back, and elevate the legs. Douse the face with water, and loosen or remove tight or heavy clothing. The person should regain consciousness quickly.

Salt or heat cramps are of unknown cause, but they may occur as a result of a salt deficiency—a rare occurrence in a woman unless she sweats profusely and deliberately eats a low-sodium diet. Cramps can be best avoided by a normal to generous salting of foods during periods of heavy activity. Salt tablets should never be administered without plentiful water consumption, and in general they are not recommended unless the person is on an extremely low sodium diet. Symptoms include severe cramping, usually in the legs or abdominal muscles, and it can last up to fifteen minutes. The soreness can remain for several days. Cramps can frequently be alleviated by stretching the muscle or by flexing it against a heavy object to get the nerves to fire in a different direction. Drinking a solution of one teaspoon of salt in a quart of water should help prevent repeated episodes.

Symptoms of heat exhaustion are faintness, rapid heartbeat, weakness, clammy skin, unstable walk, and possible nausea and collapse. A headache also may be present, and the body temperature may be normal or slightly above. Sweating and a pale skin color may also be present, but this varies. Treatment should consist of resting in the shade and taking fluids. The victim should recover fairly quickly.

The much more serious heatstroke comes about rapidly and usually occurs during long bouts in sustained, especially humid heat when sweat can't evaporate well and thus can't cool the body. Profuse sweating may cause dehydration; at some point the body stops sweating altogether, perhaps to prevent further dehydration, and the internal body temperature soars. Since fit women don't sweat as much in humid heat as men, they may be less likely to suffer heatstroke. Symptomatically, the person may earlier have felt hot, then quickly may become confused, uncoordinated, delirious, or unconscious. Usually the body temperature will be above 105°. The skin will be hot, and sweating will be completely absent. Treatment must be immediate to prevent brain damage or death. The victim should be immersed in or doused with water, preferably cold water, to bring the body temperature down as quickly as possible. Fanning helps, as does removing clothing (if dry) and anointing the body with water or alcohol. The person should be moved to the shade. If the victim goes into a coma, she should be evacuated immediately. Those who survive heatstroke may develop kidney failure and be less tolerant to heat in the future.

A slower pace helps reduce heat stress. If possible, don't exert yourself during the hottest part of the day. Wear a sun hat and light-colored, reflective clothing. Cool your forehead and body with frequent dabbings of cool water. Rest in the shade when you're tired. These are all common sense, but sometimes people drive themselves or others beyond common sense without realizing the seriousness of the consequences.

Older persons appear to be less heat-tolerant. They also start to sweat later. Following exposure to heat, it takes longer for their body temperature to return to normal. One study found that 70 percent of heatstroke victims were over sixty.[5] Young children are also less able to regulate the body's temperature, both in heat and cold, so they should be watched for signs of heat stress. The best method of adjusting to heat is the same as acclimatizing to altitude, gradual exposure of two weeks being optimum. Of course this is the least practical.

Physical conditioning that increases aerobic capacity aids heat adjustment, and specific kinds of conditioning will help the most. A training program of high-intensity workouts is more effective than sub-maximal aerobic exercise. In one study, those who adjusted to exercise in the heat the best were those who worked at 90 percent of their heart rates. They did intervals of ninety seconds alternated with thirty seconds of rest. This was done for fifty to sixty minutes a day four times a week in average temperatures for eleven weeks.[6] This kind of workout obviously requires dedication. However, the principle involved—of deliberately elevating the body's temperature to an extreme—will work in a more moderate program.

Another effective method is to train *in* heat. In one study, women walked on a treadmill at 50 percent of VO_2 max at average temperatures. Another group of women did the same thing, but in a temperature of 118 degrees. At the end of the nine-day test period, both groups showed improved heat tolerance, but those who had worked in the high temperature averaged 45 percent better.[7]

Adapting to Cold

People are basically tropical animals. Without protection such as clothing and shelter, most require high ambient temperatures to feel comfortable and to maintain their resting metabolic rates. Although we can adjust in time to slight variations of temperature, there are diverging opinions about our ability to acclimatize to cold in the way that we acclimatize to heat. The success of persons living in extreme cold is usually a question of their ability to avoid it, such as insulating themselves from low temperatures, wind, rain, and snow. Since physical activity increases heat production by as much as tenfold or more, the fit person who is able to keep active is more likely to survive prolonged exposure.

Several adaptations have been noticed in permanent residents of extremely cold areas. One is reduced heat loss through respiration. How this works is not completely understood, but it may be the result of experience, in which the person is not as anxious about the cold and so does not breathe as fast and deep. She may also have learned to breathe through clothing or clenched teeth to warm the air before inhaling it.[8] Another essential feature of long-term adaptation to cold is reduced shivering despite increased heat production. Findings show that women divers in Korea do not shiver to the same extent as those not so adapted.

A person who is accustomed to the cold can experience a one- or two-degree drop in the body's internal temperature without the vessels to her extremities constricting. Persons of different races, such as Eskimos, Caucasians, and Negroes have been tested to see if this is the result of racial body characteristics. Apparently it is not, for all three have shown an increased blood flow to their hands after repeated exposure to cold. This adaptation allows them to maintain manual dexterity despite the cold.

People do not adapt to cold in the long term by increasing their basal metabolic rate (BMR). The differences in BMR among populations in tropic, temperate, and arctic environments are probably because of the food they eat. Eskimos, for example, traditionally eat a diet high in fats and protein. Those living in tropic areas eat foods high in carbohydrates, and those in temperate areas tend to eat a mixed diet. Fats and protein require greater energy to metabolize than carbohydrates and thus increase the BMR. Should the percentage of fats and proteins decrease, the BMR will too. Eskimos who eat a European diet do not as a rule have the higher BMR.

One short-term adjustment we make to cold involuntarily is shivering, where the amount of blood flow to the shell of the body drops, thereby constricting the blood vessels in the skin and resulting in a drop in the skin's temperature. Shivering may increase the metabolic rate by two to four times. The energy expenditure of violent shivering is about the same as jogging, five times the BMR. However, shivering usually cannot occur for more than half an hour continuously before the muscles become fatigued. When that occurs, shivering stops. People exposed to cold can learn to sleep even though they're shivering. But it takes between three to ten nights to get to this point (not a pleasant prospect), and probably after this time exhaustion overcomes the extreme discomfort of shivering. Because of their generally lower skin temperature and greater subcutaneous fat, women could be compared to walruses or seals. Both of these animals conserve heat by sporting a heavy layer of fat, which provides effective insulation when their blood vessels constrict. However, in studies done of men and women immersed in cold water, the smaller women actually cooled faster, the insulating value of their fat being offset by their greater surface area per pound of body weight than that of men. This is what is meant by surface to mass. Their small size would also allow greater cooling because small masses cool faster than large ones. Another postulated sex-related difference in cold tolerance is that women's potential for heat production through shivering may be less, since they have less muscle mass than men.

Women generally have longer hair and this may be an insulating advantage, since 40 percent of the body's heat is lost from the head and neck. But Caucasian men's extra body hair may act as some compensation for the lack of what is on their heads.

The woman's lower BMR, probably the result of her smaller muscle mass, also means that she requires less food to maintain body temperature, certainly an advantage when food is scarce or when it must be carried on a backcountry excursion.

Hypothermia

When cold adaptation, both voluntary and involuntary, is insufficient to maintain the body's internal temperature above 95 degrees, hypothermia results. Far too many venturers into the outdoors die each year through lack of knowledge and foresight about this usually preventable condition. Hypothermia, or decreased temperature, has been dubbed "the killer of the unprepared," because the classic victim is caught in the elements without adequate food, clothing, heat, and shelter when the weather changes. Deceptively, the ambient temperature is usually not below 45 degrees, but added factors of wind and wetness often act quickly to lower dramatically the effective temperature. The wind-chill factor acts by swiftly convecting warm air away from the body. About two-thirds of the wind's effect on temperature occurs in the first few m.p.h. "Water chill" means that the conductivity of heat through water is thirty-two times faster than in still air, which is why wet clothing and especially immersion in water cool the body so quickly.

Another factor producing often unanticipated temperature drops is elevation. The temperature in still air drops approximately 3½ degrees for every 1,000-foot gain in altitude. A trip from sea level to

12,000 feet, for instance, involves a temperature drop of 42 degrees just from elevation alone. A perfect example of the seriousness of the combination of cold, wet, and wind was experienced by members of the 1980 American women's expedition to Dhaulagiri, Nepal, when they left sunny Tukuche (9,000 feet) one morning en route to a hillside camp at about 12,000 feet, located on the notorious Yak Pass. Out of 270 porters who had carried loads from Katmandu, all but 50 or so shook their heads vigorously when begged to carry further, pointing toward the pass and stating, "Many cold up there." Having had their thermostats set in the warm-to-hot mode for ten days, many of the expedition members started up the hill in shorts or skirts, some even in thongs. Three hours and 3,000 feet later, immersed in fog and buffeted by high winds, they struggled into camp shivering and miserable. Later, they complained that the coldest they ever got on the entire expedition was at Yak Pass. On the mountain itself, cold was expected and thus was well prepared for.

The signs and symptoms of hypothermia are well documented in mountaineering and other texts. Violent shivering, muscle fatigue, feeling cold, and perhaps slight incoordination occur early, when the core

Snow caves are excellent shelters from the winter elements. Once inside, your body heat warms the surrounding air and you stay much warmer than you would in a tent. Building the cave itself generates body heat too. Photograph courtesy of Kellie Erwin Rhoads.

temperature is above 90 degrees. Below 90 degrees two key warning signals are gross muscular incoordination, including stumbling, and mental disorientation, especially apathy. The hypothermic victim suddenly stops taking care of herself. She can't cope and can't muster the energy or the wherewithal to even button her coat or put on her gloves. Before these later symptoms occur, hypothermia can be considered mild and can be treated by protecting the victim from further heat loss, supplying food, rest, or more clothes. By the time the mental changes occur, the hypothermia is considered severe, according to Dr. Cameron Bangs, a hypothermia specialist at the Yosemite Institute's Mountaineering Medicine Symposium in March 1980. Steps must be taken to warm the victim, since she will not be able to generate her own heat. Treatment includes the classic nude-bodies-in-the-sleeping-bag rewarming method, heat supplied by warm rocks placed on the neck, armpits, and crotch, or inhalation of heated, humidified oxygen (available only in sophisticated rescue units) until the victim can be evacuated to a hospital. Bangs emphasizes that severe hypothermia should never have to result in death in the field if proper steps are taken. One classic mistake is to leave the hypothermic person alone while going for help; the victim inevitably wanders off, removes some or all clothes in a state of relaxed apathy, and dies.

Rewarming of the mild hypothermic is the utmost priority and should not be delayed. Giving fluids is important. If the victim is able, she should be encouraged to drink as much as possible. Warming the fluids will not help raise the core temperature, but it might make it easier to ingest greater volumes and it adds a psychological boost. Alcohol should not be given because it causes dilation of the blood vessels in the skin, which briefly gives the sensation of warmth, while in reality it drains away precious body heat. Food is important as an energy producer if the victim is able to eat. Prevention, as always, is infinitely easier and safer than cure. Education, awareness, and preparation are vital for prevention of hypothermia. Fitness is also important. The fit person can generate more heat longer and delay exhaustion. Cold temperatures, like hot ones, increase the body's workload (as does wind); they also decrease endurance and muscular strength, both of which can be better tolerated by a fitter individual. (For treatment of severe hypothermia, see chapter 4.)

Are women more resistant to hypothermia than men? In exposure to mild cold, probably so, because their higher fat content serves as insulation. In extreme cold, yes and no. Since women are generally smaller and have greater surface-to-mass ratio than men, they can lose heat faster. Being small means that your body cools faster, much like a small pan of water cools faster than a large one. And yet in numerous reported survival situations (being trapped in storms or snowslides), women seem to outlast men, so other factors must interplay. Despite a woman's lower skin temperature, her extremities (when size is not a factor) are not more susceptible to cold injury. The lower skin temperature is probably explained by greater subcutaneous fat deposits.

Conclusions about the subjective component of cold tolerance are difficult to make. Sedentary, indoorsy women may tend to complain about the cold, while active and athletic women may be more likely to ignore pain, having become accustomed to mild levels of it during training and high-stress endeavors. Whatever your tolerance level, vigilance needs to be high to protect yourself from serious cold injury.

Frostbite

While the body's attempt to hoard heat by refusing blood to the extremities makes biological sense, it simultaneously subjects these areas to frostbite. The body parts most vulnerable to frostbite are the feet and hands, the face, and the ears, which present a large surface area with little insulation. Interestingly, the feet are able to tolerate colder temperatures than the rest of the body without registering discomfort. This is nice while wading cold streams, but it also increases the vulnerability of these important appendages.

Frostbite is produced by direct freezing of tissues and by injury to the tiny networks of blood vessels, which stops blood supply. Skin will freeze at −25 degrees in calm conditions, but with a wind of 15 mph, the temperature need be only as low as 0 degrees. Freezing occurs at higher temperatures if the skin is wet. Factors that impair peripheral circulation, such as altitude, immobility, and dehydration, make you more vulnerable to frostbite. The classification of frostbite into mild, moderate, and severe is often impossible until weeks after the injury. The only distinction that needs to be made in the field is between frostnip and frostbite. Frostnip involves a sudden whitening or blanching of the skin, especially about the face, that is quickly and completely reversed by immediate rewarming. Frostbitten skin is white, firm, and/ or waxy and is numb to the touch. Often the first symptom of both types of injury is *no* symptom. A toe that previously could be felt wiggling against the boot is suddenly numb. At this point, immediate rewarming may prevent frostnip from progressing to frostbite. Too often the nonsignal isn't noticed until much later.

When frostbite is diagnosed away from hospital facilities, it's better to keep the injured part frozen until reaching the hospital. Thawing in the field, which is awkward and imprecise, is often accompanied by severe pain and marked susceptibility to infection, both of which are difficult to control in the field. You can walk or ski out on a frozen foot without causing further damage. But a thawed part often becomes completely unusable, meaning that you will have to be evacuated by stretcher. Hospital treatment of frostbite mainly involves elevation and disinfection. Fortunately, the days of horrific amputations of digit after digit by candlelight in a dirty tent on a high mountain have been relegated to the classic mountaineering literature. Now amputation is rarely even considered until *months* later, since an injury that initially appears to be severe may turn out to be much less so after it heals. Of frostbitten parts that do recover, some will completely heal, but many will continue to be extra sensitive to cold for months, years, or even permanently. Some will manifest pain or tingling intermittently or exhibit a reduced pain threshold to mild physical injury.

Two other types of cold injury that are related to frostbite may also occur. One, which has no particular name, involves temporary damage of the nerve branches of a finger or toe without visible injury. Pain may or may not occur initially, but subsequently the part may ache, especially when cold or bumped. Usually, normal sensation will return with time. Another cold-related injury, called immersion foot, occurs under cold and wet conditions when the temperatures are not low enough to cause actual freezing of the tissues. Mountaineers or backpackers caught in an early fall snowstorm, for example, unprepared to wade about in deep snows, may have their feet immersed in cold slush for days during exit. Eight students who were so caught during a wilderness course reported to the local emergency room with signs and symptoms of immersion foot. These included pain, decreased sensation, redness, and swollen feet. Treatment is simple—rest and elevation. But the feet may be intolerant to cold for some time. Cold injury of any severity, then, may involve permanent or semipermanent sequels and disability.

Prevention of frostbite involves preventing hypothermia, avoiding constricting boots, socks, and gloves, and staying well hydrated. Cigarette smoking, which constricts peripheral blood vessels, has been found in one study to increase cold injury in moderate smokers but not in heavy smokers. Perhaps the blood vessels of heavy smokers become tolerant to nicotine's constricting effect.

Altitude Acclimatization

From Annie Peck's first ascent of the 18,000 north peak of Huascaran in Peru in 1908, to the first female ascent of Mt. Everest by a

Japanese woman in 1975, to the 1982 American women's expedition to Ama Dablam (22,350 feet), which put all eight members on its summit, women with appropriate fitness and experience have been successfully venturing to high altitudes. Skiing, hiking, and climbing are often done at altitude (and paddle sports too, if done on the likes of Lake Titicaca in the Peruvian highlands).

As a person ascends from sea level to altitude, the amount of oxygen in the air decreases, and the body begins to compensate. The rate of breathing increases (hyperventilation), thereby more oxygen is exchanged in the lungs. The heart rate increases, so blood gets circulated back and forth from the tissues to the lungs faster. The body stores of hemoglobin, which carry the oxygen in the red blood cells, become mobilized, thus more oxygen can be carried. And soon, new hemoglobin and red blood cells are made. Meanwhile, the kidneys work to readjust the acidity of the blood, which has been altered by the changes in respiration. Initial adjustment, or acclimatization, occurs in a matter of minutes, hours, and days, but more complete acclimatization takes several weeks. Despite adequate acclimatization, activity at altitude becomes increasingly more strenuous as oxygen decreases. $\dot{V}O_2$ max decreases about 3.5 percent for every 1,000 feet of elevation gain. At 17,000 feet, for example, a person's $\dot{V}O_2$ max is only one-half of its sea-level value. By 20,000 feet, $\dot{V}O_2$ max has dropped to one-third. This explains the frequent comments that, at the highest altitudes, even tying one's bootlace is an unimaginable burden.

Below 7,000 to 8,000 feet, physiological adjustments to altitude usually involve little discomfort, perhaps some fatigue or mild shortness of breath on exertion. Above this elevation, about 50 percent of those who ascend fairly rapidly to 12,000 feet will experience more noticeable and more uncomfortable symptoms, which collectively are known as acute mountain sickness (AMS). In most people the symptoms disappear within twenty-four to thirty-six hours as their bodies acclimatize. Headache is common but can usually be relieved by aspirin, a night's rest, and/or brief periods of forced hyperventilation (breathing faster and deeper deliberately). Nausea, vomiting, loss of appetite, insomnia, and fatigue are also common. Shortness of breath may occur, and perhaps a cough. The pulse is usually rapid. At this point the malady resembles seasickness or a bad hangover, and as Dr. Charles Houston, a high-altitude researcher comments, "Though few die from it, some wish they would."[9] No treatment of AMS is necessary at this stage, except to rest and *not to ascend further* until the symptoms disappear.

Above altitudes of 9,000 to 10,000 feet, these symptoms become worse in some cases. Signals indicating that adequate acclimatization is *not* taking place are: If the headache is not cured by aspirin, rest, or hyperventilating, or by taking Tylenol with codeine, a moderately strong, narcotic painkiller; if nausea and vomiting persist or worsen; if insomnia is persistent and severe; if shortness of breath becomes marked; if the cough is debilitating or there is blood-streaked phlegm; and/or if the fatigue progresses to lassitude. These are symptoms of a serious progression of maladaptation, called high-altitude pulmonary edema (HAPE). Pulmonary edema refers to an abnormal collection of fluid in the air sacs of the lungs. The mechanism of the development of HAPE is still unknown, but it is not related to the pulmonary edema that is caused by heart failure at low altitudes. With a stethoscope, and in severe cases without, crackles in the lungs with breathing (rales) may be heard. HAPE may be accompanied by a slight fever, and often it has been misdiagnosed as pneumonia. It usually takes thirty-six to seventy-two hours for the symptoms to become obvious, so the importance of *not* ascending if you have symptoms of AMS becomes clear. Once the signs and symptoms of HAPE manifest themselves, there is a single solution for treatment: put succinctly by one author, "descent, descent, descent."[10] No amount of oxygen, rest, or drugs can be relied upon to stop or reverse the insidious cascade of events, which can result in coma and death within twenty-four hours.

Stories abound of climbing parties that left a member who didn't feel well at an intermediate camp, then returned a day later after the summit push to find her or him in a coma or dead. A simple way to be alert for the onset of HAPE has been suggested by Dr. David Shlim, a clinical researcher of altitude sickness: If you're not doing well at altitude, or if you get what you think is the flu, it's altitude sickness until proven otherwise.[11] The importance of early suspicion cannot be overemphasized. To descend a thousand feet unnecessarily may be a drag, but to miss the early symptoms of HAPE and become a stretcher case for someone else to try to evacuate is an infinitely greater one.

High-altitude cerebral edema (HACE) is another category in the spectrum of altitude illness, and the lines dividing it from HAPE are somewhat obscure. It takes slightly longer to develop (usually several days) and occurs at slightly higher altitudes (above 12,000 feet). It may occur as a progression from HAPE or independently of it, and its symptoms include severe headache, incoordination, poor judgment, stumbling walk, drowsiness, and coma. It is not important to differentiate it from HAPE in practice, except to know that a severe headache in the mountains can progress to coma and death even in the absence of respiratory symptoms. This form of altitude illness may be difficult to differentiate from hypothermia, but the setting in which each occurs should enable distinction. One important test you can perform, if in doubt about the diagnosis of HAPE or HACE, is to have the suspected victim walk a straight line, etched in the snow or ground, heel to toe. If the subject wavers off the line, she is exhibiting a reliable early sign of serious oxygen deprivation to the brain, which strongly suggests the presence of one or both of these illnesses. If this test is positive, in the absence of hypothermia and of alcohol, immediate descent is mandatory. One truly amazing (and rewarding) characteristic of altitude illness is the rapidity of symptom resolution with descent. Most conscious patients will feel great following descent of as little as 1,000 feet, and even comatose victims will usually "wake up" after being evacuated downward by a few thousand feet, with full recovery within a few days.

In the normal adult population of sojourners who ascend rapidly to 10,000 feet, about 1 in 200 will develop serious AMS. There is no difference in the incidence between females and males, but individuals less than eighteen years of age have been found to have a somewhat greater incidence (about 3 percent). While the pieces to the giant puzzle of altitude sickness are still being discovered and arranged, certain factors are felt to increase one's risk of developing it. Ascending too fast to altitude is perhaps the most important. Especially at risk are those who climb high mountains that are easily accessible from sea level. For example, an estimated one-half to three-quarters of all the people who attempt to climb Mt. Rainier in Washington each year develop some form of AMS. Also at risk are those who are transported by car or plane to an excursion at high altitude. For example, far more trekkers to Everest basecamp who fly to Lukla, at 9,100 feet, to begin their treks get AMS than those who walk up from Katmandu, at 4,230 feet.

Those who are forced to sleep at the elevation they have gained are also at increased risk to develop AMS. These include backpackers, trekkers, and alpine-style (rapid, light ascents) climbers, rather than skiers, who will often sleep at the bottoms of their respective hills,[12] or expedition climbers, who attain the next highest camp and return to sleep at the lower one. During sleep everyone's breathing rate normally decreases. At altitude this nocturnal decrease heightens the body's oxygen deprivation, which makes acclimatization more difficult and the development of AMS easier. This is why alcohol must be avoided at altitude, as well as prescription sedatives like Valium or barbiturates, which depress breathing. If taken prior to sleep, the balance can be dangerously tipped toward AMS. In some persons, oxygen lack during sleep results in irregular breathing, called Cheyne-Stokes, or periodic breathing. This phenomenon involves brief periods when breathing stops altogether, and so it has been responsible for a great deal of alarm among tentmates of those afflicted. It may be a frequent cause of the insomnia of altitude.[13]

Estimated guidelines for rate of ascent are elevation gains of approximately 2,000 to 3,000 feet per day when covering altitudes between 5,000 to 10,000 feet, with one or two rest days of zero elevation gain; then 1,000 feet per day for altitudes between 10,000 to 15,000 feet, and 500 to 700 feet per day at altitudes above 15,000 feet, with a rest day every two or three days. A party must limit its rate of ascent to what the person slowest to acclimatize can tolerate.

Heavy exertion at altitude, especially during the initial days at a higher elevation, is related to the development of AMS. Exercise causes an increased muscular demand for oxygen which decreases the amount of oxygen in the blood. This deficit contributes to AMS. Different people remove oxygen from the blood to different degrees during the same amount of exercise. One characteristic of those who acclimatize less well may be that their blood oxygen decreases more than others during exercise. One possible way to help compensate for this oxygen deficit involves choice of food. Since it takes less oxygen to metabolize carbohydrates than fats or proteins (see chapter 8), it seems reasonable to eat mainly carbohydrates on days of heavier exertion at altitude and to favor fats and protein on rest days.

Another physiological characteristic that may make some people worse acclimatizers is that, given a low level of oxygen in the air, some will naturally and unconsciously respond by hyperventilating less than others. This may partly explain the finding that some people who have had AMS are more likely to get it again. In other words, some people are HAPE susceptible.

Fitness is *not* a protection against altitude sickness. In fact, those who are most fit seem to be more prone than their less fit companions. Perhaps they find it more difficult to hold themselves back to a slower pace. However, since conditioning improves work efficiency, well-conditioned persons will still find the task at hand easier than those less conditioned and will generally perform better if altitude sickness is not a factor.

The best ways to avoid altitude sickness are to ascend slowly, avoid heavy exertion, especially early at each altitude, and if possible, climb high and sleep low. And don't smoke. Ten percent of the hemoglobin of the moderate smoker is attached to the carbon monoxide generated in the blood by inhaling the tobacco smoke. Thus the blood

Successful acclimatization to altitude, especially trekking at such celestial heights as 15,000 feet and above, requires a slow rate of ascent. Photograph courtesy of Richard Collins.

transports less oxygen. This has been estimated to translate into approximately 3,000 feet of relative elevation gain.

Another utterly important preventive of AMS as yet has no discernible physiological explanation. Mysteriously but crucially, hydration has been shown to be a key factor in those who do best at altitude. Hydration means drinking lots of fluids. This may seem to be confusing because HAPE involves the leakage of fluid into the lungs. Indeed, once the symptoms of HAPE appear, to take more fluid without simultaneously removing it with medications that increase urination would undoubtedly make the condition worse. However, to aid acclimatization and avoid AMS and HAPE, drinking copious amounts of fluids at altitude is essential. At the highest altitudes (greater than 16,000 feet), this means at least seven to eight quarts per day; at moderate to high altitudes (12,000 to 14,000 feet), perhaps a minimum of six quarts per day. One sign of good acclimatization is increased frequency of urination. When hydration is adequate to promote acclimatization, the urine will not only be frequent but also will be light in color or clear. On her first night at 16,000 feet, one woman on a Himalayan expedition noted that she had to arise four times to urinate. She was amused that every time she left her tent to do so at least one other woman in camp was doing the same thing!

Hydration is also important in the prevention of blood clots. Blood clots, although less common at altitude than previously thought, occasionally form in the arms or legs, possibly because of some combination of increased thickness of the blood from altitude and cold, forced periods of inactivity and constricting clothes.

The excessive use of salt at altitude has been discouraged by some, since it causes water retention and thus contributes to edema (swelling of the hands, feet, and face), especially in women who tend to accumulate fluid premenstrually. However, as mentioned in chapter 10, the relationship between edema and acclimatization is anything but clear. Among those who develop severe AMS, edema is often an accompanying sign. And the incidence of edema in women at altitude in one study was greater than among men. But no association has been found between edema and AMS.[14] Further study is obviously needed to make sense of all this.

Another occurrence related to altitude is retinal hemorrhages (HARH), which occur in about one-third of all climbers ascending above 17,500 feet. These are tiny leakages of blood in the eye, and most of the time they go unnoticed. Occasionally a hemorrhage will result in a small blurred or blind spot. HARHs disappear soon after descent, and persistent visual defects are uncommon. Retinal hemorrhages alone are not a *cause* for descent. If vision is affected, descent should probably be made to prevent possible enlargement of the hemorrhage. Since HARHs are so common at altitude, a history of them should not prevent a person from returning to altitude in the future.[15]

One drug that has recently been advocated by some to prevent AMS is Diamox (acetazolamide). Its actions on the body are multiple, including increased urine flow and ventilation. In one fairly large study, Diamox was shown to decrease symptoms of AMS and increase feelings of well-being during rapid ascent to high altitude on Mt. Rainier.[16] However, its use on longer expeditions has brought mixed and especially negative results. This is perhaps because its effects are transient. Large expeditions that involve extended periods at gradually increasing altitudes afford time for the body to acclimatize naturally. Side effects of Diamox are numbness and tingling of the lips, hands, and feet, muscle cramps, and perhaps some fatigue. Sometimes these symptoms are bothersome enough to discontinue use. Recent reports also suggest that a person's exercise tolerance may be reduced by taking Diamox, and this would be exacerbated as greater altitudes are reached.

Another potential problem involves *prolonged* use of the medication. One person who lost his Diamox during an ascent developed symptoms of AMS, while his companions not taking Diamox did not. Using a drug to aid mountaineering is ultimately an individual decision, but present recommendations among mountaineering physicians for using Diamox are: for those who have recurrent problems with altitude and/or are known to be HAPE-susceptible; for rescue personnel who may be called upon to make rapid ascents for rescue purposes; and for those who feel they must or can't avoid making rapid ascents of high mountains and who are willing to accept the hazards of drug reliance and side effects.

AMS, in summary, is a spectrum of maladaptation to altitude whose effects on the sojourner are "vile at best, and fatal at worst."[17] Its diagnosis is easy if signs and symptoms are watched for. Prevention is simple and treatment is straightforward. Only those who remain unaware of the threat and signs of AMS will continue to walk upward, into the arms of death from lack of oxygen.

Since women are different physiologically from men, it might be expected that in the complex process of adaptation to altitude, differences would be found among the isolated variables that make up acclimatization. Only a handful of studies comparing female and male responses to altitude have been conducted. Results are often conflicting and generalizations impossible to make. In addition, as more becomes known about female physiology, even interpretations of results within these studies may have to be revised. For example, conflicting results concerning whether women concentrate their blood better than or worse than men at altitude involve differences in the iron stores of the subjects. It is now known that the tests themselves may not accurately reflect iron stores. (See chapter 8). Discrepancies in findings about relative increases in ventilation and/or hyperventilation between men and women at altitude will need to be reevaluated as more is discovered about changes in female ventilatory rates related to the menstrual cycle. Ventilation may increase up to 30 to 40 percent in women during the luteal phase (that is between ovulation and menstruation) of their cycle.

When the whole is viewed rather than its separate parts, women acclimatize generally at the same rate and in the same ways as men. One measurement of adaptation is work capacity. In two separate studies, the amount that work capacity decreased with altitude was found to be similar between the sexes.[18] Another important indicator of the equality of adaptive success is that the incidence of AMS in men and women has been found to be the same.

While a woman's reproductive physiology doesn't impede her acclimatization, altitude may exert some interesting effects on it. A wide variety of changes in menses have been noted among women at altitude during strenuous exercise. Weight loss and stress usually accompany excursions to altitude and are thought in themselves to affect the menstrual cycle in unpredictable ways. The precise contribution of altitude to menstrual changes, if any, will remain difficult to ascertain. Normalization of the cycle usually follows upon return to normal elevations and activity.

Little is known about the effects of altitude on pregnancy. Despite decreasing oxygen available to the mother as she ascends to altitude, automatic regulation of the fetal environment should ensure adequate delivery of oxygen to the baby. A few pregnant women who have trekked or climbed to altitude have not reported problems with themselves or their children. However, babies born to permanent high-altitude residents do tend to be smaller and infant mortality tends to be higher than in culturally similar lowlanders.

The use of birth control pills at altitude is discouraged (see chapter 10). IUDs often cause excessive menstrual bleeding and may deplete iron stores at a time when they are sorely needed to aid acclimatization. Diaphragm jelly has been noted to cool to uncomfortable temperatures in the nighttime chill of a high-altitude tent. Finding a suitable means of birth control can be a problem for the high-altitude climber, although the obvious choice would be a condom. Fertility of both women and men has been found to decrease at altitude. However, this should not be relied upon as a means of birth control! Two women on a Himalayan expedition who discontinued birth control pills on the advice of a well-meaning doctor (because of the risk of blood clots) became pregnant at 15,000 feet, despite irregular periods in one woman. The highest impregnation is rumored to have occurred on a French expedition at 25,000 feet. Perhaps this event provides the best silent judgment of the similar—and most adequate—acclimatization potentials in both sexes.

Chapter 10

Ob-Gyn: Facts and Fiction

No woman wants any of her pursuits arbitrarily limited because of her reproductive system. But until recently too much inhibitive emphasis has been placed on the negative effects of exercise upon female reproductive physiology. In almost every issue of any women's magazine at least one article addresses "female" problems. At the same time it is difficult, even amusing, to imagine *Outdoor Life* or *Sports Afield* dealing with such "male" problems as impotence, decreased sperm production, hernias, and prostate maladies. And it is rare to find even a mention of the effects of exercise, stress, or environment on male reproductive physiology. Somehow a balance must be sought.

Menses

Of all the physiological factors that influence how well a female feels or performs, none seems more fickle than menstruation. Because its effects are so variable, and because it has been used as an excuse to restrain women's activities, the recent trend has been to deny its effects.

Some studies show that during menstruation no significant decrease in $\dot{V}O_2$ max, endurance, or perception of strength, and no significant increase in fatigue occurs. While this applies to the majority of females with normal cycles, cyclical changes in performance have appeared among a sizable portion of women studied.[1] For example, during the first two or three days of the menstrual period, a woman's ability to do well at high-intensity work involving heavy physical loads may decrease.[2] Or during this time it can take between twenty to sixty seconds or longer to recover normal pulse rates after exercise. However, women have set world records during menstruation. Because bleeding is accompanied by a loss of the excess water acquired in the premenstrual phase, performance may benefit.

What is agreed upon, despite the vastly different effects the menstrual cycle has on individual women, is that there is no reason other than personal choice why a woman shouldn't continue to exercise or make outdoors excursions during menstruation. If you tend to bleed heavily, demanding exercise may accelerate the flow and produce mild abdominal discomfort. Mild diarrhea is also fairly common during menses and is sometimes exacerbated by strenuous exercise and stress.

Menstrual irregularity is common during extended outdoor activities. The stress of heavy exercise and an unfamiliar and possibly threatening environment can contribute to hormonal imbalance. Some reports document early and late periods, heavier and lighter flow, or absence of bleeding altogether among women while they are in the outdoors. This is not generally something to worry about if normal periods resume once you return home.

Performance during the week just prior to menstruation, when estrogen levels are at their peak, may be slightly decreased from normal. Part of this may be caused by the premenstrual syndrome, in which some women experience tension, irritability, backache, abdominal pain, fatigue, and weight gain. One set of studies shows a somewhat lower degree of endurance strength during this phase of the menstrual cycle.[3] While there is no reason to forego a trip or stop exercising at this time of the month, neither should you feel inadequate if you aren't up to your usual level of abilities. Similar increases in estrogen caused by daily use of estrogen-containing birth control pills are also thought to contribute to decreased physical performance. Physical efficiency is perhaps highest during the two weeks following menstruation. This makes obvious sense in women who experience painful ovulation, premenstrual syndrome, and painful periods. Among women who do not have such difficulties, the data vary.

About half of all women have painful periods (dysmenorrhea). Of these, 10 percent are often incapacitated for one or two days a month. Athletic and active women tend to have fewer problems with dysmenorrhea than inactive women. It is not certain if the activity itself, the woman's state of fitness and better muscle tone, the distraction of the exercise, or the self-discipline and increased likelihood of denying pain reduce dysmenorrhea. Another possible factor may be the production of endorphins during strenuous exercise. These are natural opiates released in tiny but potent amounts in the brain. Whatever the cause, ample evidence exists that those who exercise are less likely to be incapacitated by menstrual problems.

Exercise, both mild and vigorous, is known to help relieve and prevent menstrual pain for some women. For those who do experience dysmenorrhea, a class of drugs called "prostaglandin-reducing analgesics" has given total relief to 65 to 100 percent of the women who use them, if used according to prescription. This class of drugs includes Motrin (ibuprofen), Anaprox (naproxen sodium), and Ponstel (mefenamic acid). These drugs are also useful for treating muscle soreness, tendinitis, and sprains, so they are an overall asset to your first-aid kit. They can produce stomach upset, diarrhea, or constipation and should be taken with meals to minimize these side effects. Women who cannot use aspirin or who have stomach problems may find that these drugs aggravate these conditions.

Excessive bleeding may make exercise and outdoor trips inconvenient, but it is no reason to stay home. It is more common in girls in their early teens and women approaching menopause. Exercise may help if there is a resultant weight loss, since overweight women tend to bleed more during their periods than thin women.

Endometriosis, a condition most common in women between the ages of twenty-five and forty five who have never been pregnant, can interfere with a training program. Among common symptoms is a nagging ache in the lower back, which the woman may think is caused by exercise, such as running. Another symptom, often preceding the period by more than one day, is a sharp pelvic pain that gradually worsens. Sometimes there can be pain during sexual intercourse, especially the week before your period.

Endometriosis is caused by escaping bits of tissue from the lining of the uterus that extend into other pelvic areas, such as the fallopian tubes, outer uterus, and ovaries. They can be tiny or large, and they often form cysts that are filled with a dark brown fluid. Each month they thicken and swell as if they were still in the uterus.

Treatment for endometriosis varies. Hormones to shrink the tissue are often administered over the course of a year. In some women,

Danazol, a synthetic of the powerful male hormone androgen, has been effective. If the ailment is severe and chronic, surgery may be necessary to remove the tissue, and the last resort is a hysterectomy.

Menses and Bear Attacks

No evidence exists that bears, other than polar bears,[4] are attracted to the menstrual odor, and studies have been done on precisely this subject. As a precaution, though, you may want to wear tampons to reduce the odor. You should also be extra cautious about cleanliness. Since sanitary napkins can irritate the inner thigh during heavy exercise, in addition to being more difficult to dispose of, you may wish to use tampons instead in the backcountry. Tampons and napkins should not be buried; animals will just dig them up, and they take a long time to decay. They should either be carried out or burned, if wood is plentiful enough to justify a fire this hot.

Bears do seem to be attracted to human sexual activity. Whether this is simple curiosity, some misdirected primal instinct, or the odor of semen or vaginal secretions is hard to say. At any rate, sex should be avoided in a heavy bear habitat. Perfume is also known to attract bears. In fact, one researcher is reported to use perfume to attract bears to his study areas. Perfumed soaps, lotions, and other toiletries often used by both sexes should not be used in bear country.

Some women take birth control pills to prevent or stop menstrual bleeding while in areas of concentrated grizzly bear sightings. Since a grizzly is more likely to attack than his more mild-mannered cousin, the black bear, this creature is the cause of most concern among backcountry users. If you take this route to assuage fears of "encounters," be aware that afterward it may take some time to restore the normal timing of your menstrual cycle.

Medications

When a woman prepares her medical kit for a trip, she should consider some special problems that may need treatment. Two infections that are common in women, vaginal yeast infections and urinary tract infections, often occur more frequently during trips outdoors, when hygiene is usually poorer and clothing often restrictive. The recent trend to avoid travelers' diarrhea by taking antibiotics predisposes women to yeast infections because the antibiotics upset the bacterial balance of the vagina. While both of these afflictions can be self-limiting, access to treatment can prevent hours or days of symptomatic misery. Vaginal suppositories for yeast infections could be included in your medical kit, along with antibiotics for urinary tract infections. Estrogen-containing birth control pills increase the risk of yeast infections, as does pregnancy. Urinary tract infections are common in sexually active and pregnant women. Prevention includes liberal fluid intake and frequent emptying of the bladder, especially after sexual intercourse.

Some drugs that are usually included in an outdoor medical kit sensitize the user to sunlight. Sunlight exposure is intensified by high altitudes and glare from snow fields, water, sand, and certain kinds of rock. Among these drugs are antibiotics, especially the newer tetracyclines like Vibramycin, diuretics, sleeping pills, and tranquilizers.

Fertility

Amenorrhea, which means absence of menstruation, has received considerable attention lately, but its cause remains a mystery. It is of interest to outdoorswomen because it appears to be more frequent in those who are training heavily, are stressed, and/or have a low body-fat content.

Some researchers believe that the onset of menstruation in young girls can be significantly delayed if the girl is athletic. The delay may be because of a change in the hormone levels which could interfere with ovulation.[5] A number of studies of adult women show that exercise does create changes in hormone levels.[6] Of course beginning menstruation is like menstruation itself—regular in its irregularity. Generally, menstruation should begin between the ages of thirteen and fifteen.

Amenorrheic women tend to be lighter and thinner than those with regular periods, and it is more common for thin women to have low levels of estrogen. However, thin means *really* thin. In women whose body-fat content is greater than 15 percent, no menstrual irregularities appeared, according to one large recent study.[7] Amenorrhea is also more common in women who maintain a low body-fat content plus train heavily, such as ballet dancers, runners, figure skaters, gymnasts, cyclists, and body builders. Amenorrhea is also more likely to appear after a woman has been training for six to eight years.

Recent studies of female cadets at West Point and marathon runners support the conclusion that amenorrhea is more likely the result of stress than exercise. It is possible, suggests Dr. Mona Shangold, an assistant professor of obstetrics and gynecology at Cornell University Medical College, that women who are attracted to a long-distance training program may also select stressful endeavors in other parts of their

Medical supplies being prepared for the 1980 Women's Expedition to Dhaulagiri, Nepal. Photograph courtesy of Shari Kearney.

lives.[8] As difficult as it is to pinpoint any one cause of amenorrhea, most probably several different causes act separately or together in a given person at a particular time. If stress is an important factor, it certainly helps to explain temporary irregularity in female mountaineers, kayakers, and others who take part in physically demanding or potentially dangerous sports.

It is reassuring that in one long-term study of women who were recreational joggers and increased their mileage over a sixteen-month period to complete a marathon irregularity did not occur.[9] Although there are no long-term studies to prove it, the majority opinion is that once intense training ceases, menstruation will commence again in amenorrheic women. Authorities agree, however, that long-term irregularity or amenorrhea is not a normal response to training. A woman who experiences this problem should visit a gynecologist to determine if she has a problem which is not related to her training. Says Dr. Barbara Drinkwater, a research physiologist at the Institute of Environmental Stress, University of California, Santa Barbara: "It is important that the public understand this because I've talked to many amenorrheic athletes who have been led to believe that this is a normal response to training. At this point we do not know what is causing the amenorrhea or if it is reversible."[10]

Contraceptives

Birth control pills can be both an aid and a hazard in outdoors activities. The risk of clotting disorders is 4 to 11 times greater in birth control pill users than in nonusers.[11] The excess mortality from pulmonary embolism (a blood clot, usually originating from a leg or arm, that lodges in the lungs) or stroke (a blood clot lodging in the brain) is 1 to 3.5 times greater, and it increases with age among birth control pill users.

Most clotting abnormalities appear to be related to the estrogen component in birth control pills. For this reason, most pills on the market now contain fewer than fifty micrograms of estrogen. This reduces the risk of deep vein-clot formation by 25 percent. Pills with fewer than fifty micrograms of estrogen or no estrogen at all are often referred to as low-dose pills. Their active ingredient is progesterone. Although the side effects of progesterone are not thought to be as great as estrogen, there may still be some risk involved with using these pills.

High altitudes, limb constriction by a packstrap, or other gear, dehydration, immobilization, as in a tent or on a belay ledge, and cold all add to the risk of blood clots. Every outdoorswoman should consider these before packing her birth control pills. One of the most serious, proven risks to developing blood clots while on the pill is cigarette smoking. The sensible woman will leave her cigarettes behind as well.

Another potential hazard of using birth control pills at altitude involves the confusing relationship between premenstrual edema and the development of high-altitude pulmonary edema (HAPE). Are women predisposed to HAPE premenstrually, when fluid retention occurs? Would birth control pills, which also may cause fluid retention, influence the development of HAPE? These are just a few of the questions that surround the mysteries of altitude adaptation and maladaptation. Meanwhile, anecdotal accounts of birth control pill users at altitude so far do not implicate the pills in adaptation problems. Still, because of the clotting hazards, women should discontinue birth control pills at least one week before traveling to altitudes of above 10,000 to 12,000 feet.

Some women use low-dose pills while in the backcountry because they can reduce or eliminate heavy bleeding, cramps, and tampon disposal problems. They may be used continuously simply to stop bleeding at inconvenient times or in difficult situations. However, sometimes low-dose pills result in light but bothersome breakthrough bleeding between periods, and the user may be caught totally unprepared. If you decide to use these pills, test them well before the outing. Their effectiveness in preventing pregnancy is also slightly less than the higher-dose pills. Remember that continuous use of pills can upset the long-term timing of your cycle. It took one woman a full year to restore her normal cycle after taking pills continuously for three weeks.

Two final although certainly not so serious side effects of birth control pills have been noted. Low glucose levels, which can cause fatigue and poor disposition, have been observed in women who take birth control pills.[12] They may also slightly reduce endurance abilities.

An IUD as an alternative means of birth control can present several problems. It may be less well tolerated by females who have never been pregnant and can cause severe pain and heavy bleeding. The heavy bleeding can cause iron-deficiency anemia and reduce the body's oxygen-carrying capacity. An iron supplement should correct this if an IUD otherwise suits you. Of course it is unwise to have one inserted, especially for the first time, just before taking an outdoors trip primarily because there's no way to remove it if it causes trouble. Although the chances of a major problem (such as embedment or puncture of the uterus and cervix) are small, the possible pain, infection, and bleeding may greatly interfere with your activities. Infection can become a major problem, since it heightens the risk of producing scarring of the fallopian tubes and even sterility. An IUD should be inserted at least two months before an extended trip to ensure that your body has adjusted to it.

Urination

Urination remains a major logistical problem for the outdoorswoman. Leg loops in climbing harnesses that unsnap or detach eliminate the need to untie from a safety system. But having to peel away multiple layers of clothing in subzero weather with high winds can cause substantial heat loss, not to mention discomfort. Shorts and pants with Velcro crotches are an interesting idea, but so far they have proven to be unwieldy. They tend to come apart, and they may irritate the inner thighs. Small plastic funnel devices now manufactured under the trade name Sani-fem need to be refined. If they worked properly, they would allow you to urinate while standing up without having to drop your pants. But the funnel section is not long enough to extend out of the fly of the pants. A small length of soft rubber hosing attached to the spout might be a solution. Meanwhile, they are convenient with hiking skirts and also for directing the stream into "pee bottles" in tents! A poncho can give you impromptu privacy if you have no other alternative. Those camping in large groups in which a communal latrine is dug have found that tying a bandanna to a tree or bush can indicate when the latrine is in use.

Not being able to hold urine is a more common problem in women who have borne a number of children because of the stretching of ligaments and muscles during pregnancy. Some women may develop this problem if already weak ligaments are subjected to heavy pounding, as in running. It can bother those women who tend to strain during heavy exercise and those who must remove backpacks or skis to urinate and find that privacy is not readily available. Kegel exercises, in which you contract and relax the muscles centered near the urethra, may help because they strengthen the surrounding muscles. In some cases this anatomical problem can be corrected by surgery.

Breasts

Breasts are not more susceptible to soft-tissue injuries than any other part of the body. However, all but small-breasted women will want to wear a good athletic-support bra to prevent discomfort and any potential sagging from the forces of gravity acting on the breasts' elastic tissue support. Of course exercise that works the upper-body muscles, particularly the pectoral muscle underlying the breasts, will help prevent sagging.

Athletic bras are a most welcome addition to the department stores' lingerie section. Unlike most women's underwear, they are made of cotton. Synthetics absorb and retain heat, and perspiration buildup from vigorous exercise remains trapped. This is a problem in cold weather because it adds to the loss of body heat. In hot weather, synthetic underwear sticks to your skin and inhibits the cooling process. When buying an athletic bra, look for broad straps that do not roll and seams placed where they will not rub or chafe the skin. Check to make sure that hooks aren't located where they will rub against a pack, rope, or other gear.

Bras and panties with fairly loose elastic are recommended for tick or chigger country. The constriction of tight elastic brings the blood to the surface along the bra and panty line, and the insects will gravitate to these sites.

Fungal infections most frequently affect the feet and groin, but the area beneath the breasts is also susceptible. A thorough cleansing, drying, and powdering is a good preventive measure. If an infection

Sanifem. Photograph courtesy of Blane Howell, M.D.

arises, it will cause itching, burning, and pain, which may interfere with your outdoors and training activities. It can be treated by applying a fungicide to the skin or, if absolutely necessary, taking a fungicidal drug.

While breast cancer has never been proven to occur as the result of a blow, occasionally a bruise on the breast will cause the forming of a nodule of fibrous tissue. This may remain for years, but it isn't of consequence. Occasionally, these are removed in the belief that they may be cancerous. And obviously it is better to have them checked than risk the consequences of delaying removal of malignant tissue. A good support bra can help relieve pain when cysts form in the breast, and a padded bra can be worn to prevent injuries in sports where blows to the breasts are likely.

Pregnancy

Most women now know that exercise during pregnancy is good for them. Exercise that strengthens the lower back, buttocks, and abdominal muscles makes delivery easier. Physically fit women report shorter labor and decreased pain, faster recovery, and fewer complications. Aerobic exercise such as walking or jogging improves circulation, which is important for the growth of the fetus. During the first three months of pregnancy, the fetus is well protected. Starts, stops, and motion such as jogging won't harm it if the pregnancy is a normal one. But you probably shouldn't exercise beyond 65 percent of your maximum heart rate. At this rate you should be able to exercise and not be too short of breath to talk. Although this may seem like an excessively cautious pace—since it isn't known how strenuously a pregnant woman can exercise before the blood supply to the fetus is decreased—it is better to err on the side of caution. And you probably shouldn't exercise to the point of exhaustion.

While women have climbed difficult mountains, set Olympic records, and run marathons while pregnant, there is also no question that pregnancy will slow you down and requires certain precautions and restrictions. You should discontinue physical activity and see a gynecologist if you have significant bleeding, pain, or any leakage of the amniotic fluid. Pregnancy also will require more frequent rest stops and closer attention to nutrition. An extremely active woman may find it hard to attain the estimated twenty-five pounds she should theoretically gain during pregnancy.

As to training, swimming and stationary bicycling (to preclude balance problems) are probably the best choice as pregnancy advances because they reduce the stress on the lower back and breasts. However, you shouldn't swim the first three weeks after delivery. This is to allow time for the cervix to close to avoid possible inflammation of the uterus.

One woman studied did continue to run while pregnant. The percentage of $\dot{V}O_2$ max she used increased from 61 percent in her third month to run nine-minute miles to 71 percent in her eighth month. By her ninth month she substituted walking for running. Her experience is similar to that of other women who have maintained a running program while pregnant.[13] Two other women studied continued to run right through to delivery with no complications, and their infants were normal. These women were not doing high mileages (more than fifteen to twenty per week), and they were in good physical condition to begin with. In general, it is probably fine for physically fit women to continue a similar training pace so long as they feel up to it. Those doing heavy training should probably cut back so as not to risk harm to the fetus. Women have begun running programs while pregnant and have improved their work capacity by about 18 percent over those who remained inactive.[14] But extremely sedentary women should probably confine themselves to light activity, such as fast walking or calisthenics.

Problems such as increased fatigue and pressure on the bladder are bound to hamper any training program and prove inconvenient while in the outdoors. Pregnant women should avoid long exposure to heat and should not exercise to the point that their own body temperature rises appreciably. There is a demonstrated connection between birth defects and sustained body heat above 102 degrees.[15] Pregnant women are more susceptible to soft-tissue injuries, and healing may take longer.

The ligaments, particularly those in the pelvic region, become looser during pregnancy, and the chances of dislocation and sprains of the extremities are greater. Women measured during the last three months of pregnancy, then at three weeks after delivery, showed a 31 percent increase in knee-ligament extensibility.[16] Because the possibility of soft-tissue and ligament injury is greater, warm-ups become even more important. A warm-up prepares the muscle and nerve pathways for work. It is much like reading a speech to yourself before delivering it.

The pregnant woman has traditionally been assumed to be even more frail and weak than the nonpregnant one, and vague fears of damaging her fetus have kept many a pregnant woman quarantined at home. While it is true that pregnancy imposes difficulties and precautions, it doesn't mean totally suspending outdoor activities. The uterus is one of the best protected organs in the body. The chance of injury to it, even after the belly begins to protrude, are minimal. Outdoor activities raise a few special considerations. Those that impose the risk of falling or rely greatly on balance, such as skiing, climbing, and surfing, should be approached with caution during the last three months.

The tendency for varicose veins to form during pregnancy, especially in women who have a genetic history of them, is exacerbated by immobility, such as long standing while waiting for your turn on the rope or kneeling for long periods in a canoe. Circulation can be aided by elevating your legs above your heart from time to time, or by making a special effort to move your legs regularly. Walking is an excellent preventive to the formation of varicose veins.

As pregnancy progresses, your changing shape can pose interesting problems. Carrying a pack becomes more difficult, and the hips no longer provide a resting place for the waist belt. In fact, the waist belt might not fit around you at all. A kayak that used to fit might not as you get bigger. The protruding abdomen can certainly impede progress in squeeze chimneys while rock climbing and may affect balance. Walking sticks are recommended by women who have hiked while pregnant, not only for balance, but to decrease the danger of falling, such as when fording a stream.

The pregnant traveler who leaves civilization should realize that should she miscarry or go into premature labor she might require hasty evacuation. The risk of miscarriage is greatest during the first trimester. About 10 percent of all pregnancies end this way. Miscarriage may involve severe hemorrhaging, which usually cannot be treated without hospital facilities. For this reason, it is better not to put yourself more than twelve to twenty-four hours away from hospital services during the first three months of pregnancy. The last three months is also a poor time for extended trips in remote areas. Whether premature labor is induced by a serious fall or occurs spontaneously, birth in a remote area would certainly be under less than optimal conditions and could result in infant death or harm or death to the mother should help be too far away.

Pregnant women should not use many of the medications and chemicals that are common to backcountry outings, including tetracycline for diarrhea, Flagyl for intestinal amoebas, and Diamox for prevention of mountain sickness. Check with a pharmacist before ingesting any drug. And beware of contracting bacterial or parasitic infections from areas with unsafe water supplies.

Hormones and Longevity

What does the female reproductive system have to do with longevity? Plenty. Estrogen appears to enhance the female immune system, making a woman more resistant to certain bacterial infections. Estrogen also favors women of all ages with a significantly lower incidence of heart disease. A healthy menstruating woman rarely has a heart attack. During and after menopause, however, the heart-attack rate in women doubles. Even so, although you stop menstruating at menopause, the ovaries still produce some estrogen. It takes about ten years after menopause before the risk of coronary heart disease in women begins to parallel that in men. A menopausal woman can do a great deal to reduce her risk by being careful not to become overweight and overfat. There is a direct relation between obesity and heart disease and also a relationship between keeping fit and avoiding heart disease.

How does estrogen work to protect women? When the formation of cholesterol blocks the coronary arteries, estrogen acts to produce a favorable balance of certain blood components. One, high-density lipoprotein (HDL), appears to aid the movement of cholesterol through the coronary arteries. Another, low-density lipoprotein (LDL), appears to impede it, resulting in the formation of plaque, a fatty deposit that decreases the flow of blood to the heart. In women, estrogen acts on the liver to produce HDL. In men, testosterone acts on the liver too, but instead it increases the ratio of LDL to HDL, thereby increasing the male risk of coronary heart disease.

Many fascinating studies seems to suggest that the male hormone androgen is not only related to men's superior physical strength, but to aggression as well. Although it is incorrect to assume that male hormones "cause" aggression, in all statistics of violent crime and death men are clearly and indisputably in the lead. We do not know that if women were bigger and stronger than men and had traditionally enjoyed the same position of freedom and dominance they would somehow handle power and independence in a more benign and less destructive fashion because of their lack of androgens or presence of estrogen and other female hormones. This is clearly a gray area of what is cause and what is effect. Social situations and, as we have seen, physical exercise, can alter the levels of male hormones in both men's and women's bodies. So while there is much to admire and admittedly envy in the biological makeup of the male, there is much for men to admire and envy in the biological makeup of the female.

Notes

Chapter 1

1. D.T. Badenhop et al., "Physiological Adjustments to Exercise Training at Varying Intensities in Individuals Over 60 Years of Age," *Medicine and Science in Sports and Exercise* 13, no. 2 (1981): 103.

2. E.L. Fox et al., "Frequency and Duration of Interval Training Programs and Changes in Aerobic Power," *Journal of Applied Physiology* 38, no. 3 (1975): 481–84.

3. R.M. Otto et al., "Metabolic Responses of Young Women to Training and Maintenance/Detraining," *Medicine and Science in Sports and Exercise* 10, no. 1 (1978): 52.

4. W.D. McArdle, F.I. Katch, and V.L. Katch, *Exercise Physiology: Energy, Nutrition and Human Performance* (Philadelphia: Lea & Febiger, 1981), p. 269.

5. Yoriko Atomi et al., "Effects of Intensity and Frequency of Training on Aerobic Work Capacity in Young Females," *Journal of Sports Medicine and Physical Fitness* 18, no. 1 (1978): 3–8.

6. James A. Gaughran, *Advanced Swimming* (Dubuque, Iowa: William C. Brown, 1972), p. 57.

7. Irvin E. Faria and Peter R. Cavanagh, *The Physiology and Biomechanics of Cycling* (New York: John Wiley & Sons, 1978), p. 106.

8. M. Krance, "A Superior Bicycle Tour," *Sierra* 67, no. 3 (1982): 43.

9. J.H. Wilmore, "Alterations in Strength, Body Composition, and Anthropometric Measurements Consequent to a Ten-week Program," *Medicine and Science in Sports and Exercise* 6, no. 2 (1974): 133–38.

10. Edward L. Fox, *Sports Physiology* (Philadelphia: W.B. Saunders, 1979), p. 130.

Chapter 2

1. Margaret Prouty, "Ladies I Have Known," *Summit* 12, no. 5 (Oct. 1966), pp. 26–27.

2. Anne LaBastille, *Woodswoman* (New York: E.P. Dutton, 1976), pp. 258–59.

3. Alwyn T. Perrin, ed., *The Explorers LTD. Source Book,* (New York: Harper and Row, 1973), p. 173.

4. Martin J. Blaser et al., "Campylobacter Enteritis in Denver," *Western Journal of Medicine* 136 (April 1982):287–90.

5. M.F. Weisenfeld and B. Burr, *The Runner's Repair Manual* (New York: St. Martin's Press, 1980), p. 170.

Chapter 3

1. Michael Loughman, *Learning to Rock Climb* (San Francisco: Sierra Club Books, 1981), pp. 122–24.

2. Ned Gillette, *Cross-Country Skiing* (Seattle: The Mountaineers, 1979), pp. 157–88.

3. Loughman, p. 127.

4. Polly Prescott, letter to the author, 1980.

5. L.C. Schussman, and J.L. Lawrence, "Mountaineering and Rock-Climbing Accidents," *Physician and Sports Medicine* 10, no. 6 (1982): 53–61.

6. James Glick, "Muscle Strains: Prevention and Treatment," *Physician and Sports Medicine* 8, no. 11 (1980): 73–77.

7. George Sheehan, "Ankle Sprains," *Runner's World* (March 1981): 93.

8. James Garrick, "The Athlete's Ankle," *Emergency Medicine,* 15 August 1982, p. 191.

9. O.M. Nwaobi, "Effect of Bracing, Elastic Taping and Non-Elastic Taping on Medial Stability of the Knee," *Medicine and Science in Sports and Exercise* 12, no. 2 (1980): 137–38.

10. Jack Levine, "Chondromalacia Patellae," *Physician and Sports Medicine* 7, no. 8 (1979): 41–49.

11. Richard H. Dominguez, *The Complete Book of Sports Medicine* (New York: Warner Books, 1979), p. 84.

12. Kenneth L. Knight, "Rehabilitating Chondromalacia Patellae," *Physician and Sports Medicine* 7, no. 10 (1979): 147–48.

13. B.D. Rubin, and H.R. Collins, "Runner's Knee," *Physician and Sports Medicine* 8, no. 6 (1980): 49–58.

14. Levine, p. 48.

15. Allan J. Ryan, "The Neglected Art of Massage," *Physician and Sports Medicine* 8, no. 12 (1980): 25.

16. Miriam Underhill, *Give Me the Hills* (Riverside, Conn.: Chatham Press, 1971), pp. 149–69.

Chapter 4

1. C.L. Burrell, and R. Burrell, "Injuries in Whitewater Paddling," *Physician and Sports Medicine* 10, no. 8, 1982: 119–24.

2. Karen Kotoske, "Canoe Safety," *Women's Sports* (June 1982): 47.

3. James A. Gaughran, *Advanced Swimming* (Dubuque, Iowa: William C. Brown, 1972), p. 57.

4. Ron Watters, *The White-Water River Book* (Seattle: Pacific Search Press, 1982), p. 58.

5. P. Astrand, and K. Rodahl, *Textbook of Work Physiology:* 2nd ed.: *Physiological Bases of Exercise* (New York: McGraw-Hill, 1977), p. 533.

6. Burrell and Burrell, p. 121.

7. James A. Wilkerson, ed., *Medicine for Mountaineering* (Seattle: The Mountaineers, 1975), p. 102.

8. American National Red Cross, *Canoeing* (Garden City, N.Y.: Doubleday, 1977), p. 320.

9. Payson Kennedy, "Raft Technique," in *The All-Purpose Guide to Paddling: Canoe, Raft, Kayak,* Norman, Dean, ed. (Matteson, Ill.: Greatlakes Living Press, 1977), p. 30.

10. Walt Blackadar, "Kayak Technique," in Payson, *The All-Purpose Guide to Paddling,* p. 15.

11. Ibid., p. 18.

12. Ibid., p. 21.

13. Fletcher Anderson, "Who Certifies Whom?" *Currents* 4, no. 4 (1982): 19.

Chapter 5

1. David Butwin, "Skiing in Colorado: Changes in the Status Snow," *Physician and Sports Medicine* 10, no. 1 (1982): 121.

2. P. Astrand, and K. Rodahl, *Textbook of Work Physiology: Physiological Bases of Exercise,* 2nd ed. (New York: McGraw-Hill, 1977), p. 321.

3. Erwin A. Bauer, *The Cross-Country Skier's Bible* (Garden City, N.Y.: Doubleday, 1977), p. 23.

4. Astrand and Rodahl, p. 595.

5. Edward G. Hixson, "Injury Patterns in Cross-Country Skiing," *Physician and Sports Medicine* 9, no. 12 (1981): 53.

6. D. Hodgdon, *Nordic Ski Accident Data 1973–1978* (Colorado Springs: National Ski Patrol System, 1978).

7. Hixson, p. 47.

8. Ibid., p. 51.

9. Ron Watters, *Ski Camping* (Moscow, Idaho: North Country Book Express; 1979), p. 149.

10. P. Eigenmann, and R.V. Hockey, "Cardiovascular Benefits of Cross-Country Skiing Related to Skill Level," *Medicine and Science in Sports and Exercise* 12, no. 2 (1980): 141.

Chapter 6

1. P. Astrand, and K. Rodahl, *Textbook of Work Physiology: Physiological Bases of Exercise,* 2d ed. (New York: McGraw-Hill, 1977), pp. 370–71.

2. J.L. Marshall, and H. Barbash, *The Sports Doctor's Fitness Book for Women* (New York: Delacorte Press, 1981), p. 20.

3. P.B. Sparling, and K.J. Cureton, "Biological Determinants of the Sex Difference in Distance Running Performance Among Trained Runners," *Medicine and Science in Sports and Exercise* 12, no. 2 (1980): 81.

4. V.L. Katch, B. Campaigne, P. Freedson, S. Sady, F.I. Katch, and A.R. Behnke, "Contribution of Breast Volume and Weight to Body Fat Distribution in Females," *American Journal of Physical Anthropology* 53 (1980): 93–100.

5. W.D. McArdle, F.I. Katch, and V.L. Katch, *Exercise Physiology: Energy, Nutrition and Human Performance* (Philadelphia: Lea & Febiger, 1981), p. 371.

6. J.A. Feagin, "Women at the Service Academies," *Sports Medicine for the Athletic Female,* Christine E. Haycock, ed. (Oradell, N.J.: Medical Economics, 1980), pp. 339–44.

7. J.R. Morrow, Jr., and W.W. Hosler, "Strength Comparisons in Untrained Men and Trained Women Athletes," *Medicine and Science in Sports and Exercise* 13, no. 3 (1981): 194–97.

8. Ann Oakley, *Sex, Gender and Society* (New York: Harper and Row, 1972), p. 28.

9. V. Heyward, "Relative Endurance of High- and Low-Strength Women," *Research Quarterly for Exercise and Sport* 51, no. 3 (1980): pp. 486–93.

10. R.A. Shively, W.A. Grana, and D. Ellis, "High School Sports Injuries," *Physician and Sports Medicine* 9, no. 8 (1981): 46–50.

11. P.B. Sparling, "A Meta-Analysis of Studies Comparing Maximal Oxygen

Uptake in Men and Women," *Research Quarterly for Exercise and Sport* 51, no. 3 (1980): 542–52.

12. Astrand and Rodahl, p. 124.

13. M. Melvin, "The Future of Women and Sports," *Sports Medicine for The Athletic Female,* Christine E. Haycock, ed. (Oradell, N.J.: Medical Economics, 1980), pp. 409–12.

14. J.S. Petrofsky, R.L. Burse, and A.R. Lind, "Comparisons of Physiological Responses of Women and Men to Isometric Exercise," *Journal of Applied Physiology* 38, no. 5 (May 1975): 863–68.

15. Ibid.

16. P. Vaccaro, G.M. Dummer, and D.H. Clarke, "Physiological Characteristics of Female Masters Swimmers," *Physician and Sports Medicine* 9, no. 12 (December 1981): 75–78.

17. E. Chapman, "Physical Conditioning of Women Ages 20–59 Years," *Medicine and Science in Sports and Exercise* 12, no. 2 (1980): 120.

18. P. Dranov, "New Genetic Findings: Why Women Live Longer," *Science Digest,* May 1981, pp. 32–33.

19. Ibid.

Chapter 7

1. Edward L. Fox, *Sports Physiology* (Philadelphia: Saunders, 1979), p. 12.

2. David C. Bachman, and Marilynn Preston, *Dear Dr. Jock: The People's Guide to Sports and Fitness* (New York: E.P. Dutton, 1980), p. 24.

3. A.A. Sucec, "Horizontal Treadmill Protocol for Concurrent Determination of $\dot{V}O_2$ max and Anaerobic Threshold for Male and Female Distance Runners," *Medicine and Science in Sports and Exercise* 13, no. 2 (1981): 69; and J.C. Rupp, "Anaerobic Threshold Measures: Variance Between Method and Sex," *Medicine and Science in Sports and Exercise* 13, no. 2 (1981): 69.

4. James J. Nora, *The Whole Heart Book* (New York: Holt, Rinehart, and Winston, 1980), p. 109.

5. W.D. McArdle, F.I. Katch, and V.L. Katch, *Exercise Physiology: Energy, Nutrition, and Human Performance,* (Philadelphia: Lea & Febiger, 1981), p. 204.

6. R.J. Marnard et al., "Comparison of Left Ventricular Dimensions in Sedentary and Endurance Conditioned Women," *Medicine and Science in Sports and Exercise* 12, no. 2 (1980): 129.

7. P.F. Brodal et al., "Capillaries Supply of Skeletal Muscle Fibers in Untrained and Endurance-Trained Men," *American Journal of Physiology,* 232, no. 6 (1977): p. H707.

8. Fox, p. 211.

9. C.W. Heath et al., "A Physiological Comparison of Young and Older Endurance Athletes," *Journal of Applied Physiology: Respiratory, Environmental and Exercise Physiology* 51, no. 3 (1981): 634–40.

10. Barbara Hart, "The Effect of Age and Habitual Activity on the Fractionated Components of Resisted and Unresisted Response Time," *Medicine and Science in Sports and Exercise* 13, no. 2 (1981): 78.

11. E.I. Smith, Jr. et al., "Physical Activity and Calcium Modalities for Bone Mineral Increase in Aged Women," *Medicine and Science in Sports and Exercise* 13, no. 1 (1981): 60–64.

12. J.E. Brody, "The Best Things in Life Are Free (Like Exercise) to Ward off Ravages of Aging," *New York Times* News Service, 1979.

13. R.J. Shephard et al., "The Influence of an Industrial Fitness Program upon Medical Care Costs," *Medicine and Science in Sports and Exercise* 13, no. 2 (1981): 89.

14. A. Lovell, "Body Shaping: Seven Science-Hot Breakthroughs," *Self*, January 1982, pp. 51–52.

15. Alex Ayres, "Body and Brain: The Impacts of Aerobic Running on Intelligence," *Running Times*, August 1982, pp. 21–27.

16. G. White et al., "Passionate Love and the Misattribution of Arousal," *Journal of Personality and Social Psychology* 41, no. 1 (1981): 56–62.

17. W.W. Hutchison et al., "Androgen Levels in Male and Female Athletes Participating in Different Sports," *Medicine and Science in Sports and Exercise* 13, no. 2 (1981): 135.

Chapter 8

1. M.W. Blackburn, and D.H. Calloway, "Basal Metabolic Rate and Work Energy Expenditure of Mature Pregnant Women," *Journal of the American Dieticians Association*, no. 69 (1976): 24.

2. G. Ahlborg et al., "Substrate Turnover during Prolonged Exercise in Man," *Journal of Clinical Investigation*, no. 53 (1974): 1080.

3. W.D. McArdle, F.I. Katch, and V.L. Katch, *Exercise Physiology: Energy, Nutrition, and Human Performance* (Philadelphia: Lea & Febiger, 1981), p. 326.

4. P. Astrand, and K. Rodahl, *Textbook of Work Physiology: Physiological Bases of Exercise*, 2d ed. (New York: McGraw-Hill, 1977), p. 490.

5. M.V. Krause and L.K. Mahan, *Food, Nutrition and Diet Therapy*, 6th ed. (Philadelphia: W.B. Saunders, 1979), p. 50.

6. Edward L. Fox, *Sports Physiology* (Philadelphia: W.B. Saunders, 1979), p. 67.

7. Ibid., p. 37.

8. S.K. Powers, W. Riley, and E.T. Howley, "Comparison of Fat Metabolism between Trained Men and Women during Prolonged Work," *Research Quarterly for Exercise and Sport* 51, no. 2 (1980): 427–31.

9. Arlene Blum, *Annapurna: A Woman's Place* (San Francisco: Sierra Club Books, 1980), pp. 142 and 176.

10. E.D. Schlenker et al., "Nutrition and Health of Older People," *American Journal of Clinical Nutrition*, no. 26 (1973): 1111.

11. Krause and Mahan, p. 84.

12. L. Lutwak, "Continuing Need for Dietary Calcium throughout Life," *Geriatrics*, no. 29 (1974): 171.

13. U.S. Department of Health, Education, and Welfare, *The Ten-State Nutrition Survey 1968–70*, U.S. DHEW Publication No. HSM 72–8130–4.

14. K. Nilson et al., "The Effect of Iron Repletion on Exercise-Induced Lactate Production in Minimally Iron-Deficient Subjects," *Medicine and Science in Sports and Exercise* 13, no. 2 (1981): 92.

15. D.V. Harris, "The Anemic Athlete," *WomenSports* 4, no. 12 (1977): 52.

16. D.B. Clement, and R.C. Asumndson, "Nutritional Intake and Hematological Parameters in Endurance Runners," *Physician and Sports Medicine* 10, no. 3 (1982): 37–43.

17. D.L. Costill et al., "Effects of Caffeine Ingestion on Metabolism and Exercise Performance," *Medicine and Science in Sports and Exercise* 10, no. 10 (1978): 155.

18. M.M. Toner et al., "The Effects of Caffeine on the Metabolic and Cardiovascular Responses to Exercise," *Medicine and Science in Sports and Exercise* 12, no. 2 (1980): 109.

Chapter 9

1. D.V. Harris, "Survival of the Sweatiest," *WomenSports* 4, no. 11 (1977): 48.

2. A.J. Frye, and E. Kamon, "Suppression of Sweating During Exercise in Men and Women," *Medicine and Science in Sports and Exercise* 13, no. 2 (1981): 91.

3. A.M. Paolone et al., "Cardiovascular Adjustments to Heat Acclimation of Females," *Medicine and Science in Sports and Exercise* 13, no. 2 (1981): 91.

4. P. Astrand, and K. Rodahl, *Textbook of Work Physiology,* 2d ed. (New York: McGraw-Hill, 1977), p. 556.

5. Ibid., p. 553.

6. C.V. Gisolfi, and J.S. Cohen, "Relationships Among Training, Heat Acclimation, and Heat Tolerance in Men and Women: The Controversy Revisted," *Medicine and Science in Sports* 11, no. 1 (1979): 56–59.

7. I.C. Kuppart et al., "Physical Conditioning May Prevent Heat Stress in Acclimatization," *Physician and Sports Medicine* 9, no. 3 (1981): 32.

8. G.W. Mason, "Ultraviolet, Cold, and Low Pressure," *Northwest Medicine* (October, November, December 1968).

9. Charles S. Houston, *Going High: The Story of Man and Altitude* (New York: American Alpine Club, 1980), p. 100.

10. Peter Hackett, *Mountain Sickness: Prevention, Recognition and Treatment* (New York: American Alpine Club, 1980).

11. David R. Shlim, "A Case of HACE," *Off Belay*, no. 51 (June 1980): 9–12.

12. Herbert N. Hultgren, "Sickness in High Places," *Emergency Medicine*, 15 July 1980, pp. 25–52.

13. John R. Sulton, "Sleep Disturbances at High Altitude," *Physician and Sports Medicine* 10, no. 6 (1982): 79–84.

14. P. Hackett, and D. Rennie, "Rales, Peripheral Edema, Retinal Hemorrhage and Acute Mountain Sickness," *American Journal of Medicine* 67, no. 8 (1979): 214.

15. Charles S. Houston, *High Altitude Physiology Study: Collected Papers* (Burlington, Vt.: Arctic Institute of North America, 1980).

16. Eric B. Larson et al., "Acute Mountain Sickness and Acetazolamide," *Journal of Medicine* 248, no. 3 (July 16, 1982): 328–21.

17. Drummond Rennie, "See Nuptse and Die," *Lancet* 2 (1976): 1177–79.

18. Daniel S. Miles et al., "Absolute and Relative Work Capacity in Women at 758, 586, and 523 Torr Barometric Pressure," *Aviation, Space and Environmental Medicine* 51, no. 5 (1980): 439–44; and Piro Kramar, and Barbara Drinkwater, "Women on Annapurna," *Physician and Sports Medicine* 8, no. 3 (1980): 93–99.

Chapter 10

1. Carl E. Klafs, and M. Joan Lyon, *The Female Athlete*, 2d ed., (St. Louis: C.V. Mosby, 1978), p. 38.

2. G.J. Erdelyi, "Effects of Exercise on the Menstrual Cycle," *Physician and Sports Medicine* 4, no. 3 (1976): 79.

3. L. Folinsbee et al., *Environmental Stress: Individual Human Adaptations* (San Francisco: Academic Press, 1978).

4. Bruce S. Cushing, "The Effects of Human Menstruation on the Polar Bear," mimeographed (Missoula: University of Montana, 1979).

5. G.R. Brisson et al., "Exercise-Induced Blood Prolactin Response and Sports Habits in Young Women," *Medicine and Science in Sports and Exercise* 12, no. 2 (1980): 99.

6. Klafs and Lyon, p. 38.

7. M.K. Hendrix, and T.G. Lohman, "Incidence of Menstrual Disorders in Female Collegiate Athletes and Its Relation to Body Fat Content," *Medicine and Science in Sports and Exercise* 13, no. 2 (1981): 104.

8. B.L. Drinkwater (moderator), "Menstrual Changes in Athletes," *Physician and Sports Medicine* 9, no. 11 (1981): 101.

9. Ibid., p. 104.

10. Ibid., p. 109.

11. *Physicians' Desk Reference,* 34th ed. (Oradell, N.J.: Medical Economics, 1980), p. 1869.

12. F. Haynes et al., "Substrate and Hormonal Responses During Exercise in Users and Non-users of Oral Contraceptives," *Medicine and Science in Sports and Exercise* 13, no. 2 (1981): 105.

13. P.L. Hutchinson, K.J. Cureton, and P.B. Sparling, "Metabolic and Circulatory Responses to Running During Pregnancy," *Physician and Sports Medicine* 9, no. 8 (1981): 55–61.

14. P. Hage, "Brief Reports: Exercise and Pregnancy Compatible, M.D. Says," *Physician and Sports Medicine* 9, no. 5 (1981): 23–24.

15. C.E. Haycock et al., *Sports Medicine for the Athletic Female* (Oradell, N.J.: Medical Economics, 1980), p. 335.

16. V. Brewer, and M. Hinson, "Relationship of Pregnancy to Lateral Knee Stability," *Medicine and Science in Sports and Exercise* 10, no. 5 (1978): 39.

Index

285